You're Not from Around Here, Are You?

LIVING OUT
Gay and Lesbian Autobiographies

Joan Larkin and David Bergman
General Editors

You're Not from Around Here, Are You?
Are You?
A Lesbian in Small-Town America

Louise A. Blum

The University of Wisconsin Press

The University of Wisconsin Press
2537 Daniels Street
Madison, Wisconsin 53718

3 Henrietta Street
London WC2E 8LU, England

1   3   5   4   2

Printed in the United States of America

Library of Congress Cataloging-in-Publication Data

Blum, Louise A., 1960–
You're not from around here, are you? : a lesbian in small-town America /
Louise A. Blum.
pp.   cm. — (Living out)
ISBN 0-299-17090-X (cloth) — ISBN 0-299-17094-2 (pbk.)
1. Blum, Louise A., 1960–   2. Lesbians—United States—Biography.   3.
Rural lesbians—United States—Biography.   4. Homophobia—United States.
5. Cities and towns—United States.   I. Title.   II. Series.
HQ75.4.B55 A3   2001
305.9′0664—dc21   00-011980

Parts of chapter 5 appeared in modified form in the Poetic Space Chapbook Series
(Eugene, Ore.: Poetic Space, 1993) and in *Pillow Talk,* ed., Lesléa Newman (Los Angeles:
Alyson Books, 1997).

Parts of chapters 13 and 14 appeared in modified form in *Sojourner: The Women's Forum,*
May 1996, p. 5 and July 1995, p. 11.

For Connie and Zoe, the loves of my life,

and for all the people who make up my community

Contents

Acknowledgments

I want to thank all the people who took the time to read this book in its various incarnations and give me constructive comments: Joseph Arbach, Kathy Bambrick, Bruce Barton, Fay Driskell, Jakki Flanagan, and Bill Pokorny. Belinda Thompson not only generously read several drafts, but also set me straight (so to speak) on the order in which trees and bushes bloom in the spring. Andrea Harris took time out of her summer to read my revisions and offer invaluable criticism. My sister-in-law, Nadine Sullivan, and my niece Sarah Boujais, stayed up all night to read the final draft. And of course, I must give my most heartfelt thanks to my partner, Connie Sullivan-Blum, who has read this book so many times it hardly seems fair that she had to live through it too. After eleven years, she can still turn the most mundane experience into an exciting and hilarious journey.

Special thanks go to Lyn Lifshin, who not only read the manuscript, but gave me encouragement along the way, Mary Dearborn, for her careful and thorough reading of the first draft, and Madison Smartt Bell, who has been trying to help me get an agent ever since I met him in 1988.

I also want to acknowledge Katherine Forrest, Ruthann Robson, and Judith Katz who responded to my urgent plea for advice some years ago, Sue Pierce, without whom this book might never have seen the light of publication, and Victoria Brownworth, who first suggested I write this book, and told me: "People just want to hear the story."

I am grateful to my students, who throughout the years have continually challenged and inspired me, and to Walter Sanders, who as chair has set the tone for an open and inclusive department whose members have offered me more support than I ever expected to receive. And I must also acknowledge Judith Sornberger, fellow writer, who has remained my friend through good times and bad.

Jim Glimm and Dale Witherow, perhaps more than anyone else, showed me how to live here. Jim, may he rest in peace, between his hunting, his drinking, his storytelling, and his incessant offering of advice taught me how to appreciate the wildness of this landscape and its people. Dale, as an artist and professor, showed me by example how to balance my teacing with my art. Kevin Grubb, the first openly gay person I ever met, showed me that true radicalism is sometimes just living your life.

I will always be grateful to the two doctors and all the nurses who saw me through my insemination and pregnancy and to all the people of Wellsboro, who, at their best and at their worst, make up America.

And, of course, I must acknowledge Zoe, whose presence continues to provide me with the most wonderful adventure of my life.

Will That Be MasterCard or Visa?

The rains began to fall at the end of June, hurling through the streets, flooding the rivers, and sending them running over the roads. Two inches fell in half an hour one day, sweeping a woman and her pickup truck over a bridge. The river that ran through Job's Corner jumped its dam and returned to its old course. Roads were closed permanently. We could no longer get to the mall, fifty miles to the north. Going to a movie was out of the question. We were trapped in Wellsboro, Pennsylvania, with no end to the rain in sight.

"What about this one?" Connie asked, picking up an ovulation kit in the drugstore and turning it over to read the back. "Clear Plan Easy."

"I like the sound of that," I said. Clear Plan Easy. It sounded like something I couldn't mess up.

Connie frowned at the instructions. "All you have to do for this one is piss on a stick," she said.

We looked at each other. "What could be simpler?" Connie asked.

Indeed, what could be simpler? Ten days after the start of my last period, I could begin to test for the hormonal surge that would precede my ovulation. Once we saw a blue line on the test stick, we could order the sperm. As the day approached for me to begin testing, I could feel my courage leaving me, running from me like the water that coursed down the road in front of the house, heading for the fields. I read the directions over and over: keep the test stick pointed down and avoid splashing the windows with urine. I resisted the urge to practice. The night before the first day of testing I dreamed that I was trying to piss on my stick and people kept knocking at the door, trying to get my attention. "Leave me alone!" I kept saying, moving from bathroom to bathroom in search of privacy. When I'd closed the last door behind me, I turned to find myself out on the roof of a building, with people I knew driving past on the street below. "Hi, Louise!" they called, over and over. I gave up, sank down on the toilet that sat out in the middle of everything, and pissed on my stick. There was no blue line.

There was no line in actuality, either. Starting on Day 10 of my cycle, I got up every morning and pissed on my stick, worrying about it every step of the way. Had I left it in the stream of urine long enough? Had I splashed any urine in the little window?

Every day I drove to Mansfield, the small university where I taught English as an assistant professor, braving the floodwaters that periodically submerged Route 6. I could hardly think about my teaching. My whole life revolved around the ovulation kit. I concentrated as if sheer mental energy could cause the blue line to appear, wavering and then growing solid, taking up its space in the little window that waited for it. Around me the water surged, thick and brown and furious, hurling down the hillsides, surging across the roads like cattle, leaving layers of sludge in its wake.

I drove my stretch of highway with my eyes on the pavement in front of me, barely cognizant of the churches that dotted the landscape, almost as numerous as the cows: the Valley Missionary Alliance, the Full Gospel Church, the Assembly of God, River of God, Church of God, and so on, all carefully whitewashed and maintained, every church with its own hand-lettered sign out front, the slogan changing every day. This was God's Country, as the welcome sign attested, and Connie and I were two lone lesbians, trying to conceive a baby by our own version of immaculate conception. I just kept my eyes on the road, around me the flood waters rising as if Nature herself were testing for a surge, pissing down on all of us, waiting anxiously, to see what might appear.

My luteinizing hormone surge, or as those of us in the know called it, an LH surge, showed up on Day 13 of my cycle. This meant that my ovulation would occur, just as the brochure said it would, on Day 14, exactly halfway through my cycle. I took the test stick down to the kitchen to show Connie. "Look!" I told her triumphantly. "I'm having my LH surge!" I felt vindicated somehow, more of a woman. Hormones were surging through my body, taking over my bloodstream, detectable even in my piss. I felt like an extremely complicated being.

Connie took the test stick and studied it over her bowl of cereal. "Look at that," she said, examining the dark blue line in the test window that matched the dark blue line in the sample window that showed us that we had done the test correctly. She looked at me admiringly and handed it back. "Way to go," she said. I warmed to the approval in her voice. I was worthy of this mission. I would, in fact, conceive our child. I felt like a vessel, open and pure. It felt a little bit like being a nun.

Connie brought me the phone. "It's time to call the sperm bank," she said. It felt urgent, like we didn't have a moment to lose. I dialed the number and ordered up two shots of Donor No. 9012, praying that his sperm was still available. We'd chosen him not only because his physical characteristics matched Connie's but because he'd listed interests in skiing and guitar. We'd liked his explicitness. Other donors had listed sports and music, but this was better, we agreed, because it implied that he might actually participate in these activities, as opposed to watching them on television while he opened up a can of beer.

"We'll ship it right out," the woman at the sperm bank informed me. "Federal Express Priority will guarantee that you have it by ten-thirty tomorrow morning for just ten dollars more."

I hesitated for just a moment. We didn't have to do this. I could hang up the phone right now, throw out the donor information, and our lives could just go on the way they were. I could feel my stomach plunge, as if I'd just stepped off the edge of a cliff. "OK," I said. "Send it express."

"Fine," she said. There was a pause. "Will that be MasterCard or Visa?"

As it turned out, the extra $10 was a waste of money. We lived in what Federal Express had officially classified as a Remote Area, meaning that it couldn't guarantee priority delivery before 4 P.M. I waited on the front porch with Connie, both of us watching the street. I wondered what I was doing, trying to have a baby in an area so remote that Federal Express couldn't even deliver on time. The world around us seemed full of moisture; the tops of the trees were shrouded in fog, a mist that seemed to roll up from the ground, as if we were in a jungle. I could picture elephants careening down the street, heading for the water. The petunias sprawled up the balusters of the porch, indolent in the wetness that flooded their roots. It was a jungle outside, teeming with wildness, and I was about to try to conceive a baby. I thought I must be crazy.

When the Federal Express truck pulled into the driveway, the driver hauled a large gray tank out of the back of the truck and carted it up to the porch. Connie and I studied it dubiously. It was stamped with the words **HUMAN TISSUE**. The driver looked at us, from one to the other. "You want to sign for this?"

Connie and I looked at each other. I signed my name tentatively, as if this might just be the last straw, consigning me to an instant state of motherhood from which I would never escape. The driver pocketed his pen and sauntered off down the steps, his clipboard under his arm, whistling something as he headed off to his life, leaving us on our front porch surveying our tank of sperm.

"Well," Connie said. "I guess this is it."

We both just stood there looking at the tank. Neither of us wanted to touch it.

"I guess it is," I said. "I guess it's time."

"It's time," Connie said. We looked at each other. "Let's go."

We drove at high speed, the Talking Heads' "Little Creatures" playing over and over on the cassette player. "I want to do it," Connie said breathlessly as she squeezed the steering wheel in her hands. "I want to do the insemination." She glanced over at me. Her eyes glowed, as if with fever. I wondered for a moment if she might be mad. "Then we can say I got you pregnant," Connie said. Her voice rang with satisfaction. She looked back at the road, swerved, and hit a pothole. "OK?" she asked eagerly. We passed a placard rising majestically from a hill. "The fear of the Lord is the beginning of wisdom," it read. The words were arranged on the billboard in the shape of an open Bible.

I shrugged. David Byrne's voice filled the car, ricocheting off my ears and through my brain. "Sure," I said. The rain ran down the side of the road and splashed against our tires. "Who else?" I asked. The tape switched over, the beat relentless and even. I shook my head to clear it.

By contrast, the waiting room at the doctor's office was deathly silent. Not even Muzak dented the quiet. People lined the room, looking stern and uncomfortable in straight-backed chairs that were just a little too small, their children playing on the rug. It was a practice that concentrated on the poor; the majority of the obstetrics patients were high risk, fourteen-year-olds who'd gotten pregnant by their boyfriends, or sometimes, by a member of their family. "Incest capital of the world," my colleagues used to joke. I'd always found the comment irritating, but now, looking around the room, I found it even more annoying, because I suspected that it might be true. The rest were elderly people on Medicare and Medicaid. The median income in the county was $12,000. Its population was forty-one thousand, more than forty thousand of whom were white. Most of my students were the first in their families to go to college, some already the first to finish high school. It was what I liked about teaching here, the idea that I could really accomplish something, really give my students a vision for change.

It was a lot like the work I used to do in my twenties, when I organized people in low-income neighborhoods to seek change.

Everybody looked at us when we walked in lugging our tank between us, the **HUMAN TISSUE** label clearly visible on the side. We checked in at the window, then found a couple of empty seats against the wall. People eyed us uneasily. I wanted to make some comment about the head we were taking into the office, but the remark dried on my tongue. There was no room for levity here. This was a serious business. Children played around us on the floor, their faces smudged with dirt and grime. One looked up at me, her fingers in her mouth, her eyes large and solemn. I felt a chill go through me. This was what we were here for? What had we been thinking of? The tank sat between us on the floor, ominous as a time bomb. I could almost hear it tick.

"Connie," I whispered. Connie looked at me. Her eyes were huge. She played incessantly with the keys in her hands. "I'm not even sure I like kids," I whispered.

Connie glanced around the room, leaned in closer. "I know," she said. "I held a little baby today, and I didn't feel *anything*."

"Louise Blum?" the nurse said, opening the door. Connie and I rose as one and hauled our tank across the room between us. All eyes followed us to the door. Not only did we have our own **HUMAN TISSUE** with us but we didn't have to wait. I could sense a restive stir behind us.

"Come this way," the nurse said. We followed her mutely. I didn't know her. I hadn't known the receptionist. I didn't know anybody here, except for Dr. Gordon. I felt as if I might throw up. The nurse led us to a room where we deposited our tank of sperm. She looked at us, nervousness evident in her glance. She didn't know why we were here. She didn't know what preparations to make. The two of us just stood there, the tank between us on the floor. "The doctor will be right with you," she said and backed out of the room, closing the door behind her.

I took a deep breath and turned to Connie. "Well," I said. "This is it."

Connie nodded, taking her own deep breath. "Yes," she said, "it is."

I sat down on the table, not knowing where else to sit, and glanced at my watch. I took another deep breath and tried to connect with the egg inside me. Was it in there? Was everything where it was supposed to be? I glanced at Connie out of the corner of my eye. She was looking very serious. I reached out and took her hand in mine. It was cold and slightly clammy. She looked at me and tried to smile. There wasn't anything else to say. In the end we could only sit there and wait for the doctor to appear.

We'd been through this once before, nearly two years earlier. On the recommendation of our family doctor at the time, we'd scheduled an appointment to meet with an insemination specialist in another city. I'd dressed for the appointment carefully, my pink triangle pin prominently displayed on my lapel. "You look great," Connie had said, watching me dress.

I had glanced over at her as I put on my boots. "Oh, yeah? Would you inseminate me?"

Connie had smiled at me. "In a heartbeat."

We had held hands across the seat of the truck as we drove. The city was more than an hour away, down a long and winding road that snaked through a tricky mountain pass that took several lives each year. Trailers and shacks, some sided with tar paper, outlined the road with puffs of wood smoke from their makeshift chimneys. Junked cars filled their front yards, the outhouses propped up against the edges of their fields. We passed a farmhouse with a sign swinging from the mailbox, a cow neatly stenciled beneath the words *Jesus Saves*.

We waited in the waiting room for hours that day. Pregnant women sat around us, reading parenting magazines and rocking in rocking chairs placed tastefully around the room. I picked up a magazine from the rack beside me and thumbed through its pages, looking at the pictures of babies and toddlers and happy glowing mothers. It was like an alien language. A chill shot through me. I put the magazine down. What were we doing here? We had agreed I would go first. I had the better insurance policy; I was the one with the aging ovaries drying up inside me, threatening to blow away on a puff of wind.

The hours crawled by. The longer we waited, the more nervous we both became. "I don't know if I can stand this," Connie confided. At that moment we heard the nurse call my name. We rose and marched across the room, aiming for that open door, the door that would take us into motherhood.

The nurse weighed me, wrote the information down in a chart, and ushered us into the doctor's office. We both sat down, our two straight chairs uncomfortably far apart. The moments ticked by. When the door opened again, the doctor walked in, short and stocky, his white jacket barely buttoning across his belly. "I'm Doctor Romero," he said. I introduced myself, then introduced Connie as my partner. I didn't know what other word to use. *Lover* hardly seemed appropriate, given the situation.

He nodded at me, ignored Connie. He flipped open my chart and asked me questions about my menstrual cycles, my personal history, filling in the relevant information. Then he glanced up at me. His glasses slid down his nose as if they might fall right off, given another moment. "Are you married?" he asked me.

I hesitated in confusion. Hadn't our doctor taken care of this? "Well, no," I said. "I'm not."

The doctor shut my chart and sat back in his chair. "Oh," he said. The word seemed to freeze on his tongue, like ice. "We don't inseminate single women."

I stared at him. "I'm not single," I said. I indicated Connie again, vaguely, with a wave of my left arm. "We're together."

The doctor cleared his throat and pushed his glasses back up his nose. "Let me clarify that," he said. His tone was crisp. "We don't inseminate women without husbands. It has nothing to do with the fact that you're lesbians."

We sat there for a moment. Neither of us looked at the other. "But our doctor talked to you," I said.

Romero interrupted me. "He talked to my partner," he said. "We've had a staff meeting since then and developed a policy."

"A policy," I echoed faintly. Inside I felt absolutely numb. My heart no longer even seemed to beat, as if it had dried up in there, whispered away in the chill of this sterile office with its white-jacketed medical personnel and its artificial air. I couldn't look at him. I got up and, without even intending to, walked out of the office and back toward the door.

Connie got up to follow me out. "Thank you," she mumbled as we left.

I never stopped at the desk to settle the bill. I never stopped moving until we got back to the parking lot, and by the time we were there I could feel the numbness fading away, replaced by a rage so deep I thought it might destroy me. I looked around for his car. I imagined slashing his tires, running the edge of my key along his doors, dumping sugar in his gas tank, stuffing a banana up his exhaust pipe, all guerrilla tactics I'd learned as a young community organizer, spending what free time I had reading Saul Alinsky and Franz Fanon and knocking on doors in poor neighborhoods.

That fucking little man, I thought, with his fucking sacred sperm, dispensing it only to those that he deems worthy. That fucking little shit.

We drove home in silence, me in the passenger seat, Connie at the wheel of the truck. As we began to climb the hills that led to home, I became fixated with her shifting of the gears. "Don't put it into fifth so soon," I said.

Connie stared straight ahead. "Don't tell me how to drive."

"It's my truck," I said. "I don't want you to ruin the transmission."

Connie pulled off the road, and we sat there for a moment. I felt my eyes fill with tears. Connie looked at me. "Why are we fighting with each other?" she asked. There was wonder in her voice. "It's that doctor that we're mad at."

After that experience a friend referred us to Dr. Paul Gordon, a man in his forties, known in town for being progressive. He treated the clients at the human services agency where Connie worked. Gordon was also the chief of obstetrics at Soldiers and Sailors, the local hospital right down the street from us. I knew him from the town's fitness center, a place I'd spent a lot of hours and where he worked out irregularly, though we'd never been introduced. I knew him by his body, which was short and compact, covered with sweat when he ran on the treadmill. "Just ten more minutes," he'd say, when anyone asked him how much longer he'd be. It was always ten more minutes. He used to spend an hour on that thing. I thought his heart rate must be something else. "We'll do it," he'd said without a moment's hesitation when I'd asked him about inseminating me. "We've never done it before," he added, "but we'd like to get into it." He might have been talking about a real estate deal.

"What about your partners?" I asked him.

He shook his head. "They'll be fine." He leaned back against the window and cupped his hands around its sill. He exuded male energy. I remembered him on the treadmill, his T-shirt clinging to his chest. For a moment I pictured his sperm jogging through his body, all suited up for the run, not frozen in some test tube somewhere, preserved for eternity.

"My best friend is gay," he said. "He was my best man, and I was happy when he told me he was gay—it meant he wouldn't make a pass at my wife!" I wondered briefly whether he would have any compunctions about a lesbian under the same circumstances. "As for the girls at the desk," he said, "they never have to know. It's a private matter."

"It's not a private matter," I told him. "I want everyone in the office to know." Especially, I thought, the "girls" at the desk. I wanted them to have to deal with it on their own, to have to acknowledge my relationship with Connie the same way they would acknowledge that of a husband and wife. I was tired of things being private. My relationship with Connie wasn't private anymore, and I was going to make damned sure it never was again.

Dr. Gordon nodded. "OK," he said. "Whatever you want."

When he stepped into the room now, on the morning of our first insemination attempt, I felt my stomach clench. He shook our hands as if it might be some sort of business transaction that we were just about to conduct. "OK," he said, looking down at our tank. "Have you opened it up yet?"

Opened it? I could hardly stand to carry it. No way was I opening it up alone and unsupervised. "No," Connie said brightly. "Can I?"

He nodded. "Certainly," he said.

Connie bent down and unscrewed the lid and pulled it off. Steam rolled out into the room. We all stared at it in awe. "It's like a horror movie, isn't it?" Connie joked. I chuckled wanly. Dr. Gordon only leaned back and crossed one leg over the other, cupping his hands around his knee, surveyed her speculatively, as if waiting to see what she might do next. I gripped the sides of the table with both hands. Nausea pummeled my stomach. Please, I thought, just let this be over soon.

"I'll just step out of the room for a moment and let you get undressed," Dr. Gordon said, pulling a drape from a drawer in the table and handing it to me.

Connie stepped over to me as soon as the door closed behind him. "We can do this," she said.

I looked at her. I felt as if I were drowning, as if she were the only person who could pull me to shore. "Don't forget to tell him you want to do the insemination," I said, as if I might not be able to talk again once Dr. Gordon came back in. For a moment I almost wished for general anesthesia, so that I could just wake up and have this all be over.

Connie nodded. I unzipped my jeans, slid them over my hips, slipped off my underwear. My heart beat unevenly. I pictured it in there, haggard and worn inside my chest, prematurely aged from too much adrenalin. "I'm scared," I said. The paper on the table stuck to my ass; the drape tore as I spread it over me, trying vainly for some sense of privacy.

"I know," Connie said. "I am too."

Dr. Gordon opened the door and stepped back in. He gave the impression of flowing in, snakelike, insinuating his body around the door. He listened seriously as Connie explained that she wanted to do the insemination. He nodded solemnly. "There's no problem with that," he said. "I'll just open Louise up and show you how to do it."

Open me up? Hello, I wanted to say. I'm still in the room. He pulled some cotton swabs out of a drawer and handed Connie a speculum to warm up at the sink. The two of them busied themselves with preparations while I lay back and tried to keep breathing. My whole body felt cold. I'd imagined this process as being more personal somehow. This felt about as personal as an autopsy. Dr. Gordon removed the vial of semen from the tank and slipped it into my hand to warm it to room temperature. Finally, something I could do. I lay back and held it in my hand, studying it between my fingers. No. 9012. It looked entirely innocuous, like a tiny vial of egg substitute.

Dr. Gordon slipped my feet into the stirrups and arranged the drape across my knees. "You slide the speculum in just so," he said to Connie. I felt the familiar suck and stretch, reminiscent of a pap smear. "Now you try," he said, collapsing the speculum and pulling it back out. Connie glanced at me, then slid the speculum back in. "Be careful," Dr. Gordon said. "You don't want to pinch the walls of the vagina."

No, I guess not. I could feel my whole body bracing itself, waiting for the pinch. The speculum slid into place. I could feel the air of the room slipping into my opened vagina. "See," he said warmly, "how the cervix just pops into view?"

I pictured my cervix popping into view, waving a cheery hello. The image was chilling. "You swab the mucous from the cervix," he told Connie, "and then aspirate the semen like so." There was a pause. I couldn't feel anything anymore. I couldn't see them on the other side of the drape. All I could see and feel was a bright hot light directed on my vagina. "That's it," Dr. Gordon said with enthusiasm. I could see the tops of their heads, the blond of the doctor's mixed with the brown of Connie's. "There it goes," he said. I tried to feel it, this rush of sperm, sent off like salmon on their run, swimming upstream despite the odds. "Gee," he said to Connie. "You're really good at this."

"My father's a doctor," Connie said modestly, as if this might be why, as if her father might have had her help him out around the office after school. I closed my eyes and tried to focus on my egg, tried to get a picture of the sperm valiantly making their way through my body. I could picture their little arms going up and down, their heads rhythmically tilting to breathe the air down deep in their lungs, their little faces taut with the pressure, while somewhere far ahead of them my egg danced on the waters like a shimmering sunrise, awaiting their arrival. I tried to wish them well, but it didn't feel like a friendly swim; it felt like an invasion, like my body had just been assaulted by a hostile army. It felt inexorable, like being injected with HIV. I felt sick suddenly. All that time I'd spent trying not to get this stuff beyond my cervix—diaphragm, birth control pills, rhythm method, withdrawal—and there I was, open-legged and ready, willingly admitting it.

"OK," Dr. Gordon said, sounding almost cheerful. He put my knees together gently, like closing the pages of a well-worn book. "It says here that you should lie here for twenty minutes or so, so I'll just leave you alone in here."

He closed the door behind him and immediately Connie was there, her face close to mine, her hands around mine. "It's OK," she said. "You're going to be just fine." Her face was soft, tiny lines crinkling the skin around her eyes when she smiled at me. "It's all done now," she said, and I could feel the muscles in the back of my neck loosening, could feel my breathing slow. "It's all over," she whispered, leaning closer to me, and I closed my eyes and felt her breath against my face, felt her lips brush my forehead, the touch of her tongue against my skin. "There's nothing else you have to do," she said, and together we waited out the rest of the time, until the doctor told us we could go.

"Here's the vial," Dr. Gordon said as we gathered our things together to leave. I felt light-headed, suddenly, as I walked out into the hallway. I moved carefully, carrying my body as if transporting the Ark of the Covenant. God knew what might be in there. "You'll want to hang onto this," he said.

"Why?" I whispered to Connie as we paid our bill at the window. What on earth would we want an empty sperm vial for? A little memento of the experience? Weren't we hoping for another kind of keepsake? Connie shrugged and slipped the vial into the pocket of her jeans. "Come on," she said, pulling out the keys. "Let's go home."

"Let me see the vial," I said when we got home.

"No," she said possessively, taking it out and looking at it fondly. Then she put it on the mantel. "Dad," she said, nodding over at me.

Just Don't Do Anything Stupid

Ifirst saw Connie a few months after I moved to town, over ten years ago now. I had just dismissed a class and was standing in front of the building, talking to a few students. I looked up and saw her a few yards away. Nothing struck me right away about her appearance. It was just that our eyes met, and hers were clear and crisp and full of light, and all I knew suddenly was that she was going to mean something to me and in a deeper way than I could name.

She came into my office a few days later and introduced herself. She was a nontraditional student, an anthropology major in her third year. She was four years younger than I. She had long dark hair and those hazel eyes, and I knew right away that her interest in me extended way past friendship, extended, in fact, as far as I might want to take it.

I'd had plenty of male lovers through the years, but nevertheless I found myself attracted to women, especially one, Sadie, whom I met in grad school and who used to tell people that she liked me so much that if she were a man, she'd marry me. Sadie had short blond hair and high cheekbones and glowing eyes. She'd seen *Taxi Driver* nearly a dozen times, and when I picked her up after she saw *Blue Velvet*, a film I'd recommended to her, she'd slid into the front seat and leaned toward me, whispering breathlessly: "Louise, I *am* Frank Booth!" I never asked her what she meant. We used to sit around and drink bottles of Rolling Rock together, roll joints or snort a couple lines of coke, and stare into each others' eyes. She was seven years older than I was, and when she smiled at me, the skin wrinkled up around her eyes. I used to lose myself in the way she smiled at me. When, sometime later, I suggested shyly that she might not need to be a man to be involved with me, the friendship ended. There's not really any coming back from a comment like that one; once it's out on the table, you can never walk away from it again. You can try to ignore it, but it's always there, taking up space, like a coffin in the living room. I thought I could just move away, lose myself in these foreign hills, and live my life alone, keeping quiet and writing books that would take care of everything, tell the world everything I had to say.

But here was Connie, big and loud and full of life, telling me straight out that she was gay and, if we spent any time together, people might begin to talk. Here was Connie, bringing coffee to my office when I wouldn't consent to go out for it with her and telling me she didn't wear a bra, despite her sister's admonishments. Like so many of our nontraditional students, Connie was a local—her whole family lived in the area, within, in fact, a fifteen-mile radius of each other. I'd already noticed Connie's breasts, much larger than mine, swinging freely beneath her shirt. I didn't think I cared if people talked. I didn't think they really would. We were just two people, after all, two inconsequential people. Why would anyone talk about us?

Connie and I spent more and more time together, until we were meeting every Monday, Wednesday, and Friday for breakfast and every Tuesday and Thursday night for beer in the town's one bar, Mark's Brother's, where Connie used to work as a waitress. She knew most of the people who worked there, including Ben, the owner. He was a good guy, she said, even if he did have a monopoly on the town's only liquor license. Before long we were spending every minute that we could together. I didn't think I cared about anything except getting to know her better. Nothing mattered more to me than being in her company, looking into her hazel eyes, watching for the traces of orange that lay along her pupils.

I made her wait nine months before I kissed her. I said I wanted to be sure that this was what I wanted, but the truth was I was afraid. I was afraid of making love to her, afraid I might not like doing the things I couldn't help imagining, brushing back her hair and kissing her mouth, cupping my hands around her breasts, putting my mouth on her. Especially putting my mouth on her.

It was December. The semester was over, and we were having a beer in Mark's Brother's. The bar was nearly deserted where we sat downstairs. Upstairs, male faculty members in tweed blazers lined the bar at one end, while plaid-jacketed local hunters clustered around the other, an uneasy truce between them. Connie lifted her glass of beer to her mouth, and as she did I saw the curve of her breasts beneath her blouse. I'd had just enough beer to feel brave. "Are you still attracted to me?" I asked her, forgetting that I'd vowed never to bring this up again. The effect was startling. Connie put down her glass immediately, foam spilling down its sides and pooling on the table around it. "I can't talk about this here," she said. Her eyes were wide in the darkness of the bar, like a deer caught in a spotlight. "I have to leave," she said and pushed back her chair.

I followed her up the stairs and inched past the line of professors, all of whom, it seemed, had something to say to me about the end of the semester. They'd grown accustomed to seeing us here, the only women our age who hung out in this bar. Our constant presence had given us a temporary status here. In the past nine months they'd all watched us fall in love, though I doubt they saw it that way. All this time we'd been romancing each other, right under their noses, and nobody ever caught on. Or so it seemed.

I caught up to Connie outside. The air was crisp and clear; the snow sparkled all around us. She was breathing quickly, her breath steaming the air. "Let's drive somewhere," she said.

We drove out into the country and as far as we could drive into a closed state park, skidding on the snow along the road. I parked the truck on a bridge. We both stared straight ahead, into the snow. "Listen," Connie said. "I really want to hold your hand, but I don't know how you'd feel about that." She kept on talking, tentative words that she placed before me like fragile offerings, but they dissolved before they reached my ears. I thought she might never stop talking. I could feel my heartbeat taking over my chest, urging me to take some action. We'd never get anywhere at this rate. I was getting that feeling I used to have in swim class as a child, when I was poised on the edge of the diving board, unable to go any farther, a line of waiting children forming behind me, my mother's voice in my head saying: "Just dive, for god's sake. Dive!" I turned to Connie midsentence, leaned toward her, and placed my mouth on hers. I was afraid I wouldn't know what to do next, afraid she might just keep on talking, afraid, even then, that I might be misinterpreting what she wanted, but then I found, wonder of wonders, that she was kissing me back, and after that I just stopped thinking at all.

I don't know how much time passed before Connie broke away. She stared deep into my eyes. Her breathing was fast, hot and moist against my face. "I want you to take me home," she said huskily.

"What," I said slowly. "You mean to your car?"

"No," Connie said. "To your home." Her hand on my thigh was heavy as lead. My blue jeans suddenly felt impossibly tight against my crotch. I could feel myself begin to sweat. Just because I'd kissed her, it didn't mean I wanted more. Did it?

"I'm not ready," I said. It sounded ludicrous, even to me. "Not yet." I put the truck in reverse and backed right into the No Parking sign behind us. "Maybe later," I mumbled, while beside me Connie turned her face to the window fogged with our breath.

It was six days before I took her to my home. We went shopping for a Christmas tree, dragged it back to my cabin, and propped it up outside while we went in and started up the woodstove, fed the cats, poured ourselves a glass of wine, put the Indigo Girls in the tape player, and sat down on the floor of my living room. We talked for a while, refilling our glasses from the bottle between us on the floor. The tension was palpable. I was starting to get that diving feeling again when Connie put her glass down on the floor and said: "Is this, are we, I mean—can I sit closer to you?"

"Sure," I said, and then her mouth was on mine again, searching out my lips, her hands on my body, pulling it close. First one glass fell over, then another. We never did get the Christmas tree in that night. The fire burned down, the Indigo Girls played auto reverse for hours, while Connie ran her tongue along my body, circled it around my breasts, slid it down my stomach.

The next morning we had coffee and toast with jam. I kept waiting for the wall to come up, to want her to leave. I expected that the time would come when I would want my morning back. It always did. Mornings after sex had always been the same for me. I wanted the other person to leave, so I could have my space again. But the time never came. I didn't want her to leave. We fired up the woodstove and talked all morning. When she left, I missed her. Being alone was not the same. It would never be the same again.

We spent every day together. We made out during bad matinees in deserted movie theaters up at the mall, an hour-and-fifteen-minute drive from where we lived. We drank beer and ate turkey sandwiches in a dark greasy bar called the Trojan, whose owner used to come out and sit with us sometimes. "You girls looking for jobs?" he'd ask us. "I need a couple of bartenders. It's hard to find girls with grit these days." I imagined a life for myself in which I worked nights as a bartender at the Trojan, pouring drinks for the locals, flirting with the hunters up from the city, going home in my pickup truck to my woman when my shift was over. A girl with grit. I thought that this might be my life, the one that I'd been waiting for. We stayed over at each other's place like girlfriends, ate pizza, and smoked pot and made love in all the rooms we had between us. I began to know her body as if it were my own, strong and golden and full. The first time I put my mouth on her was the first time I'd ever put my mouth on a woman, and as I ran my tongue through the hair between her legs, plunged it deep into the folds of flesh that lay hidden within, I felt as if I'd come home again. I held her hips with my hands, buried my face in her, and thought to myself with satisfaction: I am made for this. Our love seemed charmed, untouchable. At first it seemed as if we were blessed; when we walked down the street, people smiled and nodded. It was as if the whole county were turning out to applaud our union, lay its hands on us, shower us with approval. I thought I was walking on air.

Then I went back to Ohio for Christmas, to my parents' house in Chardon, the small town where I'd grown up. I was full of excitement, full of the heady power of this new love. "So," my sister said, bringing her cup of coffee into the dining room and sitting down beside me. "Tell us about this new guy you're seeing." And, just like that, I got up and left the room, my heart pounding as if my life were about to end. I could feel my sister turn to look at me as I left. I sensed her hurt and confusion, quickly masked by her anger, but all I knew was that I was suddenly so afraid I had to get away, hide myself in some distant corner of my parents' house.

I couldn't bring myself to talk about it. Certainly not to my mother, who had made her thoughts on homosexuality clear since I was in college and made friends with Patrick, the first openly gay person I had ever met, who worked with me on the student newspaper. His flamboyance had shocked me at first. I'd felt uncomfortable around him, his open sexuality, his blazing pink mesh tank tops that showed off a physique that no other guy on campus had. He couldn't even walk into the cafeteria without the fraternity boys screaming "Faggot!" and throwing food at him. As I got to know him, I forgot about his sexuality, unless he brought it up. I wondered privately why he did bring it up, even though publicly I defended him to the end. But if my feelings about him were ambivalent, my mother's were unequivocal. "It's sick," she said, not looking up from her cooking. She was slicing carrots on a cutting board. "How can you say that?" I asked. "What would you do if I brought him home for a visit?" She picked up the cutting board and swept the carrots into the pot on the stove. I heard them sizzle in the oil, then quickly give up the fight. She kept the knife in her hand as if she might need it. "I'd be nice to him," she said, not looking at me. "But I could never *like* him."

I avoided my mother's calls on Sunday mornings. I became afraid of the phone, afraid to talk to anyone. When I finally managed to confide in Roger, one of my colleagues, over a beer at the bar, he quickly said: "Just don't tell anyone—don't do anything stupid, like hold hands walking across campus or anything, and you'll be OK." He ran a hand through his hair as he added, "I understand." He was having an affair that he had to keep secret too.

Despite Roger's warning, we just weren't careful people. We just weren't good at not holding hands when we walked across campus. We weren't good about not making every meal out a romantic one. In a place with no gay restaurants or bars it was hard to fool anyone. And then there was that one Sunday afternoon in the basement of Mark's Brother's. We ordered hamburgers and beer and carried them downstairs. No one else was in the bar. We sat in low chairs in the corner, held hands and talked, kissed after careless looks up the stairwell. There was something exciting about it, kissing in a public place. It felt dangerous. It felt real. Connie sat beside me, her thigh touching mine. I fought the urge to slide my hand down her jeans. "Go pick some music," she said, dropping some quarters for the juke box into my hand.

I flipped through the choices and leaned over to insert the coins. Connie got up and came over. She stood behind me; I could feel her hand slipping into the back pocket of my jeans, her breath against my ear. Before we knew it, one of the waitresses was behind us, a woman we didn't know. I froze by the juke box. Connie turned around. "Hi," she said, taking a step toward the waitress for no apparent reason. The waitress turned and ran for the stairs. Connie turned back to me and shrugged. "I don't know," she said. "I think I scared her." I didn't think anything of it. We finished our food and reluctantly parted ways, Connie to her home and me to mine.

The next day one of my students, a self-appointed rebel, came down to my office and sat down beside my desk. "Listen," she said. "Can I be a twenty-one-year-old punk and give you some advice for a minute?"

I sat back in my chair. "Sure."

She looked at me and took a deep breath. "Be careful what you do in that bar," she said. "Everything gets out. The bartender told everyone last night—including a bunch of faculty—that he had to throw you out for obscene behavior with a woman."

I felt numb for a moment. I was gossip material. My job as an untenured professor might really be on the line. What I did actually mattered to someone other than me. It was a revelation, one of those revelations that creeps up on you like a thief and wraps its fingers around your neck and threatens to choke the life out of you unless you surrender any valuables you might have in your pockets. I called Connie. "I don't know what to do," I said. I was shaking.

"Call Ben," Connie said, "and tell him what happened." I hung up the phone. My heart thundered in my chest till I didn't think I could talk. I didn't want to call Ben. I wanted all this to go away. My fingers hovered above the buttons on the phone. My hands trembled on the receiver. I took a breath so ragged it hurt my throat. And then I took another. "Look," I said, when I got him on the phone. I told him what had happened. "I'm a professor," I said. "I can't have this. You have to do something." Ben forced the bartender to apologize to me, but it didn't matter. It had still happened, and there was no taking it back. The bubble had burst—the magic had been stolen from us. We'd thought our space was sacred, but it turned out no place was sacred for us. I thought our love had made us safe, but nothing was safe anymore.

Connie and I went for a drive, skidded through the ice and snow up Firetower Road, went as far as we could before the "No Winter Maintenance" sign. Connie put the truck in park and looked at me. I couldn't even see her sitting across the bench seat from me. "I just don't want this," I said. I thought of Patrick. "I don't want this to be my battleground. I don't want who I have sex with to matter. I don't want to start going to Gay Pride marches. All I want is to live my life, with nobody bothering me about it."

"You're a thirty-year-old single woman," Connie said. "People are going to talk about you no matter what you do. You'll always be suspect."

I couldn't even look at her, at those familiar hazel eyes, those hands on the wheel, those fingers that had touched me everywhere, taken me places I'd never been and brought me back to myself, breathless and clutching at her arms. I didn't want to be suspect. I didn't want to be anything. I just wanted all this to be over.

"I want to go home," I said, and I went back to my cabin on my mountaintop, as far away from the world as I could get, fired up my woodstove, and sat down with my cats. When the telephone rang, I didn't answer it. This isn't who I am, I thought. This isn't how I want my life to be. But Connie's words kept ringing in my ears, persistent as a virus: "They'll talk about you anyway. It doesn't matter what you do." The cabin was silent all around me. The cats purred in my lap. The snow fell softly to the ground, obscuring the tracks my truck had made in the driveway. Maybe if I was lucky, enough would fall to snow me in and keep me from ever having to go out again. I closed my eyes. The silence echoed around me, hanging in the air like smog. I opened my eyes. There was no escaping it. I was lonely. The cats just weren't as good company as they used to be. Fuck it, I thought, and picked up the phone to call Connie.

We spent a lot of money on phone calls that first year that we were lovers. We drove a lot too. It was thirty-five miles from my cabin to her apartment, and sometimes I drove there in the evening just to spend the night with her. We used to meet in Mansfield and then take one car the rest of the way to the mall to go to a movie or out to eat. En route to a movie at the mall one day in the late spring we stopped to have lunch at the Pizza Hut. We had a glass of wine. We toasted each other several times. The restaurant emptied out as the lunch rush left. The waiter, a young guy who seemed familiar somehow, brought us each another glass, on the house. We sat there for hours, holding hands under the table and staring into each others' eyes. We started talking about the future, about what we wanted. A dog, we both agreed. A house. We looked at each other. "A baby," I said. Connie smiled at me, one hand touching her wine glass, the other touching me. "A baby," she said.

We never did get to the movie that day. Instead we went to a bar and had another glass of wine. We planned out our future, planned out our baby. "He'll probably be a boy," Connie said. "You know he'll be a boy." We ended up at the mall, throwing quarters into the wishing well at one end. "For our baby," Connie said, and we closed our eyes for a moment.

"What's his name?" I asked her.

We both looked up at the same moment. A bar and a store stood before us, side by side, their names emblazoned above their doors. Maxwell's and McCrory's. We turned to each other. "Maxwell McCrory," Connie said.

"Maxwell McCrory Sullivan-Blum," I said. We studied each other for a minute.

"Let's drink on it," I said, and we touched hands, for just a moment, before we went inside.

Maybe It's Morning Sickness

After our first round of insemination I was immediately convinced that I was pregnant. We spent the next few days pouring through *What to Expect When You're Expecting,* trying to see whether I had any of the early signs. The days dripped. The house was full of bugs: ants, moths, and mosquitoes. Everything was lush from the rain, teeming with life, dense with it.

Connie made me drink a glass of milk, in case I needed the extra calcium. I immediately felt nauseous.

"Maybe it's morning sickness," Connie said hopefully.

"Maybe it's milk," I grumbled.

Or maybe, I thought, grimly, it was anxiety—if I wasn't pregnant, we'd have to go through all this again. And if I was—well, there was all of Wellsboro to face and the possibility that by our own stupidity we were bringing a child into a world as welcoming as a snake pit.

The town of Wellsboro is the most picturesque in these parts. It's the kind of town I used to dream of living in when I was a child. I used to fantasize about living in a neighborhood just like the one I live in now, with white houses and big front porches and shady backyards and lots and lots of children my age right next door.

Wellsboro is the county seat. It's where the doctors and the lawyers live, though this is a medically underserved area, so there's not too many of the former but a lot of the latter. It's a quiet little town of four thousand, full of tree-lined streets, two-story houses with big front porches, and one department store, one diner, one movie theater (all owned by the same family), one liquor store, and four of the county's eight stoplights. A chain of hills called the Endless Mountains encircles our town, hides the sun from our view, seeds our sky with clouds, and gives it a strange dark beauty that has slipped into my heart.

Ten years ago I drove into town and unloaded my pickup truck and carried my belongings up to my two-room apartment above one of the two antique stores that grace Main Street. I hung my lace curtains across my storefront windows overlooking the catalpa trees that weep their lush white flowers every summer and cover the sidewalk with petals. After I walked down the street to one of the two hardware stores to buy screens for my windows, the guy at the cash register paused in ringing me up. He looked me up and down and said: "Oh, you're the new English professor that just moved into town."

It took me aback for a moment. I'd forgotten that in a town this size everybody knows everything, all the time. "Oh, you're the one that moved in above the antique store," they'd say down at the post office. "Noticed you got a lot of parking tickets last month," they'd say over at the sporting goods store. "Gotta watch the cops when the weather's nice. You can park anywhere you want when it's raining; they don't like to walk around then," they'd caution me as they rang me up.

I liked the discourse. It never left the surface. Living in this town seemed easy. I liked not having to worry about whether I'd locked my doors. I liked being able to go running any time of day or night. I liked that I could walk down any street I chose, even if I did find myself counting the lawn jockeys that nobody's ever even bothered to whitewash. I didn't have anything to fear. I was white, employed, and as far as everyone was concerned, I was straight. No one was ever going to hurt me. I liked the gas lamps that lined the streets, left over from another era. I liked the freedom here, the wildness of the landscape, the violet blue of the mountains in the winter time and the profusion of lakes in the summer, and that nobody else I knew seemed to have any idea that this place existed. So what if the nearest mall was fifty miles away? So what if public transportation didn't exist? There was a certain peace to this small town. I liked driving down dirt roads that slipped deep back into the hills where I could see deer and bear and wild turkey and, once, a golden eagle. One night I heard the shriek of a bobcat in the woods, splitting the air like the cry of a woman. I liked the fountain of Winken, Blinken, and Nod in the center of the town that doubled as a wishing well. I liked that when I worked out at the gym, I got to know the dentist who saw his patients at the Red Cross headquarters and the attorney who got elected judge and the minister over at the Lutheran church, whose parishioners worshipped on folding chairs and whose office occupied a trailer in the parking lot. I liked that people asked me how many miles I ran and how long it took me. Nothing ever got too personal. It never occurred to me that I might be a curiosity, thirty and living all alone with no kids, no apparent boyfriend. It never occurred to me that anybody might say anything more than what they said to my face. Why would they, after all? What difference could it possibly make, how I lived my life?

After a while I moved out of my apartment to a rented cabin on top of a mountain six miles out of town. Even the locals didn't know about it. I chopped wood for my woodstove and drank water from my well. The minerals in it turned my hair orange when I showered. I took long walks down the road with a cup of coffee every morning at dawn. It was so deserted up there that grass grew down the center of the road. Only one other person lived up there, an old mountain man who let me ski on his property and canoe in his beaver pond, which never had any beavers in it. "There used to be two," he told me, "but he died, and then she took up with some other beaver down the road." At night I watched the sun set over the fields behind my cabin, burning them up before it sank behind the trees. I liked my life. I liked my job, I liked my cabin, and I liked this image of myself, alone, in blue jeans and hunting boots, wearing a flannel shirt to walk down my road, my hair cut so short even the breeze didn't touch it.

For the two weeks after our first insemination attempt, all I thought about was my body. I taught my classes, met with students, read books, tried to write, but my mind was constantly elsewhere, watching my body like a hawk, mining it for signs that it no longer belonged to me alone, that I was sharing occupancy for a time with a tenant I really didn't know, whose personal habits I had no idea how to gauge.

When Connie and I first decided to get an apartment together, a year and a half after we met, I told my mother about it nervously, at first implying that I was moving by myself back into town. "Oh, good," she said. "I hated you being up there in that cabin, all alone." During the next conversation I mentioned that Connie would be moving in with me, intimating that it was just to split the rent. "Oh, good," she said. I could hear the surprise in her voice, the slightest hesitation. "Now if you could just meet a nice man," she said. I could picture her with her lips pressed together, nodding her head, imagining me, no doubt, back in town, surrounded by two-story houses filled with eligible men, all of whom I could finally meet, now that I was no longer splitting firewood alone on my mountaintop. I didn't say anything else. There was no third conversation, no subsequent talk in which I let it drop that, in fact, there would be no Nice Man, that Connie and I were really moving in together in the most significant sense.

I didn't say anything to anyone. I kept my mouth shut. I mentioned to my colleagues that I was moving but only vaguely mumbled something about a roommate. They regarded me evenly. Most hadn't even seen my cabin. Except for Roger, with whom I seemed to have so much in common, I'd never even had a drink with most of them. Roger and I had spent many hours bellying up to the bar at Mark's Brother's with the good old boys, but with everyone else I'd kept my distance. I didn't know anything about them.

Connie and I spent the day before we were to move in cleaning the house, a sagging two-story white house with an uninhabitable second floor and a sagging front porch. The elderly woman next door stopped by when she saw us sitting on the front steps sharing a sub. "So you're the ones moving in," she said, appraising us carefully through narrowed eyes. She pulled her coat tighter and held it closed at the neck. "Well," she said. "I just hope there aren't going to be any *boys* over."

Connie and I avoided each other's eyes. "Oh, no," I said after a pause. "There won't be any boys."

Roger helped us move in. He was the only person from school I dared to ask to help us. He was annoyed by the task. "Why don't you make an announcement in class?" he asked me. "Get some strong men to help." I didn't answer him, but inside my heart was beating hard at the thought of witnesses, Strong Men moving our things around, setting up our bed. What would they think? I was nervous enough about this move. I didn't want to have to pretend in front of strangers that we were just roommates moving in together. As we were loading up the boxes from my cabin, I began to cry. I had loved this cabin. I'd lived here all alone, survived every season here. I had muscles in my arms and legs, visible badges of my competence. Connie and I had fallen in love up here, had the best sex I'd ever had on the floor of the kitchen, the couch beside the woodstove, the bed, the table, up against the walls, out in the fields during electrical storms, beneath the hot sun in the summertime. We'd taken off our shirts and walked bare-breasted, hand in hand, down our deserted dirt road. Only once did we get caught, by the mountain man driving back to his house. We dropped hands and ran, not stopping until we were safe behind a tree, holding our sides and gasping with laughter, clutching our shirts to our chests. The next day he stopped by to make small talk. "I don't know what you girls got so modest about," he drawled on his way out. "You can do whatever you want to up here, you know."

And that was how it felt. Like we could do anything we wanted, and no one would ever know. But now we were giving all that up and moving to the center of town, imprisoning ourselves in one of those nice white houses surrounded on all sides by people we didn't know.

As we moved our things into the new house in Mansfield, I escaped to the basement, sat on the stairs, and sobbed into my hands. Connie found me down there and sat beside me, nervously touching my shoulder. "I just want to go home!" I told her between sobs.

Neither of us mentioned that this was home now.

After the move we took the keys to my cabin back to my landlady. She asked me if I knew of anyone who might want to rent the place next. I shook my head. I didn't even know anyone, period, except for Connie. She surveyed me mournfully. "You hate to advertise," she said, shaking her head. "You never know who might answer it. Somebody colored might come, and then you'd have to rent to them."

I stared at her. This was the woman I'd been renting from for the last year and a half, who'd helped me split a cord of wood and showed me how to stack it? "Not that I'm prejudiced," she said quickly.

Oh, no? I thought, but she had already turned away, already moved on in her head to the next task at hand. She'd lived in this town all her life, as had the generations before her. She'd been reluctant enough to rent to me. "You're not from around here, are you?" she'd asked me, sounding just the way you might expect her to sound, like John Wayne in some cowboy movie, just before he blows the guy from somewhere else away. But she had rented to me. It never occurred to me that there might be people she wouldn't rent to, no matter what.

Neither Connie or I said anything to her. We just gave her the keys and went back out to the truck, drove back to Mansfield, back to our new life together, a conglomeration of boxes and paintings and plants so profuse we could barely get in the door, barely make a path to walk through.

Combining our households was easy—our pictures melted in together on the walls, our blankets nestled together on the beds, our sweaters soon found their way into one cupboard—though we had twice as many things as we needed: two sets of cooking utensils, two toasters, two mops, three litter boxes. What was harder was combining our lives. We were both anxious about living together— Connie because she had lived with a lover before and I because I hadn't. I had always lived alone. Even in the years of sharing cooperative households with people, I'd always had my separate room. We both hung onto things, Connie to her four inoperable vacuum cleaners and her Hollywood frame and lumpy mattress, given to her by her last lover, just in case she might have to move back out again. I hung on to the idea of my separate space, a room that would be mine, the room, I figured, subconsciously if not consciously, that I could close myself into if things between us didn't work out.

We hadn't lived together two months before we began to have fights. Fights like neither of us had ever had before, fights in which some demon seemed to come to life inside me, raising its head and sending its fire roaring from my throat. We screamed at each other, slammed doors in each other's faces. I shouted obscenities I never knew were in my vocabulary. I had never raised my voice to anyone before. I could feel my anger take me over, shake me in its grip till I feared I would lose my soul. I could see her through the anger, see the hurt in her face, but I couldn't get to her, couldn't move past the desperation that held me like a straitjacket. Inside me, it seemed my body, my solid oak door of a body, had turned to ash; there was nothing left for me to get my hands around.

One day at the end of the semester a friend of ours stopped by. Connie had known Rick for years; they'd gone on archaeology digs together, spent late nights drinking scotch and playing poker and smoking cigarettes together. They both saw me at the same time after I moved to town. "She's something," Rick said, according to Connie. "I'd like to sleep with her."

"You're not her type," Connie said.

Rick just looked at her, Connie told me. "You want to bet?" he asked her.

"What did you say?" I asked Connie, fascinated, when she related the story to me over breakfast months after we'd gotten together.

"Nothing," she said, stirring cream into her coffee and lifting the cup to her lips. "I didn't think you'd want to be the object of a bet," she said, surveying me above the brim.

"Of course not," I said, turning away. Inside I felt mildly disappointed. Something in me kind of liked the idea, that two people would compete for me. It made me feel like a fairy-tale princess, watching the battle from the sidelines, marrying the victor. It just wasn't a way I was accustomed to feeling.

Besides, both of us found Rick sexy. He was a Vietnam veteran with black hair and a thick moustache and a slow easy body. He used to wait for me at the door of the English building in the morning, smoking a cigarette outside on the steps. "Morning, Beautiful," he'd say as I walked past, and I'd feel a flush of excitement roll through me, warm me somewhere deep inside. He'd taken one of my classes, and every time I turned to write something on the chalkboard, I was conscious of his watching me from behind. I wrote a lot of stuff on the board that semester.

On this visit he had a friend with him, Carl, whom he introduced as a gentleman. Carl was tall and gangly; the slightest southern accent graced his words. His hair was nearly white, his demeanor deferring. I offered them a beer; we shared a joint in the living room, waiting for Connie to come home. "Remember those tight jeans and high boots you used to wear?" Rick asked me, nearly moaning. "Why don't you put them on?"

We often wondered, Connie and I, how we could find Rick so attractive.

When Connie got home that night, we went out to Mark's Brother's. Everyone was there, celebrating the end of the semester. Connie and Rick stood a little to one side, their arms around each other, both impossible flirts, while I sat at the bar drinking a glass of beer from the pitcher that we shared. Carl looked at me, his tongue just lightly stroking his upper lip. He looked like one of our cats, ready for a night of canned food and Pounce treats. "I think you're hot, Louise," he said. "I mean, really," he added, as if I might have thought he would be lying.

I turned away. Maybe he'd just go away if I ignored him long enough.

Carl leaned slightly closer to me. Rick might have introduced him as a gentleman, but I knew it wasn't true. "I'd really like to sleep with you," Carl said. His hand touched my thigh, hesitant at first, then growing heavier, firmer, as if I were a piece of furniture he had every right to touch.

I pulled back. "No thanks," I said.

He leaned closer, his hand caressing my thigh. "Why not?" he asked. "You're really sexy."

I looked down at his hand, then over at Connie, where she stood with Rick at the end of the bar. He had one arm slung across her shoulder, hers circled his waist. They resembled each other a little, dark, somehow Italian looking, though Rick was swarthier, older, coarser than Connie. He was full of edges, in his old faded blue jeans that had somehow grown to the shape of his body in that way that men's jeans do, as if he never took them off. I knew that at home his wife was probably cooking his dinner, watching his kids. Neither of them looked at me. Their heads were so close together, they looked as if they might kiss, given another minute or two. I pushed Carl's hand off my thigh. "I'm with her," I wanted to say. But I couldn't. I couldn't claim her. Carl had more right to touch me in this bar, amid this crowd, than I had to touch Connie. I felt solid and heavy, rooted to the bar stool as if at any moment it might pull me through the floor and leave no visible sign that I had ever even been there, ever lived my life at all.

Carl followed my gaze. He poured himself another glass of beer from the pitcher on the bar and refilled my glass as well. I was losing count of my drinks. Was this my third? He took a sip, let it rest in his mouth and travel down his throat like brandy. He nodded over at Connie and Rick. "They're real special friends, aren't they?"

I felt the hair on the back of my neck prickle. A sense of deadly caution came over me, draped me like a second skin. A darkness seemed to fuse through the room. "Yeah," I said slowly, taking another sip of beer. "As a matter of fact, they are."

Carl leaned in close. I could feel his breath, stale with beer, against my cheek. "Does it piss you off?" he asked softly.

I took another sip of beer, then drained the glass. Carl poured me another. I wanted to throw it in his face. I wanted to walk down the bar and put my arm around Connie, pull her to me. I wanted to hold her, the way that Rick could hold her, in that easy sensuous way. As if I were entitled to. But I didn't. I just took hold of my glass again, to lift it to my lips. It trembled in my grip. "No," I said. "It doesn't."

Carl nodded, took a long slow sip of his beer. "I've been watching you," he said. His face was so close to mine that his hair, gray with middle age, brushed my forehead. "Trying to ignore them."

I pulled back as far as I could before I bumped into the person on the next stool. "I've been giving them space," I said.

Carl looked at me anxiously, worry creasing his brow like a stain. "Gee," he said. "I hope I didn't piss you off."

Go fuck yourself, I wanted to say. Get away from me. I wanted to push him off his stool, stride past him the length of the bar, grab Connie, and take her with me, out of the bar, back into our life together. But I didn't. I only put down my glass and got up. The floor tilted a little beneath my feet. I steadied myself on somebody's shoulder, summoned up my balance, and made myself walk over to where Connie stood. "I'm leaving," I said. I could hear my voice trembling. "I'm getting out of here." Connie looked at me with surprise, then back at Rick. I turned, left the bar, and stomped out into the snow. I could hear her footsteps behind me, slipping a little on the ice.

"Wait a minute," she said, catching up to me. "What's the matter?" Her words slurred. She reached for my shoulder and missed.

I couldn't even answer her. My jaw was so tense it ached. I felt full of fury. I wanted to hit something. I got to the truck and tried to open the door. It was locked. I wanted to put my fist through the glass.

"Hold on," Connie said, digging in her pocket. "I've got the key."

"Forget it," I said. "I'm walking home." I turned and left her in the snow beside the truck and made my way through the snow and slush on the sidewalks. I felt dead inside, like I wanted to cry but had run out of tears.

Connie was home when I got there, waiting on the front porch. "What the fuck is going on?" she said. I pushed past her, tried to open the door. It was locked too.

"Open the fucking door," I said.

"You open it," she said, throwing me the key.

I threw open the door and stomped back to my room, the place where I had set up my computer, the place I tried to call my own. But none of the doors shut tightly in this house. I had nowhere to go, no place that was safe to hide. I began to cry. I cried until I couldn't breathe. I cried myself to sleep that night after hours of fighting with Connie. The next morning my head ached. I couldn't quite remember everything that had happened. But I remembered the feeling, that helpless feeling of having to be someone else in public, someone not in love with Connie.

We fought all the time. The more we drank, the worse we fought. "Fine," I'd say. "Let's just break up."

"You always want to break up!" Connie would say. "You're always ready to give up."

It was true. I was always ready. All I could think was that if I could just get back to my cabin, things would be OK. I'd been wrong about this love. It wasn't blessed. It wasn't magic. I couldn't do it, and I didn't know why I had ever thought I could.

One day Connie brought home the business card of a therapist who had been hired to do workshops with the staff of the agency where she worked. "He's really good," she told me, watching me earnestly. Her eyes on mine were steady. "You could talk to him."

I could talk to him. Just the thought of talking to him made my stomach churn. I kept the card in my room, on top of my desk. Now and then I fingered it cautiously, as if just to touch it might suck me into therapy and never let me go. Deep inside I was afraid that if I went to see him, I'd have to come to grips with being crazy, that all this fighting was because I was insane, unable to live in the regular world, conduct normal relationships. I thought if I walked into his office I might never come out again. But I kept the card anyway, looked at it every single day, imagined dialing his number, giving myself over into his hands.

Connie and I fought about everything. We fought about things we'd despised in former lovers, about fears we didn't know enough to voice. And as we fought, we grieved everything we'd ever lost, every sacrifice we'd ever made. We grieved our pasts. And most of all we grieved the silence, the inability to tell anyone what was happening with us. "My god," we would say to each other after each fight, our eyes red, our faces bloated from tears. "If we were straight, we could go out and say to the neighbors, the waitress at the diner, people at work: 'I'm upset because I had a fight with my husband.' And everybody would understand. Everyone would empathize." But as it was, we could tell no one, and I used to pull my grief around me like a blanket, use it to cloak myself as I left the house, tried to hide within its folds, suffer my life in silence. If I were a man, I used to think, I could go to Mark's Brother's and order a drink and say: "Oh, *women!*" And every man there would understand. But we didn't have that consolation, and, in the end, as I watched my straight friends' relationships fall apart as easily as ripe fruit, I think that that was the thing that saved us.

My period that first month came like a geyser. My uterus felt like someone was wreaking havoc in there, ripping unused lining from the walls like wallpaper and hurling it out through the cervix. The days were dark and full of rain. I was so menstrual I felt like a gasoline tank waddling down the road—one misplaced match and I'd burst into flame, explode all over the street, detonate the entire town.

I wasn't pregnant. There was no baby inside me, no new life taking hold and kicking its way into the world. I wasn't pregnant.

It felt like my fault, somehow.

"You need to have a ritual," said Deborah, one of my colleagues as she bought me a martini that afternoon. Deborah was one of my best friends, one of the first people I'd come out to after I realized I was gay. "Something to mark your completeness as a couple." She clicked her glass with mine. I raised it to my lips, felt its burn in my throat. I thought it could never burn enough to take away the pain I felt inside. "You know," Deborah said. Her eyes were full of sympathy, soft and blue and completely surrounded by the folds of her skin. "How you don't need a baby to make you whole."

I took another sip of my drink and nodded glumly. "It should be the opposite of planting and growing," I said. "More like tearing something out and burning it."

Deborah nodded. "In a sense that's what menstruation does," she said.

I nodded again. The day dripped down around us, a faucet you couldn't close tight enough. Deborah touched my hand. "You could weed," she said.

Connie and I bought a bottle of champagne, lit the candles at the kitchen table, and toasted our two-ness. "To us," Connie said.

I touched her glass. "To us," I echoed. We drank, not taking our eyes from each other. To look away was a Slovenian curse. We took our rituals from many cultures. The champagne filled my mouth, warmed my throat as I swallowed. Eleven days until we could start the ovulation kit again. The champagne soothed my stomach, rippled through my limbs. This time it would work. I set down my glass, worked my finger around its rim. Somewhere deep inside I knew that that this time it would work. This time, for sure, I would get pregnant.

For a while we had considered asking male friends to give us sperm. I balked at spending the money on something that might never even work. Besides, there was so much sperm in the world. Did we really have to pay for it?

Every male friend became a potential donor. We drew up lists, tallying up our friends' good points (appearance, intelligence, etc.), then charting out the bad. "Count him out," one of us would say, drawing a line through a name. "High blood pressure." "Scratch him off the list," the other would say. "Manic depression in his family." Our male friends began to avoid us, crossing the street when they saw us coming. I found myself weighing every man I met in terms of sperm potential. "He's attractive," I'd think, shaking someone's hand. "I wonder what his sperm count is."

Sometimes men would volunteer information, nervously, it seemed to me. "I had a vasectomy," one friend told me, quite unsolicited. "But I'll be glad to put in a word to somebody else for you." Even our women friends became edgy around us. "My husband's not on your list, is he?" Deborah asked us, her jaw set. I wasn't sure which response would be more offensive. None of the men we knew felt comfortable just giving us sperm. "Why?" I asked Connie with annoyance. "They think nothing of spreading it all over the place, but when somebody actually wants to put it to use, they get all territorial!"

"I don't know what the big deal is," Patrick wrote to me. "If I weren't HIV positive, I'd give you mine." I couldn't think of anyone's sperm I'd rather have.

"What about Jesse?" Connie asked. Jesse was a gay man who worked with Connie down at human services. He had two children, both beautiful; he was HIV negative. He was intelligent and handsome. "He'd be great," Connie said, putting down her pen.

I thought about it. He was tall and dark-haired. He had always reminded me of Connie, had the same expansiveness about him, the same love of attention. Having his genes would be like having Connie's. Besides, he was a great father. Not that that mattered. All we wanted were his genes. "I'll talk to him at work," Connie said, "and see if he'll come talk to us."

We invited him over for lunch, sat him down in our kitchen while I served him chili and cornbread. I had spent all day making lunch. It felt like the old days of trying to impress boyfriends with my domesticity. I felt a little uncomfortable about it. It was the first time in a long time that I'd wanted something from a man. One of the best things about being a lesbian was that I felt at ease now with men, able to be friends with them, able to appreciate them for who they were without wanting them to be something they weren't. Now that was gone. The balance of power had shifted in their favor, and I didn't like the feeling.

He sat at the end of our kitchen table, big and male, eating our chili. I sat at the other end toying with my spoon. We talked about the weather, about Clinton, about the situation in Bosnia, till I couldn't stand it anymore. "What about the sperm?" I asked.

Jesse put down his spoon. "I think I'd want to be involved," he said. "I don't think I'd feel right about it otherwise." We all paused for a moment, the chili cooling in our dishes. "And I don't know if I want another child." He looked at us, his eyes large and dark. "I need more time to think about it."

After he left, Connie and I went for a walk. It was spring in Wellsboro. The snow was gone from the yards. Crocuses peeked out around front walks. Neighbors planted bulbs around their trees. The bite was gone from the air, replaced by a soft warmth, a gentle breeze. It hadn't occurred to me that the baby might have a father. I wasn't sure I wanted that. "What would it mean?" I asked Connie. "Does that mean his partner would want to be involved too?" I shivered, even in the warmth from the sun. Jesse was one thing. I could almost imagine him involved with our baby. But his partner was another. I didn't know him at all. Besides, four people, all with equal say in the baby's welfare, all making decisions, all having to consult each other first. It reminded me of living in cooperative households, deciding everything by consensus. It used to take hours just to determine whether the windows should be open or closed. Did I really want to take the already stressful situation of having a child and make it even more complicated?

"I can't eat anything," Margie said, pushing her pizza away and sitting back. She looked terrible, drawn and tired and, at four months, barely appeared to be pregnant. "The nausea just never stops."

"Margie lost fifteen pounds," Julie said. "The doctor threatened to put her in the hospital."

I looked at them uneasily. This was the first time we had met Margie and Julie face to face. They were a lesbian couple from a nearby city and they'd heard we were trying to get pregnant. They had gone through six months of insemination, and now they were finally pregnant. We were sitting at a Pizza Hut. It was packed with kids racing through the aisles, crowding the tables. I felt out of place. This was a family restaurant. We didn't belong here, Connie and I. I fingered my pizza. It was cold. I reached over and put my hand on Connie's thigh. She reached down and squeezed my fingers. A child pushed past me, putting its greasy hand on my arm for a moment to steady itself. I resisted the urge to shudder.

Across the table Margie was shaking Tums out of a roll. She put one hand on her chest. "You wouldn't believe the heartburn," she said confessionally, popping half the roll into her mouth. "I just can't wait till this is over." I watched her surreptitiously. I felt pity for her somehow. I would never say I couldn't wait till my pregnancy was over. This was my first and last shot at it. We'd already agreed that Connie was going to go next. I was going to enjoy my pregnancy, treasure every day of it. I took a sip of my diet Pepsi.

"What have they got you on?" Margie said, chewing her Tums. "Clomid?"

I looked at her blankly. "Nothing," I said. I felt uncertain, suddenly. Should I be *on* something?

Margie stared at me. "Nothing?" she said. Her eyes narrowed. "Huh."

"Margie was on Clomid," Julie said unperturbed as she poured herself another diet soda from the pitcher between us. "We had a friend doing this in Florida. She didn't have any money to waste, so she got the doctor to give her a shot of HCG." She reached across the table and refilled our glasses. "She got pregnant the first time."

Margie nodded and pushed the roll of Tums back into her pocket. "Get 'em to give you an HCG shot!" I glanced at Connie. I didn't even know what an HCG shot was. "Have they done a fertility workup on you?" Margie asked. I shook my head. She stared at me in horror. "But how do you know you're fertile?" she asked.

"Margie had hostile mucous," Julie said, placidly sipping her soda. "They finally did an intrauterine insemination and she got pregnant right away."

"Get 'em to do it intrauterine," Margie said, nodding her head. "Don't waste any money!"

"Intrauterine?" I said weakly.

"They take an extra long tube and stick it right into your uterus," Margie said. She shuddered vigorously. "It hurt like hell!"

"And it costs more too," Julie said, "because you have to get the semen washed. And that's, like, what? Another hundred dollars, hon?" she asked, turning to Margie.

I could feel the panic rising in my stomach. Maybe I wasn't even fertile. We could be throwing all this money away. We had only so much saved up. What if we ran out and then they found out I was infertile? I pushed my plate away. Now I felt as if *I* might be sick.

"With an HCG shot, your egg'll be right there," Margie said, shaking a few more Tums out of her roll.

I could feel myself sweating. The Pizza Hut seemed incredibly warm. The press of kids was overwhelming.

"We were committed to this," Julie said. "We didn't know if we'd have enough money, so the last time we were at the doctor's we stole angiocatheters in case we ran out of money and had to do it ourselves."

I nodded, dazed. What were they going to do—hold a man hostage and force him to jerk off? I imagined us kidnapping a man and forcing Dr. Gordon to come in and test him for HIV and genetic diseases. I imagined it on the evening news, the reporters interviewing Dr. Gordon as he came out, snapping his little bag shut. "They're two desperate women," he'd say, shaking his head. "Two good girls gone bad." The lesbian hostage crisis, they'd call it. We could get the lesbian avengers to come in and fight for us. Women everywhere would start forcing men to come at gunpoint. "Just empty it into this little jar," they'd say, "and you won't get hurt."

Margie shook her head. "I've got to go," she said, putting her hand back on her heart. Beside her, Julie swept up the check.

"We'll get this one," she said, pulling out her purse. "I know it's hard when you're going through the process."

Margie staggered to her feet, one hand on the small of her back. She stopped for a moment and laid a hand on my arm. "Are you using Ovuquick?" she asked.

"No," I said hesitantly. It sounded like something you might mix with milk.

"It's what the sperm bank recommends to test for your ovulation," Julie said, scrawling her signature across the check and tossing it down on the table. "It's supposed to be more accurate."

More accurate. I wondered what she meant. I mean, either you were ovulating or you weren't. There either was a blue line or there wasn't. Right?

"Wal-Mart will order it for you for only fifty dollars," Julie said. "Much cheaper than anywhere else."

"We'll call you," Margie said, "and see how you're making out."

We watched them leave. Connie exhaled sharply. "Wow," she said.

I looked at her. My stomach ached. I wondered, not for the first time, just what we were in for.

I'm Gay!!!

We paid an extra $15 that month for the privilege of making a special trip up to the airport, an hour and a half away, to pick up the sperm, because Federal Express didn't deliver to Remote Areas on Saturday, when my LH surge had decided to appear. After we got back, the tank of semen sat in the living room, its **HUMAN TISSUE** sticker cheerfully plastered down its side. I sat down on the couch and stared at it. Why was I even doing this? Who wanted a fucking kid? What was the fucking point? I wondered if Connie and I should talk about it, sit down and figure out once and for all whether we really wanted to keep this up. There was no support for us. We had no legal protection by way of marriage laws. No one supported us in this—not our parents, not our society. Even my best friend, Deborah, gave me a hard time about it. "It's really hard to write once you have a child," she said again and again, until I had to ask her not to. "It's hard enough to write now," she cautioned. In front of me the tank seemed to glow with its own light. Inside were semen, frozen midswim, packed in dry ice, waiting to be brought to life. I wondered why we were doing this. I thought of our friends' children, with their eating disorders and learning disabilities and criminal records, dropping out of school, holding up convenience stores, getting pregnant, attempting suicide. My stomach churned. My shoulders ached. The tank just sat there. It had no answers. It just was. Outside, birds fluttered through the trees, and squirrels sought nuts among the leaves. A chickadee hovered in the window for a moment, then disappeared. In front of me, the tank sat, squat and gray. I sighed and got up. I didn't know why we were doing it. We just were. I looked back at the tank. The hell with it.

⁘

Connie and I stayed in the closet for a year after we moved in together, seemingly invisible people in the center of town. I taught classes as if I were a paper cutout, someone with no life at all. While my colleagues regularly speckled their discussions with references to their spouses and children and relationships, I built a fortress around myself. I taught courses in creative writing, where students would read aloud terribly personal, often painful things that they had written. A moment of silence always followed. I ached to tell them something about myself, to respond to them from my heart. But empty spaces punctuated my presence. It was as if I'd led them to a cliff and then just pushed them over, without ever teaching them to fly.

Empty spaces filled my writing too. I was going to write great books. Now it seemed I had nothing to say. The computer screen blinked back at me, dark and empty. My writing hand felt leaden. I could barely make the pen move across the paper. Suddenly, everything was dangerous. What could I write about, when there were so many things I couldn't say?

I tried the words out in my head, trying to make them fit. *Gay. Lesbian. Bisexual.* None felt right. "Do you think I'm gay?" I asked Connie over dinner, not for the first time.

"What do you think?" she asked me seriously. To her credit she never laughed.

I had no idea what to think. All I knew was that the word *lesbian* scared the shit out of me. I hadn't told anyone but Roger about Connie. I had decided not to tell my mother. She doesn't want to be close to me anyway, I told myself. I didn't have to tell her anything.

Then one day I tried to show a film in class, *I Heard the Mermaids Singing.* The sound quality was bad; students heckled the screen when they couldn't understand the words. By the time we got to a scene in which two women kiss, I couldn't stand it anymore. One of the boys whistled in derision. "Whoa!" another one said, as if this might be a porno flick we were all going to watch together. With shaking hands I shut off the VCR and dismissed the class. I couldn't look at them as they left. My heart was beating too hard.

The next day one of the students came to my office and, shutting the door behind him, sat down beside my desk. Scott was a quiet student, an excellent writer. I knew from his writing that he was bright. His eyes blazed at me across the classroom, full of the things he had to say, even though he never opened his mouth in class. "I wanted to talk to you," he said, and then he stopped and looked down at his hands spread out across his knees. "I'm gay," he said, looking up at me. His eyes were huge, so dark brown they were nearly black. "And when you tried to show us that movie, I guessed that you are too." His face shone with expectation. His lower lip quivered, just a little. It was as if he'd given me a gift, laid it out on the desk between us, waiting to see if I'd accept it.

I took a breath, the kind that expands your entire rib cage. "Yes," I said. I cleared my throat and glanced at the door. It stayed resolutely closed. No one else was around. There was no way out of this. "I'm gay too," I said. And there it was, out there on the table. I glanced around me tentatively. Nothing had changed. I'm gay, I repeated, to myself. I'm gay. It felt like a load had lifted from my shoulders. Of course. I was *gay*!

"Oh, god," Scott said, exhaling explosively. "I've been here four years and I've never met anybody who was gay. Do you know any other students I might be able to talk to? Anybody I could get to know?"

The phone rang. When I picked it up, it was Connie, her voice a little breathless. "Hi," she said. I could almost feel her breath through the phone curling seductively around my ear.

"Hi," I replied, without even thinking about it, in that telephone voice reserved for lovers. I glanced at Scott. He smiled and looked away, as if to give me privacy. "I'll call you back," I told her. I looked at Scott after I hung up. "My lover," I said. My lover. I was talking to my lover. He nodded. While I was talking to a student, I got a call from my lover and I didn't have to pretend that it was anybody else. I felt light-headed from the freedom of it.

At home that night I felt reborn. I was gay. "I'm gay," I told Connie exultantly over dinner.

She nodded. "Congratulations."

Connie had always planned to go to grad school, to pursue a doctoral degree in anthropology. Originally, she had planned to go right after getting her bachelor's, but getting involved with me had put that on hold.

As we took a walk down our street one day, we talked about our future. Now that I knew I was gay, it seemed like the next thing we should do was leave. Wasn't that what gay people did, after all? Figure out they were gay and then pack up and move to San Francisco or New York or at least Northampton, Massachusetts? They didn't stay in God's Country.

We walked along our street, past tiny ranch homes that grew smaller and newer the farther we walked from the college. Four blocks was all it took to get to the end of any street in Mansfield. Could we really stay here, knowing we were gay? Could we even *be* gay in Mansfield? Not many people were, as far as I could tell.

"I don't know," I told Connie. "It just seems like we *should* go somewhere else." I thought of all the people I knew—the judge and the minister at the fitness center, the guy who changed our oil, our insurance agent. I thought fondly of my gym, our mountain bars, these streets where I could walk at any time of day or night, of the miles and miles of countryside that lay only a few minutes away, waiting for us to plunge deep into their depths, full of trees and streams and mountains and lakes. My tenure-track union job, which paid me more than anyone else I knew was earning. I liked it here. I liked the challenge of this mountain place. Even now that I was gay. It took guts to live here, didn't it? Not like all those women in Northampton, who were interviewed on *20/20*.

"I'm not ready for grad school right now, anyway," Connie said. "Let's not move right away. Let's stay here for a while."

I thought of Patrick, back in our little private college deep in the farmlands of Ohio and how he used to have to take a deep breath every single time he went into the cafeteria. I thought of how much courage it must have taken him just to live his life. He couldn't have hidden his sexuality. He wouldn't have. It was who he was. And all of a sudden I understood. I understood the marches, the support groups, the activism. "Patrick just lived his life," I said. "People harassed him all the time and he didn't care. He lived his life anyway."

Beside me Connie was silent. I thought of Patrick, striding into that cafeteria day after day after day, even when he must have wanted to run in the other direction. I thought of his dark blond hair and his deep brown eyes, how he'd confided to me as we stood in line how much easier it was when he didn't have to walk in there alone. I could be like Patrick. I could walk into that cafeteria too. I didn't have to eat alone in the safety of our dining room. Patrick had survived. I could too.

When we got home from our walk, I got out a bumper sticker I'd hidden away some time before, "Action = Life, Silence = Death," a pink triangle on each end. I looked at the back of my truck, bare except for a fairly innocuous Amnesty International bumper sticker. I looked at Connie. The pink triangles burned my hands. I'd never seen one on any car in God's Country. "I'm doing it," I said. I stepped forward, pasted it on the back of my truck, then stepped back and looked at it. The pink triangles glistened in the sunlight, slightly crooked there on the back of my truck. My stomach went a little soft. I wondered, suddenly, where this truck might take me now. Connie watched me nervously.

"What if I don't want to come out the way you do?" she asked me. Her voice shook a little.

I put my arm around her, there in front of our house in Mansfield, in full view of our neighbors. "I don't know," I told her, tightening my grip around her waist. My heart beat a steady rhythm in my chest. "We'll just have to wait and see."

—❦—

I got my period a week or so after the insemination, as the flash floods from Hurricane Chris tore through the area, submerging the fields. Hurricane Chris. What a wimpy name for a storm, I thought, not like Agnes or Camille. I went to sleep and dreamed that a crowd of people was storming the house. We tried to lock the door but because of the rain none of our doors and windows shut properly anymore. As the crowd kicked away the screens and tore the doors from their hinges, I realized there was no way we could ever make the house secure, we could never be safe from them, no matter what.

Getting a Double Dose of It

So what's it like, living there?" my old friend Jill asked me on the phone. I knew Jill from my days as an organizer. Those days seemed like a different world now, like they belonged to someone else's history, back when I was fresh out of college, with long wild hair and a penchant for peasant blouses, sleeping with men, and organizing other people for better lives while having virtually no life of my own.

"OK, I guess," I said. I felt hesitant confiding to her. I knew she lived in a community of lesbians, went to lesbian parties, lesbian restaurants, lesbian bookstores. I wasn't sure she knew what it was really like here, in this forgotten mountain range. I twisted the phone cord around my fingers. "I don't really have any friends, though, other than Connie."

Jill laughed, that wry mocking laugh that I used to love when it was directed at somebody else. "Well," she said dryly. "You'd better get some."

I wanted to come out to Deborah. She had wild curly hair and deep lines around her eyes, and she'd tried to make friends with me before, but I'd always shrugged off her attempts, burrowing deep inside myself to avoid giving her any clues to who I really was. Now I watched her walking through the halls, her full skirts and shawls billowing out around her. She could be a friend, I thought to myself. I heard Jill's mocking laugh and thought of Patrick throwing back his head and striding through the door to the cafeteria. I could do it.

I invited Deborah and her husband, Wayne, over for dinner with Connie and me. I didn't come out to them with words; instead, we just made no attempt to hide our relationship. The evening went smoothly, even easily. Maybe this wouldn't be so hard, after all, I thought. I hadn't even had to say anything. Deborah and I began to read each other's work, the first overture of friendship. I wrote seven more stories that summer, all with lesbian protagonists in small towns in rural Pennsylvania. "Gee," Deborah said, after she read them. "If you ever publish them in a collection, people will think there's some small town in Pennsylvania that's just chock full of lesbians!"

She used the word. *Lesbian.* I hadn't used it about myself yet. I hadn't actually said it to anyone. And I hadn't said it to anyone at the college. As far as anyone else knew, I had no life at all, except for a couple of pink triangles fading into the dust on the back of my truck. It wasn't really coming out, I sensed, to sport a symbol recognizable only to other gay and lesbian people.

———

Aline studied me, her eyes narrowed and her scissors poised. I'd gone to her for a haircut because every woman in town with a good short haircut told me they went to her, but now that I was in her studio I wasn't so sure. It was crowded with women, all in their mid-fifties, all with hair molded into helmets around their heads, lacquered with spray. My image in the mirror looked startlingly out of place in Aline's salon, surrounded by pink hair curlers and advertisements for Retin-A cream, all autographed by Aline's mother— "This really works! Ask me!!" she had written. I stole a glance in the mirror at Aline's mother. Her face was a mask of wrinkles. "How do you want it?" Aline asked me, drawling all the words together till they sounded like one.

"Oh," I mumbled, avoiding her eyes in the mirror. "Short." My stomach tightened. I wondered whether I would recognize myself when she was through.

Aline stepped back, satisfaction stamped on her face like a brand. "Finally," I imagined her thinking, "something besides a wash and set!" Behind us the women sat beneath driers and watched *The Prince of Tides* on her VCR. I wondered if, when they died, wash and sets would become a thing of the past, while the grandmothers of the future sprayed up their high hair. Aline put down her scissors and reached for the clippers, which were off to one side and covered, I imagined, with dust. She gunned them up beside my ear. "But not too short," I said. It was too late. The clippers had already cut a swathe through my hair as if it were a wheat field. I sat back in my chair and tried to relax, strapped in for the ride. A woman behind us turned up the sound in time to hear Nick Nolte describe someone as a fucking asshole.

"Oh." One of the women shuddered. "I just hate it when they talk like that."

All the women nodded in unison. Close to my face, intent on her job, Aline pursed her lips. "I've never understood it," she said, guiding the clippers along the edge of my sideburns. "Why can't they just say something else besides THAT word?" The other women clucked in agreement. Aline leaned in closer. "Why can't they just say: That idiot asshole?" she said. "Or something like that." Her breath was hot on my face and smelled faintly of wet dog.

"My daughter-in-law talks like that," one woman said, fumbling to adjust her head inside the tank of the hair dryer. "Every other word."

Aline swiveled me around so sharply I nearly flew out of the chair. She lifted the scissors off the counter, spun them around on her fingertips. "I slapped a girl's face once for saying that in front of me," she said, pulling the hair off my forehead with a comb and brandishing the scissors dangerously close to my eyes. "She never said it to me again." She closed the blades around a lock of my hair, which instantly turned into history. It was a lock I'd liked.

Something happened on the television and there was a moment of silence while it registered with everybody. "Have you seen this movie before, Louise?" Aline asked me. I told her I had, as a matter of fact. Connie and I had watched it the week before. "How does it end?" she asked.

I hesitated. Was this a trick question? Would I be punished for withholding information? My dedication to art won out. "I can't tell you that," I said.

The salon was silent for a moment. I wondered whether it would all be over soon. No one even breathed. Then Aline clapped me on the shoulder so hard I could feel the bruise beginning to form. "Good girl," she said. She winked at the others. "She's not going to give it away."

"She's a good girl," her mother said, nodding in agreement.

A good girl. I fingered the cape Aline had tied around my neck. It was so tight I could hardly breathe.

Behind me the women were intent on the screen again. "That really is her son in real life, you know," one of them said, nodding at the character playing Barbara Streisand's son.

"No," said Aline's mother, sweeping feverishly at the pile of hair around my chair, a mix of the last three customers. "Who's his father?"

"Elliot Gould," Aline said, misting my hair with her spray bottle.

One woman snorted. "So he got a double dose of it," she said. "Poor kid." She glanced around at the rest of us. "What's her name in the movie?" she asked. "Epstein, Goldstein—it's a Jewish name."

I kept my eyes on the mirror, while Aline dusted me off with an old towel that had obviously seen a lot of necks that day.

Aline's mother stopped sweeping to study the screen again. "Look at that nose," she said.

I didn't say anything, just dug in my pockets for the money to pay Aline. My neck felt naked, raw to the touch. I imagined a gun was trained on it, ready to go off at any time.

⚬⚭⚬

Connie and I sat in our truck parked on the side of the road and stared straight ahead. "Could you mirror what I just said?" Connie asked me. Her words were slow and careful, her jaw set like iron. I studied the windshield, feeling resistance deep inside my stomach, as if I were eight years old again, folding my arms and sticking out my lower lip. I didn't want to mirror her. We'd been arguing for an hour, starting at the house and continuing as we drove. We were supposed to be meeting Wayne and Deborah for brunch. Now we were pulled over on the side of the road trying to use the techniques we'd learned in couples counseling. I knew we had to do it. I knew we had to get to the core of this fight now, or we'd never make it through the brunch. I gripped the steering wheel tightly in my hands. Outside, a soft wind stroked the trees, combed through their branches slowly, shaking out the leaves. I sighed.

"You said . . ." I repeated her arguments back to her, keeping my voice as level as possible. It was a draining, tedious process, but it kept me from using the time while she was talking to formulate my own arguments. It meant I had to listen to her. This was the way we fought now. Gone were the screaming irrational bouts of the past. Now we fought in measured careful tones, not stopping till we'd said everything we needed to say. We dealt with issues as soon as they came up, no matter where we were. We fought at the automatic teller machine, in the Chinese restaurant, in an aisle of the supermarket. Oh, great, I'd think each time. We have to go through this again? But every fight was a little less scary than the last. The quicker we got to it, the quicker it was over. And anything was better than those fights, when I'd had no idea what might come out of my mouth from one moment to the next.

A car pulled off to the side of the road behind us. Deborah appeared at the window, peering at us worriedly. "We saw you sitting here," she said. "We thought you might have broken down."

"Oh, we're fine," I said. "We're just finishing a fight." It sounded like it might have been a meal we'd sat down to. I glanced at Connie. "We're almost done."

"OK," Deborah said, backing up. She looked apologetic.

I turned back to Connie. "All right," I said. "Where were we?"

———

Three times a week I worked out at the fitness center in Wellsboro that was owned by the same family that owned everything else in town. It was the only fitness center in the county, and the lack of competition showed. For $300 a year you could work out with anybody else in town who could afford it in a tiny room crowded with mediocre weight machines and trotters. I alternated between hating the little room with its grimy facilities and enjoying the company of the other members. Doc, an elderly man who'd been born and raised in Wellsboro, went there nearly every day, more to talk than anything else. He used to pick a machine and sit on it, breathing heavily, holding court to the people waiting patiently for him to move. I'd been working out with him for two years. I felt a certain fondness for him. Doc was a fixture at this fitness center. At least he was hanging out here, not down at the diner with the other men his age, packing his arteries full of cholesterol. Today he was comfortably ensconced on the biceps machine, both hands planted on his knees.

"How ya doin', Doc?" asked the only other person in the room, a young guy working his abdominals on the incline. I sat on the floor, stretching out my calf muscles, feeling them between my hands, solid and strong.

Doc leaned back, rolling his tongue from one side of his mouth to the other like he was working a wad of tobacco. "Well, I'm worried about Clinton," he said. "What with this gays in the military stuff."

I froze on the floor, my hands around my leg. My muscles suddenly felt leaden, as if they might be pinning me down instead of making me strong.

"They can't fight," Doc said, slapping his tiny wizened thigh. "I was in the navy in World War II," he went on, "and we had one of 'em on the ship with us once." He glanced around the room at us, as if to make sure he had our full attention. "We took care of him," he said. His laugh was almost a cackle. "He couldn't cut it." Doc stretched back against the machine. "None of them could cut it."

I stayed where I was on the floor, bent over my body as if I might be able to disappear, if I could only stretch out far enough. My heart beat its ragged steady beat. I've got to say something, I thought. I've got to. Over at the biceps machine Doc coughed a cough that went on just a little too long. He wheezed at the end of it. The other man in the room looked at me. Our eyes met for a moment. Neither of us said anything. "Pansies," Doc said over in his corner of the room, holding his chest. I got up from the floor, my heart pounding. I've got to say something, I thought. I'm gay, I said in my head. I willed myself to say it out loud. I'm gay. I'm gay. My tongue felt swollen in my mouth. I looked at Doc, sitting on his machine, staring contemplatively at the floor. "Goddamned fairies," he said. His breathing was heavy. We all stayed where we were, surrounded by images of ourselves in the mirrors around the room. Say it, my head urged me, but I couldn't do it. I picked up my towel, left the weight room, and went into the locker room to shower. Go back in there, I told myself, toweling off and putting my clothes back on. Go tell him. I studied my face in the mirror above the sink. It regarded me solemnly, short hair sticking up in every direction. I looked like a kid. I picked up my bag and went out into the hall. Go back in there, I told myself again, almost pleading. I could hear Doc's voice coming from the weight room. He'd moved on to a new subject now. I stood there for a moment, listening to his voice, talking about the air show up at the mall.

Suddenly, a new voice sounded in my head. He's just an old man. You don't have to tell him, it said. Just let it go. I went back outside, started up the truck, and pulled out onto the road.

Turn around, the first voice said. Go back there and tell him you're gay. That's all you have to say.

What's the point? said the other voice. It won't change anything.

I didn't turn around. I kept on driving, all the way back home. I felt sick inside. I thought about it all night. I could barely sleep. The next day I got up, dressed in my workout clothes, and went back to the gym. The fitness center was empty. I worked out anxiously, stealing furtive glances at the door. When he came in I would tell him. As soon as he came in, I'd say: Doc, about yesterday . . .

The door opened and another guy came in, a dentist I'd known from working out here as long as I'd known Doc. "Hey, Louise," he said, seeing me. He walked over to one of the machines, put his towel down on it, and strapped on his weight belt. His biceps bulged. "Did you hear about Doc?" he asked me.

My whole body felt cold. "What about Doc?" I asked him slowly.

"He died last night," the dentist said. "Full cardiac arrest." He snapped on his weight-lifting gloves and rubbed his hands together. "That'd be the way to go," he said, looking over at me. He screwed some weights onto the bar and stretched his body out along the bench. "Fast. No messing around." He lifted the bar in his hands, grunting with the effort.

I got up and left the room. Doc was dead. My throat ached. Doc was dead, and I'd never had the chance to tell him how I felt. I went outside and started up the truck. Wildflowers bloomed along the road. Doc was dead. I'd never said what I'd needed to say. I'd never have another chance.

"I've got to go see my mother," I told Connie, furiously throwing clothes into my duffle bag.

"Are you going to tell her?" Connie asked, watching me go through the medicine cabinet and pack up the essentials.

"I don't know." I had no idea what I would do. I only knew suddenly that I had to go. I threw my duffle bag in the back of my pickup truck and drove the three hundred miles west, to my hometown in Chardon, Ohio.

I was there three days before I could get up the nerve to broach the subject. She's nearly eighty, a voice in my head kept insisting. Give it up. She'll never come around. You can't expect her to. But I knew I had to. I couldn't talk to her at all now. How much worse could it be? I'd taken her to a movie, then out to dinner in a vegetarian restaurant in the Coventry section of Cleveland, a place I'd been before but now seemed to be seeing for the first time. Women with short haircuts and jean jackets populated the restaurant. The male servers wore double earrings. My mother and I made small talk over our tofu burgers. I couldn't make myself say anything. Ask me, I found myself thinking, staring at my mother wordlessly. Ask me if I'm gay. Please, just *ask* me. If all I had to do was nod, I thought, I could do this. I could come out.

I was driving back from the restaurant when my mother cleared her throat. Maybe now, I thought, tension mounting in my throat. Maybe she'll ask me now. "If only you'd meet someone there," she said of the place that she must envision as a vast wasteland, sparsely populated by people without names or faces, for all I'd told her about it. "Some nice man."

The road flashed by, punctuated by the lights from passing cars.

Outside all was darkness, heavy and languid against the glass that held us in. My heart beat so fast I thought my mother might be able to hear it. My throat ached from the pressure. "Actually," I said, "I have met someone." I stared straight ahead through the glass.

My mother shifted in her seat. I could feel her caution; I could smell it on her, sniff it out as if we were two animals, warily circling each other in the darkness of some jungle. "Oh, good," she said carefully. "Who is it?"

I kept on driving, my fingers knotted around the wheel so tightly I thought for a moment I'd never be able to let go when we got back home. "It's someone you know," I said. My mouth felt dry. The lights of the oncoming cars seared my eyes.

For a moment we were silent, there in the darkness of the car. Then my mother spoke. "Is it Connie?" she asked softly.

Inside me, something let go, just let go, and I could feel everything rushing to the surface, washing from my pores like blood. My heartbeat slowed, my hands relaxed on the wheel. I thought, for one brief moment, that I might lose my grip altogether, send us flying off the road, careening off into the night. "Yes," I said. "Yes." The word felt like a dove, leaving my tongue as it might a branch, searing off into the air, bearing a message in its beak. "It's Connie."

"I had a suspicion," my mother said, nodding to herself.

"I've been wanting to tell you," I said. I could feel the words spilling out of me. "I've been wanting to be honest with you. I didn't feel like I could even talk to you before." I stole a look at her. Her profile was soft, in the darkness of the car, nestled into the collar of her coat. "You don't care?" I asked her. I could hardly believe my good fortune.

My mother didn't look at me, just kept on staring straight ahead. "There's more than one kind of happiness in the world," she said.

I felt something melt inside me, just like that. I reached for her hand and held it the rest of the drive home.

When we pulled into the garage, I turned the engine off, and we sat there for a moment. Then my mother looked at me. "But what will happen," she asked, "when you part ways?"

I didn't understand. "What do you mean?" I asked her. "We're not going to part ways."

"But I thought Connie wanted to go to grad school," my mother said. "What will happen then?"

I looked at her. There was the slightest line, between her eyes. "Well," I said. "I'll go with her." My mother didn't say anything. Her hands were clasped in her lap. "It's like we're married," I told her carefully.

"We'd better go in," she said. "Dad will wonder why we're out here."

I helped her out of the car and shut the garage door solidly behind us. Inside I felt light as the night air. We walked together back toward the house. The stars glistened overhead, bright against the blackness of the sky. I felt as if they held my soul, as if everything I was had spun out into the distant corners of the world, fused with the stars and the trees and the night around us. My mother was silent as we walked. I took her hand and squeezed it. Her fingers were limp in mine. If her silence touched me in any way, pressed just ever so slightly against the edges of my joy, I put it from me. "There's more than one kind of happiness," I repeated to myself. I took a deep breath in. The night air filled my lungs. I could feel myself expanding. This happiness is mine, I thought. That night I slept for hours in the bedroom where I had spent my childhood, in the farthest corner of the house, away from the rest of the family, and in the morning I packed my duffle bag again and began the drive back home.

She Should Keep It in the Bedroom

W e have no reason to believe you're infertile," Dr. Gordon told me patiently over the phone. I had called him to request an infertility workup after the second insemination failed.

I hung up and paced the kitchen. Outside a light rain fell. A fog lifted off the street. A woman from up the hill sauntered down the sidewalk with her toddler. They held hands beneath their umbrella. I watched them through the window as they faded from view, a vision of what I wanted to be. Except, of course, that she belonged here. Except that she deserved a child.

"Listen," Connie said. "We just have to trust them." She put her hand on my arm. "Remember?" she said. "Didn't we decide that?" I looked down at her hand. She was right. We had decided that. We had talked about this over and over. It was true—we had no reason to suspect infertility, but deep inside I was convinced. We were throwing our money away. Inside, my eggs felt like party goers at the end of an evening, cheerfully donning their coats and hats and heading out the door. "See ya!" they'd be calling, pulling the door shut behind them and putting their arms around each other on their way down the steps. Meanwhile, I was left inside an emptying room, endlessly mopping up, watching the ranks thin out, waiting for the moment when I was in there all alone, with no more eggs to party with. I knew we had to trust them. I wanted to trust them. I wanted to stop worrying about it. There was enough in this process to worry about without obsessing about infertility.

Connie moved behind me and massaged my shoulders gently. "Why don't we set a deadline?" she said. Her hands worked my muscles. I could feel myself surrendering to them. "After three more tries we'll insist on a fertility workup."

I closed my eyes. For three more months we wouldn't worry about it. I took a deep breath. "OK. It's a deal." I could feel something in me lift. We'd been granted a reprieve. We looked at each other for a moment, then Connie pushed back her chair. After all, our lives had other aspects besides the race for pregnancy. We had dinner to make, for example. The house needed to be cleaned. That load of whites just kept getting larger. The endless details of life kept mounting up, no matter how much our quest to become parents kept crowding them out. The chores were all still there, just beneath the surface, threatening at any moment to break apart, really screw everything up, if we didn't pay enough attention to them.

During the next insemination Dr. Gordon showed me the sperm under his microscope. "If you'll look closely and just adjust this knob right here," he said, guiding my hand, "it will bring the sperm into focus."

I peered through the microscope, turned the knob a quarter turn, and waited patiently for the blur to clear. Margie and Julie had suggested that we ask to see the sperm, to make sure of their motility. "Besides," Margie said. "It looks neat." I wasn't expecting much. To be honest, I didn't really believe in our sperm. I didn't really believe that anything was in that little vial, nothing capable of creating life, at any rate. I turned the knob another quarter turn and there they were, millions of tiny sperm, squirming around the petri dish like bugs that couldn't get off their backs. "Wow," I said aloud. I couldn't help myself. They were so much more active than I'd imagined them. Up till now I hadn't been entirely sure that they were moving at all.

"You've probably got eighty or ninety percent motility there," Dr. Gordon said. He sounded proud, as if he were somehow responsible.

I looked back at the sperm. Some were actually moving across the slide as I watched, from one end to the other. I began to feel hopeful. If they could move like that under a bright light, think what they could do in the dark and secret caverns of my body. Millions wriggled around in circles, flopping like beached fish. "There's a lot of them!" I said despite myself.

Dr. Gordon laughed and put his hand on my arm. "That was so innocent!" he said in a tone of pure appreciation. I looked at him out of the corner of my eye as I stepped back to let Connie take her turn. Dr. Gordon probably thought it was the first time I'd ever seen sperm. I fought the urge to set him straight. Let him think he was the first person to get sperm between my legs. What did I care? "I'll leave the room so you can get undressed," he said, removing himself discreetly.

Connie took my hand. "Look at them," she said, awed. She looked back at me and squeezed my hand. "They're really moving!"

I took off my clothes, climbed back up on the table, and spread my little paper napkin across my thighs just in time for Dr. Gordon to come back into the room. He flipped to a new page on his clipboard and laid it on the sink, ready for his next notation. He turned to the table, pulled the stirrups out, took my feet, and carefully wedged them into place. I watched passively. I'd given up trying to move my limbs myself. Apparently once I was on this table, my body was his. He put my feet into the stirrups, he spread my knees apart, he opened up my vagina, and god knows he knew his way around my cervix. He took a syringe, aspirated the semen from the vial, pulled up his little stool, and bent toward his work. Connie stroked my hair and looked deep into my eyes. We'd given up having her do the inseminating. Who actually got the sperm inside me seemed irrelevant. I wanted Connie up with me. She took my hand and squeezed it in hers. Her touch was like a benediction. "I love you," she whispered.

"I love you too," I whispered back. The fluorescent lights buzzed. I could feel Dr. Gordon slipping in his speculum, turning the screws. Connie's eyes held mine as determinedly as if we had been toasting.

"There we go," he said. I imagined him whistling, dusting off his hands, another good day's work completed, another batch of motile sperm sent off on its expedition. He brought my knees together gently. Connie squeezed my hand.

"I'll just leave you alone now," he said, closing the door behind him gently. Connie bent forward and kissed my lips. Her tongue touched my teeth. I caught hold of her hand and guided it between my legs.

"Come on," I said, pressing her hand into place. "Make me pregnant."

It was thirty minutes before anybody told us that it was time for us to go.

Branches swollen with green leaves waved triumphantly along the bike path, leaning out to brush our faces as we walked along it holding hands. The smell of them clung to the air, reminding us that the summer was nearly over, about to surrender to the fall, the start of our second year of living together. Crickets hummed along the trail. Beside us in the creek bed turtles sunned on a fallen tree. Connie was tall and strong; her hand held mine as if she had a right to. Now and then, when someone else appeared on the path, she dropped it. Each time I felt a pain in my heart, searing my chest.

Connie glanced at me as a few kids tore past on bicycles. "I'm sorry," she said.

I didn't answer her at first, just watched the squirrels rustling through the leaves in the woods beside the path. Clouds arched through the air. A light breeze touched our faces. I turned to Connie. "I don't want you to let go," I said.

"I know," Connie said. We walked along in silence for a while, feeling the sun burn itself into our skin. "I don't know what to do about it," she said.

I looked at her. Her eyes were green in the sunlight, set off by her tan. "I just wonder what you'll do," I said carefully, "when we have a baby with us." A bird trilled as if carried away by its own song. "I just want to know," I said, "if you're going to claim us."

We stopped for a moment. A toad hopped out in front of us, then quickly turned back, losing itself in the leaves beside the path. "I don't know how to do this," Connie said, reaching for my hand again. A couple appeared on the trail ahead, coming toward us. I held her hand tight. I could feel her fingers tremble as they walked past. She didn't let go. "I want to be able to claim you," she said.

We walked along in silence for a while. "Straight people do things in a certain order," I said, thinking out loud. "They get married first, in a public ceremony. They declare their commitment in front of everybody. They put on rings. Then they buy a house. They get some stability. Then they have kids."

We looked at each other for a moment. A frog sang in the creek beside us, then stopped as suddenly as it started. "There's a process to it," Connie said.

"There's a process for a reason," I said. It made sense somehow. We turned to each other at the same time. "Let's get married."

As a child Connie had had visions of getting married, walking down the aisle in her long white dress, her bouquet gripped firmly in her hands, leaving in her wake a diaphanous trail of white, a wash of admiring onlookers, the pews packed with family and friends. I, on the other hand, was barely eight years old when I announced at a summer camp that I would never get married *or* have any kids. There was a moment of silence from the other children, an instant of held breath. The camp counselor, an athletic young woman with deeply tanned skin and short blond hair, looked at me admiringly. "Good for you," she'd said.

I lived my life on the presumption that I would never marry. I notified every boyfriend in advance that this was temporary. I don't need that shit, I consoled myself through grade school, through high school, through college. I'd watched my mother deferring to my father through the years. My life is more than that, I thought. I'm going to be a writer—not somebody's wife. Only with Sadie had I had a sudden vision of a *life* together, as we mixed our gin and tonics in her kitchen or cooked Thanksgiving dinner for our friends. The vision was so clear that for a moment I could taste it on my tongue, mixing with the gin, acrid as communion. I gazed at it longingly, shimmering before my eyes for a moment before it disappeared.

But now, after a year of living with Connie, I knew that this was what I did want. Marriage *and* kids.

"I don't want to invite my family," Connie said, as we went though our invitation list. We were sitting at our dining room table, the cats asleep in our laps, the setting sun sending its last light shimmering through the window that overlooked our backyard. Connie's parents were Irish Catholic, so Irish Catholic that they'd had thirteen children before her mother had had to have a hysterectomy. I could picture her uterus caving in on itself from the effort. Her parents had a long tradition of exiling their children, particularly their daughters, for transgressing the family dictates. Connie's favorite sister had earned the first sentence by announcing at the age of eighteen, when Connie was eight, that she was a lesbian. Their parents forbade Connie to see her again. She was uneasily reclaimed into the fold when she renounced her lesbianism and married a man, was born again, and had two children. When Connie herself left home at age eighteen to join a Pentecostal church, her mother threw open the door dramatically. "If you walk out that door," she said, "don't ever come back." When Connie renounced the church in favor of her lesbianism four years later, she went back home. A mutual silence assured her reception. Connie never mentioned being gay, and her parents turned a blind eye to the various girlfriends that she brought home with her for the holidays.

"OK," I said. "Don't invite them." I went through my list, adding names and addresses. I was confident of my mother. She would come. I knew she would come. Finally, I was getting married, the one thing she'd always seemed to want for me. I wasn't nearly as sure about the rest of my family. I wanted to invite them, but I didn't know if they would come. Unlike Connie's family, we didn't have dramatic confrontations, only silences. My older brother disappeared to Canada to avoid the draft in 1968 when I was eight. The waters closed above his head with barely a ripple. If there was talk in the town about it, there was none in our house.

"But I want to invite them," Connie said, putting down her pen and looking at me.

"OK," I said. "Invite them."

Connie wrote a letter to every member of her family and enclosed it with the wedding invitation. I just put my invitations in the envelopes alone and sent them off to my family with no explanation. That was my coming out—an invitation to my wedding. It reminded me, a little uneasily, of when I had first announced my vegetarianism to them when I was twenty, over Thanksgiving dinner.

I waited for my mother to mention the invitation on the phone. She didn't. Connie waited for her parents to call and confront her. They didn't. We regarded one another uneasily, across our silent telephone. "What now?" Connie asked.

I shrugged. I didn't know. It felt like we'd just lobbed a ball into the other court, and our opponent had just walked away. We waited a few weeks and checked off the RSVPs as they began to come in from our friends, if not our families. Finally, I called my mother. "Are you coming to my wedding?" I asked her.

"I don't know," she said. "I've been very busy lately."

We had a hundred things to do before the ceremony. We had to order rings, arrange the flowers, and buy alcohol and paper plates and cups. We had to buy our dresses, though we'd also discussed twin tuxedos. We contacted a real estate agent at the same time and started looking at houses. We looked at houses right up until the day before the ceremony. We began to contact doctors about insemination. Everything was starting to come together.

"We want to order flowers for a—uh, ceremony that we're having," Connie said. I didn't say anything, just stayed where I was, a little behind her, a little out of sight of the woman at the florist shop. A Ford pickup in the parking lot bore a bumper sticker. I could see it through the window. It said, "Buy American. Bring them to their Japa-knees." I drew a little closer to Connie.

The woman took us over to her books and began to pull them out. "What kind of ceremony is it?" she asked, opening a book.

I felt myself freeze. Connie took a breath. "It's for a wedding," she said. Her voice trembled. "Our wedding."

I waited, resisting the impulse to turn and run for the door. The woman looked up at us and smiled. "I only meant formal or informal," she said gently.

"Oh!" we said in unison. "Informal," Connie said. "Formal," I said. And all three of us laughed at the same time.

I called my mother every week or so as the wedding date approached, to ask whether she was coming. Her response was always the same.

"I haven't had a minute to think about it," she said. My older sister was expecting a baby, and I knew my mother wanted to be there when she gave birth. Still, I was conscious of an ache deep inside me, as if a wound had healed badly and left a lump of scar tissue that never really went away.

"Mom," I said. I took a deep breath. I had months of therapy under my belt, months of practicing assertive wording, but it didn't make it any easier. "I perceive you would be taking this a lot more seriously if I were marrying a man," I said.

"Well, yes," she snapped. "I probably would."

I took another breath and reached deep down inside myself and screwed up all my courage. "Mom," I said. My voice caught a little, climbing from my throat. "Mom, when you say that, I feel . . . I feel . . ." I started to sweat, my heart began its steady drumbeat, gradually picking up its tempo. Even after months of rehearsing my feelings it wasn't getting any easier. "How you feel is not important," my mother used to tell me again and again and again as I was growing up. "Other people are what's important." I took a deeper breath. My hand, clammy with sweat, slipped on the receiver. "Well," I said. "I feel, I guess I feel—angry." I closed my eyes. There. I'd said it. There it was—my anger with my mother—out on the table. I opened my eyes again and took a firmer grip on the receiver.

"Well, *don't*," my mother said.

And that was it. I stared at the telephone. One thing I'd never learned from therapy was what to do with the other person's response. I guess that's not the point.

My parents didn't come to our wedding. Neither did Connie's. I called my brother in Canada to invite him but told him almost in the same breath that I didn't expect him to come all the way out. Connie did the same with her sister in Texas. She turned to me after hanging up the phone. "I told her I knew she wouldn't be able to come," she said. She looked puzzled. "Now why did I say that? I'd expect her to fly out for anybody else's wedding."

It was hard to take our own wedding seriously at times. Though it felt more real and more crucially important to me than any other wedding I'd ever been invited to, I simultaneously felt like apologizing for it, adding the footnote: "Of course, it isn't really *legal.*" On the invitations we had put *commitment ceremony*, not *wedding*. As I looked down at our copy now, I wondered why. Why was it so hard for me to claim this wedding? And if I couldn't fully claim it, how could I expect my family to?

My father never responded to the invitation. I never called him on it. I thought about it every day, then put it at the bottom of my list of priorities. I knew in the back of my mind that if I let it go long enough, eventually it would be too late. And, eventually, it was.

On May 15, 1993, three years after we met, we exchanged vows before seventy friends and family members at a ceremony officiated by our couples counselors. I liked the irony of it—the '90s version of shamans and priests. Or maybe the gay and lesbian version.

Two members of my family did come. My oldest brother, Bob, drove from Ohio with one of his sons, a twenty-one-year-old man I realized I didn't even know. I felt a swell of pride when I saw them. I did have family after all. Mrs. Kovac, the eighty-year-old who'd lived across the street while I was growing up, came on the arm of her daughter, Carol. "Your mom wanted to come," Carol told me the moment she saw me. I turned away. I didn't want to believe her. I was convinced my mother could have come, if only she had wanted to.

I invited nearly all my department colleagues—and all of them came. Friends came from as far away as Boston and Milwaukee. I hadn't even realized that we had so many friends between us, but we did, nearly all a product of coming out. All seven of Connie's brothers came, if none of her sisters, all with their wives or girlfriends. Her parents didn't come, and in the end she only felt relief. "Mom and Dad said they disapproved," one brother told her seriously, taking her aside just before the ceremony began, "but that they understood if the other kids wanted to go." My emotions fought with each other. As happy as I was with the people who were there, I still felt full of grief at the absences. When we lit a candle for those friends and family who were unable to attend, I couldn't stop myself from remarking caustically, "Of course, whose fault was that?" One of my colleagues laughed appreciatively, even as I cursed myself for allowing sarcasm to intrude on one of the most important moments of my life. Some people, after all, really hadn't been able to attend. My sister, for instance, happened to be in labor throughout the ceremony, surely a valid excuse. Those friends and family who were there overflowed the house, spilled out onto the porch, and down into the yard. I wondered when it would be enough for me, when I'd just be able to be happy with what I had.

When I slid the ring on Connie's finger, I almost expected it not to fit, though we'd tried them on a dozen times before this moment. But it slid on smoothly, and after Connie had slipped on mine we looked at each other. Her eyes shone. A breath of wind moved the wind chimes gently on the porch. The breeze ruffled the curtains, filled the room with clean spring air. Crying, we kissed each other, then turned to the rest of the room. A friend who'd spent the morning programming our new CD player hit the button, and Bonnie Raitt flooded the room: "Let's give 'em something to talk about." People began to congratulate us as we moved through the room. We had done it. We had gotten married. We'd come out to our families. We'd taken one huge step in the process, one huge step into the rest of our lives.

We spent hours outside posing for the family photos. I stood there on the front lawn with my arms around Connie, surrounded by her brothers and their wives and girlfriends. I felt a rush of excitement; my face burned with it. These were my in-laws now. I was one of the family. They considered me family. At least some of them did. We posed with Bob and my nephew and pulled Mrs. Kovac and Carol into the picture. I'd grown up with them. Mrs. Kovac had taught me to make bread when I was ten and had followed the progress of my writing through my life. I felt a surge of love for them, swiftly followed by a wash of grief. I'd wanted my mother to be here. I'd wanted her to witness this, this success I'd achieved with my life.

A neighbor strolled by, pretending to be out for a walk. He pointed at me. "Is she getting married?" he asked Deborah's husband, Wayne.

"Yes," Wayne said, smiling over at me.

As Connie joined me on the lawn, the neighbor squinted over at us. "Is she getting married too?" he asked.

Wayne hesitated. "Yes," he said, turning quickly away.

Rain fell off and on through the day, weighing down our unsteady porch roof and trickling slowly into the gutters. "It's good luck," somebody said, "to have rain on your wedding day." We stood there on our porch, toasting with champagne, laughing with our guests, until the rain on the roof reached a pivotal weight and crashed through the rotted ceiling, drenching our family and friends.

⎯⎯∞⎯⎯

Julie and Margie sent us down a handful of pregnancy test kits that Julie had lifted from the doctor's office where she worked. "You don't have to wait till your period's due," Margie told me enthusiastically. "We started testing the week afterward." I repressed a surge of annoyance. I felt envious of Margie, with her baby deep inside her belly. I felt envious of their nursery, which they had showed us proudly on our last visit. I felt envious of their lives, secure in their pregnancy, about to change in ways I couldn't fathom, couldn't even begin to predict.

I tried to wait for Connie to come home from work before I did the test, but I couldn't. I put my cup of urine on the sink, dropped a drop into the test circle, and waited. It was a long two minutes. I felt a quickening within me, a hope as clear as prayer. I couldn't leave the room. I stayed right next to the test, as if my very proximity might somehow influence the results. I looked at my face in the mirror. I thought of the mothers that I saw in the supermarket every time I went. They looked different than I did somehow, older, more mature. I didn't look like a mother. I looked like Louise. I felt like I was only just figuring out my own life. How could I think of starting someone else's? I had shadows beneath my eyes. My face looked tired. I glanced down at the pregnancy test, the tiny circle still blank. I had thought I'd be immune to this. I never thought I'd get obsessed with this insemination process, entirely and absolutely obsessed, letting it take over my life the way it had. I thought I could stand apart from it all and watch the waters rage around me without ever getting wet myself. But I had. I lived my life for these tests of my urine—in the middle of my cycle for my ovulation, at the end for the possibility of my pregnancy. I spent my life counting down the days either to or from the first day of my period. I could no more keep my head above this process than I could if a river were roaring all around me, carrying me to the falls. I wondered for another moment, before I looked down at the test again, what other things I was going to be susceptible to, what other things I thought I'd never do that I would end up doing.

When I looked down at the test, it was negative. I closed my eyes and let the sorrow roll through me. In its wake I felt relief. I had stood behind a screaming little boy in a shopping cart earlier that day and felt only horror. I had been spared again. It was over for another month. I dropped the test in the wastebasket. One more month under our belt. I wondered how many more we'd have to go through before the inevitable came to pass.

⚬⚬⚬

The rains continued, bringing us from summer right into fall with no discernible difference. It was like living on the ark. Rain fell every day, as regular as a promise. I leaned back in my chair, poured myself another glass of wine, and looked around the room at my colleagues. We were celebrating the Labor Day holiday by not laboring. We all had the day off, and Rhoda, another member of the department, had invited us over to her house for dinner. I took a sip and felt myself relax. One thing about a negative pregnancy test was that it meant that I could drink. I was always menstruating, ovulating, or counting down the days between the two. I felt the calmest after I'd gotten my period, when the press of despair was lifted and I still had a few days before it was time to start the process over again.

Rhoda came into the room with another bottle of wine and set it down on the coffee table. In the kitchen I could hear Deborah asking whether the girlfriend of one of the male professors was coming.

"I don't know," Rhoda called back, filling her wine glass. "I'm just afraid she'll call and want to bring her kids."

I set down my wine glass. I could feel something in me catch and tighten warily, as if my sentries were on post. Rhoda doesn't want her to bring her kids, I thought. I looked at Rhoda, who was taking a sip of her wine and turning to talk to someone else. The realization hit me like a wave of nausea. When I had kids, I would lose these friends. I took a swallow of wine. It burned in my throat. I'd rather have kids, I thought, determinedly, but the realization clung to me uneasily. What was this going to mean? Things would change that I couldn't possibly foresee. There would be no way to plan for this. Rhoda smiled over at me. "More wine?"

I gave her my glass, watched her as she filled it, wondered when to tell her that it would be enough.

Welcome to Satan's Playground

Connie and I found the house we wanted in June, a month after our commitment ceremony. It was a yellow, steeply roofed place at the top of a hill in Wellsboro and surrounded on three sides by towering pines. The woman who lived there told us her son had planted them when he was five. "He's fifty now," she said, following one of the trees with her eyes from its base to its top. The trees stood there, flooded with calm, simple with magic, as erect and fine and proud as hawks, soaring on a breeze. We stood there for a moment, the three of us and the real estate agent, our heads tipped back as if in prayer, a salute to some new religion or some old one, where trees carried life and soaring hawks were still a reason to take pause.

The old woman looked at us more closely, narrowing her eyes. She touched Connie's arm with spotted fingers. "Do you like this house?" she asked us. Her lips were thin, stained from cigarettes. "I can't stay here anymore." The house had been for sale for a while. Her husband had died years before. "I'm moving in with a friend," she told us. "We've got a duplex together." She sounded like a kid planning her first apartment. She took us around back, to the yard that stretched out to where the cemetery started, on the other side of the old Catholic church. She looked around, as if for eavesdroppers, then leaned in conspiratorially. "I buried my dog back here," she said.

Connie smiled at her. "That's OK," she said, putting her hand on the old woman's arm. "As long as you didn't bury your husband."

No one said anything for a moment. The old woman peered at us, her brows together, and then she laughed. We all just stood there laughing, while around our heads a breeze picked up and shook the limbs of the trees like shaking hands, until it seemed the trees were laughing too.

I went in to the bank alone to apply for the mortgage because Connie was unemployed at the time, but it didn't feel right. "I don't want just my name on the loan," I told Connie, looking over the stacks of paperwork the loan officer had given me. She gazed at me steadily.

"It's your money," Connie said. I was a professor, after all. Connie had worked with developmentally disabled adults for years before we agreed she had to take a break. Her salary had barely paid for her share of the bills.

"It's our house," I said. We looked at each other for a moment. I reached across the table and took her hand. Her wedding ring grazed my finger, cool and firm against my skin. "Let's apply together," I said.

The loan officer at the bank in Wellsboro surveyed us quizzically across her desk. "I don't understand," she said. She looked at Connie, then back at me. "She has no income, her student loans total seventeen thousand dollars, and she has debts on two credit cards." We studied each other. I could feel myself begin to sweat. The loan officer put her pen down on her papers. "Why would you want to co-apply?"

I mumbled something about our cohabiting the house; it should be in both our names.

"But she can just pay you rent," the loan officer said.

Back on the sidewalk outside the bank Connie said, "It's humiliating." She folded her arms across her chest. "They'd never ask a husband and wife why they wanted to co-apply."

I glanced up the street. It was June; flags the size of coffins hung from the gas lamps that lined the street in preparation for the Fourth of July. It looked like footage of Nazi Germany, except that the colors were different. "I don't know," I said slowly. A couple of middle-aged women walked past us, turning their heads to glance back at us as they went. "She doesn't know that we consider ourselves married," I said. I looked at Connie. Her face was tanned from the sun, radiant in the morning light. "We never told her about our relationship." We walked toward the truck. "We didn't give her a chance." The sun shone brightly. A sudden breeze ruffled the flags, nearly bringing them to attention, like multi-colored erections, all up and down the street. The truck sat there patiently waiting for us, dotted with rust, the small pink triangles discreet on the left bumper, just beneath the "Question Authority" bumper sticker I'd added the previous week. Connie and I looked at each other as we opened our doors. "We're going to have to be honest," I said.

We stopped for gas on our way to the next bank, Elmira Savings Bank in Elmira, New York, the nearest thing resembling a city. A man filling up a much bigger pickup truck than ours nodded over at me from the next pump. "Like your bumper sticker," he said.

" 'Question Authority.' That's a good one." It occurred to me that this was probably a popular message in this area, which was solidly for Ross Perot in the '92 election. He glanced at the other bumper sticker, then screwed the cap back on his gas tank, strode over to the store, and reached for his wallet from the back pocket of his jeans. He probably didn't know what the pink triangles stood for, but I hoped he'd equate them with a philosophy he liked.

When the loan originator asked us for our marital status, I reached for Connie's hand. "We're together," I said.

The loan originator didn't blink an eye. "Legally, though?" she asked.

"Legally, we're single," I said, but my ring burned my finger like a small wound.

"It's just a technicality," she said.

We got the loan, closed on the house, and moved in a week after the Fourth. A small plastic flag was still waving on the front lawn when we backed the moving truck in. I took it down first thing and threw it in the trash. "Oh, great," Connie said. "Now everyone will think we're communists." It took us less than two hours to move all our belongings in. We sat on the porch, sharing pizza and watching the pine trees wave in the wind.

We shared a bottle of champagne that night, out on the back porch, watching the lightning bugs flicker in the night. Connie looked at me, her eyes deep and impenetrable in the darkness. "We'll have to make love," she said leaning closer, until I could feel her breath against my face, "in every room of the house." Her tongue circled my ear, a feather of a touch. "To christen it."

We melted right into life in Wellsboro. We held hands as we took our evening walks down side streets satin with the leaves of trees, glowing with the light from the streetlamps, coming on with the dusk, going off with the dawn. We drank beer on our front porch, barbequed burgers on our back porch. We kissed each other on the front porch in the morning over coffee, kissed again at night before bed. Wellsboro seemed like the most tolerant place in the world. People waved at us as they drove past and called hello from their front porches as we strolled past. "This is great, isn't it?" we used to say to each other. "Everyone's fine with us." The elderly couple across the street, Effie and Leon, regularly had us over for drinks. It felt like living in a scene from some movie, green trees, blue skies, languid summer days. "And people are afraid to come out," we marveled to each other as we put our arms around each others' shoulders on the porch, slipped our hands into the pockets of each others' jeans. "Cowards."

We made no effort to hide our relationship, but when classes began again in the fall, I found myself in a constant state of discomfort. I was teaching a beginning creative writing class that involved extremely personal freewriting on the part of the students. I'd advertised it as a class in which we would cut to our truth as human beings, yet I was as far from sharing my truth with them as I ever had been. When my old friend Jill asked me how out I was, I didn't know. "It's not like I've ever stood up in front of a class and said, 'I'm gay' or anything," I said.

"Well," she said, "I'm not sure that would be appropriate."

I was startled by her tone. "Appropriate." What was appropriate, anyway?

I wrestled with it daily. How could I ask my students to reveal themselves when I was safe behind my podium? I believed, as Natalie Goldberg had once written, that "a teacher transmits nothing more or less than his or her being." That was how I wanted to teach. But how could I, when I was hiding my being deep inside me? An essay I had put on the syllabus was Audre Lorde's "The Transformation of Silence into Language and Action." We had read parts of it at our wedding in May. But when I picked it up again to read it for class, I couldn't put it down. I thought she was speaking directly to me. I didn't have to wait for the fear to go away before I could talk; I could talk anyway, despite my beating heart. Every class period I got a little closer to revealing myself to my students. Every class period I left without doing it. Finally, I assigned them in class to write for twenty minutes about their greatest obstacle. As they wrote, I joined them, as I did every class, freewriting in my own journal. I found myself writing about falling in love with Connie, about how that had initially seemed an obstacle but had in fact become my greatest gift, how it kept me from taking anything for granted, such as marriage and family, and how it forced me to become an adult, separate from the family of my childhood. When we were finished, a few students read theirs aloud. I sat in my desk in the circle, nauseous and afraid. I wanted to read mine aloud, but I couldn't bring myself to do it. My heart beat so hard I was suddenly afraid that they could see it leaping from my chest.

I dismissed the class. When I went home that night, to our little house in Wellsboro, I fought with myself about it. *Appropriate.* The word resounded in my head. "That wouldn't be appropriate." But what about me *was* appropriate? I had wanted to share myself with my students, and I hadn't because I felt afraid. I felt like a coward. Connie took my hand over dinner. "Just because you didn't read it today," she said softly, "doesn't mean you can't read it at the next class."

I couldn't make myself eat anything before the next class. By the time I got there, my heart was pounding again, and I felt so light-headed I thought that I might faint. I waited until only a few minutes were left of the class. "I wanted to read what I wrote last time," I told my students, "but I didn't because I was afraid." I paused and glanced down at my notebook. For a moment I thought I would not be able to do it, would not be physically able to do it, that my heart might beat so hard my voice would never be able to sound above it. At first my voice shook as I read. I felt cold right to my core. My throat ached. But as I read, I could feel my voice coming back to me, rising above my fear, filling me with warmth. By the time I was finished, my voice was as strong as if I had felt no fear at all. But I still dismissed them quickly. I couldn't make myself look at them. I went back to my office feeling almost dead inside. I didn't know for sure how they might react.

A student came to my office later that week. "I wanted to read you something that I wrote," she said, sitting down beside me. She opened her notebook. "When Louise read to us about being gay, at first I was shocked; I thought she couldn't be gay. And then I felt proud, proud that she would share that with us, proud to be in class with her." The student looked up at me. "I just wanted you to know," she said.

After that I came out to my classes regularly, despite my beating heart. "Appropriate," I thought every once in awhile, remembering Jill's warning. I had no doubt that what I was doing was appropriate, even though every time I did it my throat threatened to close entirely, choking my words before I could even sound them with my lips. Gay and lesbian students began to seek me out, to talk to me about their lives. Everybody seemed to breathe a little easier. Straight students came to talk to me about their gay friends and family. I moderated a campus forum on gays in the military. One hundred people came, and though I thought at first my heart might detonate in my chest, I managed to do it anyway. At the end one of my senior colleagues said, "On behalf of those of us who weren't raised with gay people, I'd like to say: Be patient with us." I looked at him and said, "On behalf of those of us who've been shoved in the closet for four hundred years, I'd like to say: Get over it." Granted, he never looked at me while I was talking, but at least I did say it, and, more important, I felt no fear in saying it. I started to see the power of coming out. In October, after much deliberation, we sent a notice of our wedding to the nearest daily newspaper, the *Elmira Star-Gazette*. "They'll never print it," Connie said, watching me lick the envelope.

"I know," I said. "But maybe, just maybe . . ."

Several weeks later I got a call at my office from the features editor of the paper. "We wondered if we could do a feature story on the two of you," she said. "As part of our 'Families' section."

"Sure," I said without even thinking about how Connie might react. I was too excited to analyze it at all. We were being included in the "Families" section. We were a family. What an open-minded place this was, I thought exuberantly, this little collection of hills in the middle of nowhere.

"That's great," Connie said when I told her later that day, as we took our walk through the streets of our town. She took hold of my hand and squeezed it in hers. We walked a few more blocks in silence, the October wind whipping up the leaves and scattering them around us. Then Connie turned to me. "But what will my parents say?" she asked.

The reporter came down to interview us shortly after the spring semester started, on a cold and sunless day in January when the streets were clogged with old snow and ice and the light from the gas lamps was still visible when I left for work in the mornings. Connie barely looked at me as we drove to my office to meet the reporter.

"Are you nervous?" I asked her. She stared straight ahead in the driver's seat, her eyes on the road.

"I just don't know why we're doing this," she said. Her jaw was set. "I mean, what are they going to say?" She glanced at me. Her look was bitter. "What is my family going to do?"

I looked away, back out the window at the frozen landscape flashing past. "Do you want to change your mind?" I asked her. I held my breath. We had come this far together. I didn't know what it would mean if we stopped now. I didn't know if I could stop. Something in me was just barreling on through the woods, cutting trail with a scythe, stomping it down beneath my feet. I didn't know why I needed to do this. I only knew that I did.

Connie looked back at the road and downshifted for the hill into Mansfield. "I'm just scared," she said.

I put my hand on hers as she cupped the gearshift. "So am I," I said.

By the time the reporter arrived at my office, I was so scared I could barely breathe. I was almost relieved when the phone rang as she walked in the door—it gave me another moment before I had to face this interview. A man's voice came over the line, deep and harsh. "Get a man," it snarled, hanging up before I could reply. My hand shook as I replaced the receiver. I was aware of the reporter looking at me. I made myself look back at her. Inside I was shaking. "Wrong number," I said as casually as I could, keeping my face expressionless. Fear gripped my rib cage, squeezing it until I thought it might cut off the air supply to my lungs. Stay calm, I told myself. I must not be afraid, if only because Connie was so nervous. If both of us were afraid, we might not do this. And somehow, for some reason I could not put into words, I knew I had to do this.

The days before the story appeared grew into weeks. January stretched into February; February gave way to March. We thought we might not be able to stand it. "Why aren't they printing it?" Connie asked.

I called the reporter and the features editor who had initially contacted me, but both assured me that the story was scheduled to appear soon. "They're losing their nerve," I said, hanging up the phone. Connie and I looked at each other.

"What do you think will happen after the story comes out?" Connie asked me.

"I don't know," I said. But I could imagine. I imagined all kinds of things late at night. I imagined vandalism, firebombings, public ostracism. Some nights I envisioned a cross burning on our front lawn, sending its sparks high into our starlit sky. We were already getting obscene phone calls, which had started right after we moved to Wellsboro, when the new phone book came out. I imagined the calls accelerating, becoming increasingly personal. Right now it was just one guy, who unimaginatively whispered, "Pussy, pussy, pussy" over and over again into the receiver. We'd never reported them. I was too embarrassed to, I didn't want to admit that they frightened me.

One day late in February we drove down the street to the drugstore. Walking back to the truck we passed a station wagon parked outside the department store. We both noticed the bumper sticker at the same time: "Clinton's parents should have been gay."

We stopped for a moment, transfixed. "But what does that mean?" I asked.

"It means they wouldn't have had him," Connie said flatly.

"But why not?" I said. "They still could have *had* him."

Connie glanced at me sideways. "I know," she said. "But they don't."

We kept on walking toward the truck. Suddenly, the town seemed to be populated with senior citizens, tall, thin, refined people with white hair and taut lips, arms folded across their chests as if keeping tense might keep them safe. Suddenly, they seemed to be lining the streets, leaning up against the storefronts, chewing grass between their teeth. Suddenly, they all seemed to be looking at us, the dykey-looking women with the short straight hair and the hard-to-place clothes. "Clinton's parents should have been gay." Did that mean they would approve of us as gay parents? That they would approve of gay parents, period?

"It means," Connie said, apparently reading my mind, "that gay people don't reproduce, so in some cases we're preferable, because the line stops here."

When we reached the truck, I opened my door with a sense of relief. The truck, at least, felt safe. I glanced at Connie. "What were we thinking of?" I asked her.

Connie shook her head and started up the truck. "God knows," she said. "I certainly don't."

The story appeared March 8, 1994, on the front page of the Sunday paper. It almost didn't appear at all, the reporter confided to me later. "The advertisers threatened to pull their business," she told me. "And a top editor decided to pull the story."

"What happened then?" I asked her.

"The publisher stepped in," she said. "And told him he had to run it."

The story was incredibly positive. "Lesbians Find Love, Tolerance, and Acceptance in Wellsboro, Pa." read the headline that ran across a huge color picture of Connie and me walking through the streets in our winter coats, cheeks red from the cold. The town of Wellsboro appeared to be a small Mecca buried deep in the hills of this part of Pennsylvania that no one's ever seen.

Connie and I read the story together over breakfast, devouring our own lives with fearful fascination. We sat back at the same time and reached for the coffee. "Well," I said, buttering a piece of toast. "What do you think?"

Connie looked at me. "I don't know," she said doubtfully. "It's awfully positive. How could anybody complain?"

The article was so positive, in fact, that it almost presented a direct challenge to the town: Go on, prove us wrong! I could feel an unease deep in my stomach that this was a set-up, somehow.

The letters to the editor started with the next issue of the paper. "Story Sickened and Enraged Me," wrote one woman, the wife of a local professional. "Story on Lesbians Belongs in the Trash," wrote another. "We Have Become a Sick Society," claimed one letter. "Why don't you publish a story about a Christian family for a change," asked one writer, "so outsiders will not get the impression that Wellsboro is just a homosexual community?"

"Why do they assume we're not Christian?" Connie asked, laying down the paper.

I shook my head. I didn't know why they assumed we were sick either, but I knew that they did. All I really knew was that inside I was so anxious I could hardly bear it.

We read every letter. We couldn't stop ourselves. We bought our local newspaper, the *Wellsboro Gazette*, every week because people kept up the discourse there long after the letters to the Elmira paper had begun to trickle down. I compulsively clipped each letter and saved it, Scotch-taping it to a sheet of paper and filing them in a folder marked "The Article." I could feel a trickle of fear at the back of my neck, as if I were in the sights of someone's rifle. It's stupid, it's ludicrous, I tried to tell myself. It's obvious that they're morons. But deep inside I knew that they were the people who made history, that the outcome of civilization had always been determined by the mood of the mob. And I knew from my days as a community organizer that the mood of the mob was easily directed by a few individuals who knew exactly what buttons to push. I put the paper down, tucking it circumspectly away beneath my elbow every morning, after obsessively devouring every bit of news that concerned us, taking another sip of coffee, and trying to pretend that it didn't bother me.

"We won't tolerate them in our town," wrote one Wellsboro woman, whom we happened to know had carried on an affair with a local attorney for years, even though both were married. "Sodomites," one man wrote. "We don't want them in our home-towns," said one woman adamantly. "Or in any hometown across

America," she added, apparently forgetting that we must have been born somewhere.

"We've all lived here since the 1800s," one woman wrote. "And we're all related to each other."

"You got that right," I mumbled over coffee.

"We will continue to fight for what we believe to be right," the writer continued, "whether it's to elect male, Christian, NRA members to political offices, or to say we do not agree with the homosexual life-style."

"No person, no government can legislate me to believe or to teach my children to believe that same sex marriage is a natural or lawful institution," wrote one man. "If that should come to pass in this Tioga County, this oasis in a world gone mad, well, I've packed my bags before, I guess I can do it again."

"Fine," Connie said as she stirred oatmeal at the stove. "I won't stand in his way."

" 'Diversity' is fine," cautioned a local doctor, "as long as it's not Satan's playground."

"Satan's playground!" I said to Connie. It was almost too much to take seriously. But even while one part of my mind imagined Wellsboro as a carnival of ferris wheels and merry-go-rounds, with a sign over the entrance reading "Welcome to Satan's Playground," another part of my mind curled up and tried to hide its head, wishing we had never done this, wishing it would all just go away.

Late one day in April we read in our local paper that a man had gone to the regular meeting to confront the county commissioners. "I'm just worried about those lesbians on Pearl Street," he said. "I don't want Tioga County to become the San Francisco of the East Coast."

"They wish!" Connie said, putting down the paper.

"They'd have to open a few more restaurants first," I said.

One commissioner's response was, "I can only speak for myself as an individual, but I agree with you one hundred percent." The other two commissioners, one of whom we knew to be gay, were silent.

On the surface I tried to act as if it wasn't bothering me, but inside I felt like crying most of the time. People wrote positive letters too. Once the phone rang late at night. I picked it up gingerly, anticipating another obscene phone call, but it was a woman's voice on the other end: "I just wanted to tell you that everybody in

Wellsboro isn't like those people writing letters. Some of us support you."

One day a woman came up to us in the supermarket, as we stood in line at the cash register, her bag of groceries clutched in her arms. "I just wanted to welcome you to the community," she said. She shifted her groceries to one arm, shook our hands with the other. "I've got a sister who's gay," she said. The other people in line looked at us, then looked away. I felt a swell of gratitude. We had been publicly claimed.

Shortly after that I was referred to the ophthalmologist for eye problems I had been having. I sat in the waiting room for hours, surrounded by people in their eighties, in for glaucoma and cataract surgery. The wait was endless. I imagined a wizened old man sharpening up his little knives, rubbing his hands together in anticipation of strapping me into his chair, urging me to repent while he chiseled out my irises, blinding me in the name of God. When the nurse called my name, I was surprised to find that the ophthalmologist was young and pleasant. His gaze was steady, his hands gentle. "A lot of people support you in this town," he said softly. "Are you aware of that?"

I could feel something open up in me, as if my heart had split apart. I wanted to take his hand and place it there, let the warmth of his touch heal my wounds. "No," I said. "I'm not."

"You have a lot of friends here," he said. "I attend Quaker meeting," he added, as if that might explain things. I closed my eyes for a moment. He wasn't going to hurt me. I was safe here. This, at least, was one place where I would be safe.

But most of the time we only felt afraid. Wellsboro became an entity that had initially been friendly to us and had now betrayed us. I felt afraid of everyone. Connie and I stopped kissing on our front porch, stopped holding hands on our daily walks. I continued to clip the letters and clap them into my file folder as soon as they appeared and file them away. As long as I kept them in their manila folder with its proper heading, I thought, I would be safe. If I could just keep track of all those scraps of newsprint, I could keep this under control.

It seemed important somehow that I act as if it didn't bother me. I'd been raised with the idea that I not let people know how I was feeling, as if any show of emotion might be enough for them to get their knife between my ribs. As a child I'd been fascinated by the Stoics. Surely, this was a model of how I should live my life, surely this was what my parents meant. Unfortunately, my face had always given me away, every emotion clearly visible to all the moment that I felt it. The other children used to taunt me on the school bus just to watch my expressions change. When I first began to teach at Mansfield, a student told Connie that I was so vulnerable that she could tell by my face what I was feeling. The idea had galled me—my *students* could tell? I must not be fooling anybody! And still, despite therapy, despite all my attempts to be open about my life, a part of me thought I should hide myself away. If I could just keep a part of me private, I might survive. I looked at the headlines in my manila folder and wondered if I'd just given that last part of myself away.

Preachers spoke against us from their pulpits; a public prayer vigil was organized on the town green, beside the fountain of Winken, Blinken, and Nod. "Come join us on your knees!" someone urged in the Letters to the Editor column. Neighbors left us letters in our mailbox, telling us that they were praying for us to repent. When I went to bed at night, I imagined their prayers outside my windows, beating at the glass like wings, seeking entry. We lit our candles, burned our incense, said our own prayers, held them against our hearts like amulets, and hoped the protection was enough. It was hard enough to live together as a gay couple with no support at all, I thought, let alone to have whole churches praying for the end of our relationship.

The reporter who had done the story confided to me that the paper had received dozens of calls denouncing the story, accusing her of being a lesbian. It wasn't just our story, she told me. She'd covered a local bar mitzvah the next week and a man had called her a communist. He hung up before she could get his name.

It was about two months later, when I first heard of the organization of a local chapter of the Christian Coalition, that I realized it had finally gone beyond any illusions I might have had of control. The manager of the Comfort Inn advertised the meeting in the local newspaper, urging all members of the community to join him in combating "these 'politically correct' trends." He gave them free meeting space in one of the hotel's conference rooms, something he hadn't even given to the nonprofit agency that Connie had worked for.

"I can't believe this," I said, putting down the paper. I looked at Connie. Snow clung stubbornly to the branches of the trees, melting and freezing with the temperature, forming little cones of ice.

I could feel something growing in me, cold and final, my own pocket of ice closing off the valves of my heart, one by one. "We can't let this happen."

Connie only looked at me, her spoon poised above her cereal. The moments ticked on. "I've got to go to that meeting," I said. I couldn't swallow. I wasn't even conscious of breathing anymore. I only knew I had to go.

The night of the meeting was cold and dark. The gas lamps fought with the darkness, shedding an eerie light that wavered up and down the streets. I imagined my neighbors silently donning their coats and hats, taking up their walking sticks, and stealing out to the organizational meeting of the Wellsboro Christian Coalition. I stood in our kitchen waiting for Connie to get home. I made myself a cup of coffee and tried to face down my fear, which prowled rampant in my chest, speeding up my heart. "Why would you go?" asked one of my colleagues, a man who knew, as one of the county's only Jews, how hard it was to live here. "What good would it do for you to be there?" I wondered the same thing to myself. But I remembered my days as an organizer, the rush I used to feel before an action. I felt some of the same excitement now. Of course, in my organizing days I'd been surrounded by dozens, if not scores, of other people. Now I was very conscious of being alone and on my own.

When Connie got home, she came right to the kitchen. "I don't want you to go to that meeting," she said, pulling off her hat and gloves and stuffing them into the pocket of her coat. "Please don't go." She took my shoulders in her hands, stared deep into my eyes, and began to cry. "I don't want to be married to a martyr," she said. "I want to be married to Louise. I want to be married to you for a long, long time." She laid her head against my chest and sobbed until I thought she might never stop.

I felt torn. A part of me longed to fight despite my fear, to see my enemies face to face, to die, if need be, in a spray of bullets. The other part of me wanted to stay at home and write my books, have a baby, if I could still think of doing that here, and confront the world in a different way, a softer way, through my writing, through the way I lived. I didn't want to be a coward. But I didn't want to give my life up either. I'd done that once already, been the unhealthy starving activist, all too eager to martyr herself for the cause. I'd fought too hard to get where I was, standing in my kitchen holding Connie, feeling her hair against my face, tasting it in my mouth, here in this house we'd bought together. I brushed her hair back and looked down into her face. Her eyes were red and swollen, her cheeks stained with tears. "All right," I said and kissed her cheek. Her tears were salty in my mouth. "I'll stay home."

Several of my students went to the meeting and called me later that night to report that it was long and boring and we had nothing to fear. But I knew in my heart that we did have something to fear, that the real battle in this town would be waged in school board elections, the race for county commissioners, the election of judges. I knew that there was a lot to organize against, and I also knew I didn't want to be the one to do it. I only wanted to be, to just live my life, write my books, teach my students, and love Connie the best way I knew how. I wasn't an organizer anymore. I was just Louise, just a person trying to live her life. I hung up the phone and turned to the window. Outside the gas lamps glowed. The neighbors' houses remained silent, lit from within. I didn't know who had gone to the meeting and who had stayed at home, but I suspected I'd find out soon enough.

A few nights later a car full of teenage boys drove past. It was Friday night, the night all the kids cruised up and down Main Street in their Trans Ams, making illegal U-turns at the end of the stretch of gas lamps and circling back through a town that had nothing else for them to do. We could hear their brakes screech outside our house, could hear their beer cans hitting the pavement, could hear their shouts through our open windows, that sound of out-of-control hormones that struck terror into my heart every time. "Go away!" they yelled. "Go home!"

My stomach lurched. I ran downstairs to find Connie peering through the curtains of the front window. She turned around to face me. "I want to go find them," she said, "chase after them and hurt them." Her face was tight with anger.

I nodded. "I know," I said. My voice shook despite myself.

Connie sighed forcefully. "At the same time," she said, "it makes me want to hide."

I knew. I knew absolutely. Like the only thing I wanted to do was go inside and lock the doors, shut us both away, keep us safe. We waited to see if they'd come back, but the street stayed silent, empty. "Let's go outside," I said. We went out onto our front porch and stood there in the quiet night. "What do they mean 'Go home,' anyway?" I said. "We *are* home." I glanced around cautiously, then reached for Connie's hand. She hesitated for a moment, then tightened her fingers around mine. We stood there holding hands on our front porch, watching the stars come out. Inside I was still afraid. We were so small next to all those stars. So insignificant. What did our lives matter, when all was said and done?

The Guys at the Sporting Goods Store Think You're the Greatest

People are just bored," Roger said of the letters to the editor. "When spring comes, they'll get busy in their gardens and stop writing letters." He had stopped by my office to see how I was doing. I told him I was fine. It was what I told everyone, as if anything other than that would be unacceptable, open me up to something worse than anonymous phone calls and community meetings. Everyone knew where we lived. The paper had published a full-page picture of us walking our dog up Pearl Street. I was conscious of that, all the time. He turned to go, then stopped at the door. "By the way," he said, glancing back at me. "The guys at the sporting goods store think you're the greatest."

Spring, which didn't come to our part of Pennsylvania till early May, brought with it a sense of softness. Blocks of snow broke up as the temperatures rose, melted beneath the sun, and disappeared down the streets in muddy rivers. Grass began to stretch tentatively toward the light. People emerged from their houses slowly, hesitantly, like bears taking their first halting steps after months of hibernation. Someone left a batch of hot cross buns in our mailbox for Easter, along with a photocopy of the relevant Bible passage, "He has risen," highlighted in yellow. I made myself eat them, one after the other, after testing a bite on the dog to check for poison. I choked down every bite while standing on my front porch in full view of every car that went by, until my stomach bulged from the effort. Rebirth was on everyone's mind. Christ had risen. So could we. I was standing across the street chatting with our neighbor Leon, when he cleared his throat and looked at me. "Looks like you'll be wanting to paint soon," he said, indicating our house.

"Really?" I replied, glancing over at it. The yellow shone in the spring sunlight, the five-foot freedom flag on the front porch waving gently in the wind. Looking at it, my heart beat a little faster. Our house. Our little yellow house sparkling in the sun. Our refuge from the world. Paint it? Why would we need to paint it?

"Look up above the porch roof," Leon said, gesturing at it. His hand was wrinkled, covered with age spots. I wondered how he'd gotten to be so open-minded, talking to me out in the street like this, in full view of everyone, as if the past few months of warfare hadn't even existed. We never said anything about it, but he and Effie had continued to invite us over for drinks, if anything, even more than before.

I looked at the house dubiously. It did look like the paint was peeling, now that he mentioned it. From over here in front of his house, in fact, it looked pretty bad. "Mrs. Dolliver painted a side a year," Leon told me. "Looks like this side's ready."

"Huh," I said. A truck barreled past, sending a spray of slush up over the sidewalk. We both took a step back to avoid it. "When do you think we need to paint it?" I asked.

Leon looked at me. His eyes were dark, slightly watery with age. "Yesterday," he said, not breaking my gaze.

Ernest Henninger strode into the conference room of his offices on Main Street and shook our hands in greeting. He looked like an old-time Protestant minister, slightly frightening, standing there at the head of his boardroom table with his wire-rimmed glasses, solid and austere. I felt a tightening in my throat. He's not a minister, I reminded myself fiercely. He's an accountant. He doesn't care about our lives. All he's going to do is figure out our tax return. That's all. We had spent all the money we had, and then some, buying this house. We needed expert assistance, to get as much money back as possible.

Connie stood beside me with her hands folded, not looking at me. Around us the wood paneling emitted the smell of furniture polish. A furrow appeared in the accountant's brow as he glanced at us, and I felt my stomach churn. We had decided to go to an accountant this time, see if we could file our return jointly. The house was in both our names; we had joint checking and savings accounts. All the bills were in both our names. We were creating a paper trail. If we couldn't marry legally, we could do everything else together to show our commitment. Someday, when we got around to it, we were going to hyphenate our names. We had made our decision to file jointly with determination, but when the time came to go to the accountant for this appointment, I found myself quailing in fear. "I don't have time for this meeting today," I told Connie irritably as we drove to his office.

Connie looked over at me. "When you say that, I perceive you think it's my fault we had to do this today," she said. Her voice had an edge in it like a tire iron. "And that pisses me off."

I forced myself to mirror her, to respond to her reasonably, but inside I was in turmoil. My stomach churned. Everything—every interaction with other people, bank tellers, doctors, accountants—had become a coming out experience, and I was tired of it. Just once I wanted to be able to do something as simple as meet with an accountant and not have it require a monumental act of courage. Just once I wanted to be a normal person, without having to worry about a reaction to my very existence.

Henninger nodded at us, and we all sat down. I took a deep breath. "We want to see about doing a joint tax return," I said. "And we want to get an idea of our refund."

He nodded and glanced through our files. "Let me just go through this," he said, reaching for his calculator. He tapped out the numbers, and I sat back feeling relieved. It looked like it might be all right. I glanced at Connie across the table. She smiled at me.

Henninger scanned the papers in his hands. "According to this," he said, "you should have a refund of about eighteen hundred dollars."

I refrained from kicking Connie under the table. Eighteen hundred dollars! Who cared about filing jointly? We could paint the house, finally recover our standing in the community. Connie and I looked at each other at the same moment. Or we could use it to buy sperm.

———✎———

I was home from school one day when the phone rang. It was Karen Barber, the editor of Alyson Publications, a small gay and lesbian press in Boston. My first novel, *Amnesty*, had been accepted for publication. My heart pounded. "We can give you a three thousand dollar advance," Karen said offhandedly.

My mouth went dry. Somebody was going to publish my book *and* give me money! My palms began to sweat; the receiver slipped in my hand. I forced myself to breathe evenly. Bargain, I told myself. Don't just leap at the first offer. Besides, I knew my fellow graduates of the Iowa Writers' Workshop, where I'd attained my master of fine arts, routinely received advances of $20,000 or more. Of course, I had always had trouble *giving* my stories away. Be strong, I told myself. You're worth it. "Three thousand dollars," I said, fighting for a tone of nonchalance. "I don't know . . ."

"To be honest," Karen said, "that's a pretty good advance."

"OK," I said. "I'll take it."

⸎

We were ready to go. Between the tax return and the advance for the novel, we had enough money for nearly a year's worth of insemination. It had all come together. It was going to happen, and now I felt as if I might throw up. Suddenly, insemination felt like a sentence, a looming reality as stark as a firing squad. I was going to be inseminated. There was no getting around it anymore. After years of discussion, months of active pursuit, we were going to begin the process.

"How's the rewriting coming?" Connie asked me.

I had only to do the revisions the editor had asked for, and they'd mail us the check. "It's not," I said. The truth was, I couldn't do it. Every time I sat down at my computer, my fingers froze. My brain emptied out. As soon as this is done, I'd tell myself, we can start the insemination. And then I'd stare at the keys. I couldn't write a word.

Connie smiled at me. She laid her hand on mine. It felt soft and warm, the skin still smooth, untouched by age. I clutched at it, as if it might save me. "We don't have to do this," she said.

I looked at her. "I know," I said. I felt as if I were slipping away. I squeezed her hand tighter. "But I want to."

Connie eased her fingers from my grip, lifted my chin in her hand, and looked into my eyes. "Let's take a trip," she said. "When you've got the revisions done, let's just take a drive, get out of town."

"But what about painting the house?" I asked her.

"Screw the house." We looked at each other for a moment. "Where do you want to go?"

I studied her, sitting there beside me, soft and warm in the light from our kitchen window. I thought of the past few months of letters to the editor, of summoning up all my courage every time I went into town. "San Francisco," I said. "Somewhere where there's lots of gay people."

When I finished the revisions, I took the manuscript down to the post office and mailed it off. It didn't feel nearly as momentous as I once thought it would. It didn't feel like the culmination of a lifetime of wanting to have a book published. Instead, it just felt like something I had done, like sanding down a piece of wood, staining it deep and rich and dark, then nailing it up somewhere. I got money back, an even trade. It felt like the most honest work that I had ever done. "So when do we leave?" I asked Connie.

We traded in the truck for a new Toyota, a regular car with four doors and a backseat, ready for an infant carrier. We got a joint personal loan from the credit union and paid off all our credit card debts. We put the tax return and the first third of the advance in our joint savings account. We stood in our front yard surrounded by our flowering trees and looked up at our house, its paint job flecking off into the wind. It figured that Mrs. Dolliver had started with the damned front side. If the back of the house was peeling, nobody would know. A soft breeze ruffled our hair and sent the stripes of our freedom flag shimmering. "Let's go," Connie said.

We made it nearly to Chicago on the first day, crossing the rest of Pennsylvania, Ohio, Indiana, and as much of Illinois as we could. We drove with alacrity. We spent the first night in a Day's Inn on the highway, the second in Avoca, Iowa, where we made love in a tiny little hotel whose concierges were sure they had seen me before. The phone book was full of Blums. I wondered briefly whether I had some family here, if some relatives had stopped off here after getting off the boat from Germany. We walked hand in hand beneath the elm trees, down streets thick with azalea, past huge white houses with porches wrapping all the way around. The breeze touched our faces, smoothed back our hair. "What a beautiful little town!" I exclaimed to Connie. "We could live here!" I added, forgetting for a moment that we already lived in a beautiful small town and knew its limitations.

We drove through Nebraska as fast as we could, stopping the next night in Laramie, Wyoming. We could live here too, I thought as we drove into town; I was picturing a place where people rode down the streets on horseback, hitching up outside the drugstore. "Dykes!" a carload of teenagers, two boys and two girls, screamed at us through their open car windows as we carried our suitcases up the rickety stairs to our one-star AAA motel room. I felt a catch in my chest. Connie froze beside me. I measured the distance between us and the door to our room, between us and the street, and wondered if we could get inside in time. It's just like Wellsboro, I thought. It's just like fucking Wellsboro. Worse, because I had no turf established here, no property, no job, no claims of ownership, nothing to protect me, to show that I was just like everybody else.

Connie looked at me. Her eyes were huge. "Can we just keep going?" she asked softly.

I shook my head. "Let's just get inside," I said. We locked the door behind us and drew the curtains. "Let's just go to sleep," I said, "and get up early."

When we crossed the Golden Gate Bridge into San Francisco, I knew without a doubt that we could indeed live here. We spent our days walking the streets, our nights in the Mission District, sipping beer at lesbian bars and watching women play pool. We drank the best coffee we had ever had in our lives. We fantasized about living in San Francisco, in a community of gay and lesbian people, raising our children with like-minded neighbors in a city so open that it even listed the Castro District in its tourist information. "We'd be happy here," I said, imagining our baby starting off to a school where she wouldn't be stigmatized for having two lesbian parents.

"We're happy in Wellsboro, aren't we?" Connie asked me.

I thought about it. We had been. But were we still? I thought of the image I had had of Wellsboro as a friendly, open-armed town, waving us in off the highway, turning down our bedsheets for us, tucking us in. Now I pictured Wellsboro standing at the door, her arms across her chest and her lips pursed, shaking her head. "I don't know," I said. "Can we really raise a child there?"

"I don't know," Connie said. We walked along in silence for a while, sipping our coffee, thick and hot in our takeout containers.

"We could raise one here," I said.

Connie nodded. "I know."

We were barely out of San Francisco when we passed a succession of white wooden crosses staggering up a hillside. "Repent and Be Saved!" they proclaimed, the black lettering stark against the white. I shuddered in fear. They were the same crosses that we had on our hillsides at home. "What is this?" I asked Connie. "Isn't there anywhere we can go and be free of this?"

Connie looked at me. "No," she said. "There isn't."

Only the Castro District, I thought, thinking longingly of the good coffee that we'd just left behind. Only San Francisco. The rest of the country was a sweep of Christians, passing referenda forbidding us even to meet with each other in public meeting rooms. Repent and be saved. I could feel my heart beat, ragged in my chest. We had left our safe place. We were like mice now, loose on the jungle floor, at the mercy of animals much more powerful than we were.

Outside Fresno we swerved around a blond suntanned boy skateboarding unafraid into traffic, stooping down to swoop past our car and over into the next lane. I watched him go with awe. His image stayed with me, his thin, strong body surfing through the traffic with absolute confidence, doing things I would be afraid to do. That was the kind of kid I wanted to raise, one that would be absolutely without fear. I wondered if I could do that in Wellsboro.

We kept driving east, crossing the Mojave Desert for hours. A billboard of Anita Bryant welcomed us into Missouri. "Still America's Sweetheart," it said. Her face, cracked with age, smiled at us. She gestured at us with her glass of orange juice, her hair swept back in its fifties swoop, high off her forehead. "*Still!*" I said, gunning the accelerator. "Do they mean since she crucified gay people in the seventies?" I suddenly remembered my mother standing with a group of women after a church service. "Anita Bryant's a real hero," she'd said.

"Drive faster," Connie urged me, taking a sip of coffee out of her McDonald's container and wincing. She eyed the speedometer. "Let's get out of here."

We had planned to stop in Indianapolis for the night, but every hotel room was filled. "What's going on?" I asked a hotel clerk at the fifth place we stopped.

"It's a revival," she told me, her eyes shining. "There's fifty thousand people in town!"

Connie was waiting for me out in the car. "What is it?" she asked.

I got in and slammed the door behind me. "A revival," I told her. It just figures, I thought, starting the engine. We drive all the way across the country to find freedom and get bumped by an evangelist.

Connie just stared. "You're kidding," she said. She shook her head. "I can't believe it." We stopped at motel after motel. Every room was taken.

"How can there be so many Christians?" I asked Connie.

"The world is full of them," she said. She turned on the radio. "The homosexuals are taking over," the voice said, "with their secret agenda. Their sinful lifestyle is an abomination to the Lord."

"What the fuck is this?" I asked. We both stared at the radio.

"It's him," Connie said. "The evangelist."

His voice cracked with feeling: "We must stop the homosexuals." The car filled with noise. "Is that static?" I said.

"No," Connie said. We both listened for a moment longer. "It's applause." We drove 900 miles that day. We drove until I could no longer tell the difference between the brake and the accelerator. We didn't find a room until we hit Dayton, Ohio.

We collapsed on the bed, not even taking off our clothes. I lay with my eyes closed, my brain pulsing. Wellsboro is everywhere, slamming the door in our faces in every town across America, I thought. I pulled the pillow over my head, trying to shut off my mind. We'll never get away from it. We'd have to live in a gay ghetto to ever get away from this. That wasn't what I wanted. Was it?

It was mid-June when we got back home. The azalea and rhododendron were past their prime, their blossoms rotting into the soil around their roots. The sun was high in the sky. The peeling paint glistened beneath it. We carried our suitcases back into the house and unpacked our things. "We're home," I said. I looked around at our things, solid and familiar. We were home. We were back in the place we lived. The cats rubbed against our ankles, demanding their food. I opened a beer, handed it to Connie, and opened another for myself. I caressed its neck for a moment, feeling its chill. We were home. We were home, and we were going to have a baby.

I took a sip of beer and glanced around the house. Could we really have a baby here? I wondered. I thought back on our journey across the country, one conservative town after another, large and small. I took another sip. Could we have one anywhere?

Connie turned to me and took my hand in hers. "We're home," she echoed, looking so deep into my eyes I could feel my stomach lurch. A little thrill started up around the base of my spine. "Let's go upstairs," she said.

I drove past the university provost's house the next day on my way to Mansfield. I glanced up at it. It was covered with peeling paint. I felt vindicated. Forget the paint job, I thought. We're having a baby. I tightened my grip on the wheel. One way or the other we were having a baby. Money, I sensed, was the least of our problems.

"OK," I said, turning from the class to the board and picking up a piece of chalk. **GAY PEOPLE,** I wrote on the board. I turned back to them. "Who do you know?" I asked.

The class looked startled. "Oh, I don't mean personally," I said, smiling at them. "You don't have to out your roommates or anything." A few people exhaled, apparently in relief. "I mean, historical figures," I continued. "Or famous people now."

It was the first night of "Gay and Lesbian Literature," the first time such a course had ever been taught on this campus. I felt electric, like I could do anything. I'd just been inseminated for the third time, and I *knew* this time it would take.

I was actually teaching this course. I'd proposed it the previous spring, and the moment it appeared in the course schedule four students had signed a letter of protest to the editor of the student newspaper. "This course shouldn't be taught just because of one person's sexual preference," the students wrote. "She should keep it in the bedroom." Thanks to the ensuing controversy, the class filled up on the first day of registration. Now, as I faced the roomful of earnest students, I felt a twinge of excitement. I was doing it. I was teaching right from who I was, just the way I wanted to. Outside, campus police patrolled the halls. The department chair hadn't wanted me to teach the class at night, though he never said why. Nor did I ask him. It was as if we had silently agreed that not voicing something would negate its existence. Several students had confessed to me that they'd been a little afraid to come to class, let alone carry the books around. But here they were, their notebooks open and their pens poised, ready to learn about gay and lesbian literature. It was the closest I'd come to feeling like a revolutionary since I'd left organizing.

One student, an English major, raised his hand tentatively. "Oscar Wilde," he said.

"Audre Lorde," said another.

The class began to loosen up. I could see their postures relax. A few took off their coats, as if they thought they just might stay a while. "Kurt Cobain was bi," somebody said.

"The bassist for the Breeders," somebody else said. "What's her name?"

We went on and on, until the board was filled with names. I surveyed them with satisfaction. I was in good company. I put down my chalk and faced the class. "I'm a lesbian too," I told them. My heart gave its familiar heightened skip, as if it might flee my chest in another moment. I took a deep breath. "And I have to tell you that when I say that I feel afraid. I feel afraid every time I tell somebody I'm gay."

The class surveyed me cautiously. I turned back to the board and drew a triangle in pink chalk. "OK," I said. "Who can tell me what that means?"

Nobody could. I felt a tiny burst of pride. If anybody needed a class like this one, it was the students on this campus. I had full confidence in them. All they had to do was learn more about gays and lesbians—then they would accept us. It was all about education. I inhaled deeply. My body felt tense with excitement. I was doing it. Finally, I was teaching a course that had some relevance to me.

⸺⸱⸺

I was sitting at the desk in my office, shortly after the failure of the third insemination, struggling to make sense of the tenure application I was expected to complete this semester, when a colleague, a senior professor who'd been teaching here for many more years than I had, knocked at the door.

"I just want to take issue with the quote you have up on your door," he said, pointing to Albert Einstein's words: "Imagination is more important than knowledge." I lay my application paperwork aside and cursed my open door. Why hadn't I closed it when I came in here? "The problem," my colleague said, pausing for emphasis, "is that the kind of students we have here won't understand what it means." He gazed at me.

I could feel a surge of anger as he left. Outside, the rain fell in torrents. It was so cold I was already wearing a sweater, and it was only the middle of September. I went back to my tenure application. Surely, they didn't mean that I had to include a syllabus and handouts for every single class I'd taught in the last six years. Our regular course load was four classes each semester, after all. I only had an hour or so before the gay and lesbian literature class—I needed to put this stuff away and start preparing. I still had a stack of papers to grade. I picked one up.

"I don't see why gay people always have to talk about it," was the first sentence I read. I put the paper back down, took off my glasses, and rubbed my eyes. I felt that familiar irritability, like the hair was rising all along the back of my neck. I'd spotted a little blood yesterday, but so far today there'd been nothing on my tampon. My stomach felt like it was full of glass. I glanced out the window. Rain was sliding down the glass, obscuring everything else. It was like living in a submarine. I put my glasses back on and picked up another paper just in time to hear a student knock at the door.

"Excuse me," the student said. She was a lesbian; I knew that from the grapevine. I'd read her paper yesterday. She'd written that she didn't understand what difference your sexuality made. I wondered what reality she lived in. She stood before my desk now, her hair in her face and her shoulders slumped. "You said we could ask you for help if we wanted to form a support group," she said.

I did say that. I dimly remembered saying it last week, when I'd had more energy. Last week, when I could imagine the sperm still coursing through my body like suckerfish in earnest pursuit of my beckoning egg; last week, when I could still believe, despite the odds, that I might, just might, be pregnant. Last week I'd felt like Joan of Arc, floating about the campus eagerly dispensing of myself wherever needed. This week I couldn't imagine caring less. "Oh," I said masterfully, laying aside my student papers yet again. "Well." I longed to tell her something important, something that would make her stand up straight and throw her hair back off her face, or, better yet, clipper it all off, but when I reached deep down inside myself, I couldn't muster up anything of any worth. "Really, all you'd have to do would be put up signs all over campus," I said, "with the time and date of the meeting."

She surveyed me through her hair. "What?"

I fought the urge to shake her. "You know," I said. "Just pick a time and day when you'd want to meet and then post signs all around." I could see the confusion passing across her face like the shadow from the wing of some huge bird.

"You lost me," she said. "What am I supposed to do?"

I put down my pen. Exhaustion spread through me like a growing wind. Organize your own fucking support group, I wanted to scream. Just leave me alone! I closed my eyes for a moment. Guilt flooded me, filling my brain. What was the matter with me? I did *want* to be a role model, didn't I? My tenure application lay accusingly on my desk next to my stack of student papers, waiting for me to provide appropriate documentation for every committee I'd been on in the last twelve semesters. There were so many things I hadn't done. I'd wanted to organize a caucus of the lesbian faculty from all the campuses of the state university system, but I'd lost the energy to do it. A women's conference was coming up, but I had to get this tenure stuff in and be inseminated again at the same time.

There just wasn't enough time in my life to get it all done. I opened my eyes and looked back at my student. She was gnawing on one of her fingernails. "Look," I said. "Can we talk about this after class?"

That night I showed the class a movie by Harvey Fierstein, *Torch Song Trilogy*. I'd shown it before in other classes; I knew how to lead discussion of it. I could hear myself talking in patient measured tones, as if someone else was speaking. All along I worried that at any minute some demon would rise from my throat and choke somebody. A student raised her hand. "It's so great when straight actors play gay characters," she said. "Especially men—it must be so hard on them!"

Why? I wanted to shout. Why would it be any harder than it would be to play a straight character? I knew that I should say it aloud, that I should lead an intelligent discussion of this issue and all its implications, but inside I felt too personally insulted to be able to. I couldn't imagine myself saying anything more enlightened than "You moron." Instead, I dismissed the class and walked out to my car alone, the rain cold and persistent around my neck. So many of the papers I'd just read had hurt my feelings. Maintaining my persona as the professor of a literature class was harder than I had expected because, as a lesbian, I took the homophobic comments so personally. It might be all about education, but did I have to be the one who did the educating? I pulled open the door of my car. The rain beat down against the hood as I started the engine. I'm not the person I thought I was, I thought dully, maneuvering the car out onto the road. I'm not the person I wanted to be. The rain pelted the car. The sound of it lulled me. All I had to do right now was drive back home. I could feel the panic in my chest, as if everything were breaking up inside me. I was tired of people's need. All I wanted was to be left alone. All I wanted was to find a space inside myself and crawl inside and just die in there, just rest.

───※───

"So the letters to the editor have really slacked off, haven't they?" a male colleague asked me one afternoon when he ran into me on the stairs a week or so after the fourth insemination.

"Yeah," I mumbled, unimpressed. It was true. Now they appeared only occasionally, usually after a particularly heavy rain. My colleague glanced at me.

"You know," he said slowly, stroking his beard, "I think everybody's really OK with it." He nodded at me cheerfully. "The vet came out to see our dog the other night, and he brought his boyfriend, and we didn't say anything about it and neither did he."

"Uh-huh," I said, looking for an exit. I was tired of this, of every moment offering a reason to make a stand.

"I really think everything would be OK if we all just practiced live and let live," he said. "Why make such a fuss about it?" I felt behind me for the door to the stairwell. It must be here somewhere. "You know," he said. "I don't go around saying I'm heterosexual all the time."

I could feel something snap inside me. How dare he presume any connection between us? How dare he say everybody was *OK* about gay people. "Oh, really?" I said carefully. I looked pointedly at his hand. "Do you wear a wedding ring?" I asked him. He looked startled and took an almost imperceptible step backward. I barreled on, unable to stop myself. "Do you ever mention your wife in a public setting?" I said. "Do you ever hold her hand while crossing the street?" I took a step closer to him. "Well?" I said. "Is she covered under your insurance policy?"

"Well, gee," my colleague said, feeling behind him for the door. "I guess I never thought of it like that."

"No," I said grimly. "I guess not." I felt as if a cobra were coiled up inside me, and at any moment she might strike out with her fangs bared, and I'd have no control over her. Dumbly, I watched him leave. My body ached. My legs felt drained of energy.

And then it hit me. Just like that. A body blow, right to the stomach. I had PMS. There was no way around it. I was going to get my period, for the fourth time since we'd begun insemination. How long was I going to bang my head against the wall before I gave it up?

The flashing lights behind me sent my heart into overdrive. I didn't have to watch for cops quite so vigilantly now that I was an adult in my thirties and was working diligently to get all those past speeding violations off my record. But the sight of a cop still filled me with terror every time. It was beyond traffic tickets. Ever since my days in the neighborhoods, organizing sit-ins and demonstrations, the sight of those flashing lights was enough to make me want to run. I'd been arrested more than once, and I knew it had little to do with breaking any law. I pulled over to the side of the road and waited for the officer to make it to my window. I could see him in my rearview mirror. He got out slowly, hitching up his belt as he glared around and shifted his gum from one side of his mouth to the other. I didn't think I had been speeding. I lunged for the glove box automatically, dug out for my papers, rooted around in my wallet for my driver's license. My hands felt clammy. My fingers shook a little. I swallowed hard.

"License and registration, ma'am," he said, peering into my car. I could see myself reflected in his sunglasses.

"Was I going too fast?" I asked, handing him my documentation. I remembered that my straight female students told me they often got off by looking sweet. My reflection glared at me, my hair clippered so short I looked like a convict. There was no point in my even trying to look sweet.

The cop inspected my registration and held my license up to the light as if checking for its authenticity. "No," he said, "not really." My stomach clenched. He pulled his ticket pad out of his back pocket and scrawled something on the top sheet and tore it off. "I'm giving you a warning," he said. "You weren't going fast enough for a ticket." He stuffed the paper in my hand and nodded at me. "You have a good day now," he said. "We'll be seeing you."

I watched in the rearview mirror as he strode off, his long-legged swagger eating up the road between our cars. "We'll be seeing you." I put the car in gear and pulled out carefully, conscious of his car still parked there, as if waiting to catch me again the next time. Anger flushed my skin. Son of a bitch. In the months after the article came out, I'd been pulled over three times. "Thought your inspection sticker was overdue," one commented, "but I see now it's not." Another took his time circling the truck, checking every inch of it, until I was noticeably late for class. "Thought your vehicle might match a description of a hit-and-run," he said, working his way around to my window. He squinted up at the sun, then back at me. "'Course, that automobile had New York plates," he drawled, taking an easy look around the interior of my car. "And it was a different color." He tipped his hat to me, a gesture these guys must have picked up from an old Clint Eastwood movie. "You have a nice day, now."

Oh, sure, I thought grimly, now back on Route 6. The fear was gone. In its place was a hot quick anger. "Lose the Grateful Dead sticker," one of my students had told me. "And that 'Thelma and

Louise Live' sticker," another told me, shaking his head. "That's got to go." I glanced at the speedometer and slowed down a little. "Have a nice day." My heart pounded. I tried to draw a breath, but I couldn't get the air into my lungs. What was I doing? What the hell did I think I was doing?

The next morning I poured myself a cup of coffee and opened up the *Star-Gazette*. The same reporter who had done the feature story on us earlier had written an article about the forthcoming publication of my novel. I leafed through the local section looking for it. Maybe that would make me feel better. Some aspect of my life was still functioning, after all. There I was in Section B, smiling earnestly at the camera, looking like I didn't have a care in the world. Nobody would ever know how many rolls of film Connie and I had gone through to get that shot. I read through the article eagerly. Information about the publisher, information about me. I took another swallow of coffee. There I was—a real writer— discussing her first novel. Then came an interview with the owner of the nearest bookstore, in Corning, New York. He said his store wouldn't be carrying my novel, as there was no interest in "that" in this area. I put the newspaper down and stared into my coffee. All my life I had dreamed of walking into a bookstore and seeing my book on the shelves. Now it wasn't going to happen. At least not in the place where I lived. I read through the article again. Grief tore at my chest. What did he mean, I wondered, by "that"? Did he mean the things I was writing about—loss and grief and hope and pain? I put the paper down again. I knew what he meant. I knew exactly what he meant. And deep down I feared that there would- n't be any interest in it in any area, not just this one.

I poured out the rest of my coffee. Fog clung to the streetlamps. The cold gripped my bones. I made myself a pot of tea and climbed back into bed and buried myself in the quilts. My period came with a vengeance, rolling out of me in waves, as if to say, "See? You thought you could plant a baby in here. Well—I'm tougher than that!" I wrote in my journal for hours. I never did make it in to work that day. It was as if I were already distancing myself from my job, making room for new priorities. I watered the plants, made a batch of muffins, read a novel, went to the gym. Slowly, I could feel myself growing stronger. I walked back from the gym and let the rain wash over me. I could do this. I could live my life. I could teach my classes and write my books and love Connie and apply for tenure and keep on living my life. I inhaled deeply. The scent of the rain wound its way through my nostrils, full of dirt and earth and growing things. Inside, my body sloughed off old tissue, prepared itself for new beginnings. I picked up my pace. I could do this. I could keep on doing this.

———— ⟡ ————

"Look at this," one of my gay students told me, slapping a flier down on my desk. I shoved my tenure application aside and picked it up. It was an advertisement for a romantic getaway weekend sponsored by the Christian radio station and the Comfort Inn— for traditional married couples only. I felt a flush of anger and then, just as quickly, a sense of exhaustion. I was too tired to fight these battles anymore. I put the paper down and looked at him.

"Well?" he said. "What are you going to do?"

"I don't know," I said. I looked at him harder. "You could try entering," I said, "and see what happened."

He stared at me. "Oh, no," he said. "Not me."

I looked back at the paper and sighed. Of course, not him. I was the one who should do something, but inside I could feel myself sagging. I just didn't have it in me anymore. I glanced at my watch. Only a half hour until my next class. I still had to prepare. I was just going to have to pick and choose my battles, that was all. And this just wasn't going to be one of them.

———— ⟡ ————

"Let's try a different guy this time," Connie said. "The last one had two chances. It's time for a change." We got out the sperm catalogue and pored through the information again, even though we nearly had it memorized by now. "What about the Jewish doctor?"

I shook my head. "He doesn't have proven fertility," I said. A shame, I thought. I looked at the sheets more closely. No. 9164 kept catching my attention, but I kept pushing it away. He was Jewish, but he was also German, and I was determined not to curse my child with any more German heritage than was absolutely necessary. My own was enough, I thought. Enough anal attention to detail. Enough sense of dread and persecution. More than enough. My mother had called me after I'd sent her a copy of the article about us. "Your father doesn't think it's a good idea for you to have a baby," she said. I'd flushed with anger. My father, who'd never taken an interest in anything I'd done. How dare he? I scanned back through the sheets again. No more German blood. I had to dilute my father's heritage. But 9164 stood out so starkly it might have been printed in different colored ink.

"It's the numbers of my birth year," Connie said. "1964."

I threw down my pen. What the hell. "OK," I said. "I give up." I pushed the papers toward Connie. She re-read his donor information.

"He's a med student," she said. She looked at me. "I say we go with him."

I nodded. The German Jewish med student it was. It felt a little like playing Russian roulette, this choosing of sperm. Who knew what chamber might come up?

My hormone surge finally showed up on the fourteenth day of my cycle. We'd already ordered the sperm, already set up the doctor's appointment. The weekend had been approaching, and we'd either had to take the chance that I would ovulate eventually or risk missing another cycle. Sometimes I felt like the whole world was conspiring against my getting pregnant—faulty ovulation kits, inaccessible doctors, hostile receptionists, inadequate money supply, sperm banks that didn't ship on Saturday, an LH surge that always seemed to show up over the weekend or on holidays (except when it didn't show at all). I sat and sipped my decaf coffee and smoothed open my newspaper and thought that this month I didn't want a baby at all. Why would I want *kids*? My God, I had no time and energy now—why would I want to throw kids into the equation?

I put down my newspaper and glanced out the window. The day was gray and rainy, the way that all the days this fall had been, somehow beautiful, a dark, aching day full of clouds and fog that gave way to blue in the points of higher elevation along the road I took to work. The air was full of a cold dampness. Connie sat down at the table with me and picked up a piece of the paper. Anxiety tore at my gut. What would a child do to the order of our lives? I glanced at the clock. At two o'clock we would be inseminated. I wondered if I was especially afraid because this was the fifth time. The odds of conception were getting better every month. Maybe this time it would actually work.

I glanced around our clean kitchen, our thriving ivies in the windows, our coffee brewing on the counter.

A part of me hoped it wouldn't.

Connie glanced up at me and smiled. She touched my hand for a moment. Her fingers were warm and gentle, soft as rain. She went back to her paper.

I wondered whether I was crazy. This wasn't exactly an accident. We were going about this with cold calculation, counting days and testing urine, using speculums and angiocaths, swabbing off mucous to give the sperm a clearer path, aspirating excess semen in an effort to cram in every last expensive drop of the stuff, lying in wait for half an hour with my hips elevated to ensure the sperm had the proper start. No one could say we hadn't asked for this. No one was holding a gun to our heads. Connie tightened her hand around mine.

"Are we crazy?" I asked her. "What are we doing this for?" I took another sip of decaf. "I don't think I can stand much more of this stress."

Connie nodded and took another sip of her coffee. "I know," she said. "No wonder it usually happens through sex. That's the only way people can get over the anxiety."

Of course, I thought. "If everybody had to do it the way we're doing it, how many people *would*?" I looked at Connie. "We'd be a world populated by lesbians."

"Yeah," she said, pushing back her chair to retrieve the coffeepot. "Only two women could do it."

I wondered how many women were dissuaded by this and gave it up before they ever got pregnant. For every lesbian who actually conceived a child, there must have been a hundred who wanted to.

Connie poured the rest of her coffee into a travel cup. "We'd better get going," she said, glancing over at me. She smiled. "It'll be OK."

I drained my cup. I wished I could be that sure. I really wished I could.

The first insemination of the month went smoothly. For the first time I felt cramps as the semen entered my body. Dr. Gordon informed us that that was a good sign. The uterus was contracting because of the prostaglandin to pull the semen upward. I didn't understand it—I mean, I'd never had cramps during sex, but I was willing to accept anything that could be construed as a good sign. As I prepared for the second insemination the following morning, I felt a kind of peace settle over me, like anything was possible, like I would write another novel, grow a child in my belly, make soup and bread and spend long hours reading, make fires in the fireplace and feel myself begin to nest, settle into myself, like a bird. The morning was quiet; I could hear the water moving through the radiators. The house was settling all around me, a kaleidoscope of small soft sounds. Cars moved down the street, their tires spinning on the rain.

Connie and I drove to the office in silence, holding hands across the front seat. I was filled with a new and quiet calm. When the time for the insemination came, I lay down on the table and parted my thighs and let the doctor do his work while outside the rain fell and Connie held my hand.

As I drove to work, I felt full of peace. All I had to do was go to a lecture by a guest speaker and teach my class that night. The insemination was over. The hardest part of the day was over.

⸻

The North Dining Room, which doubled as a lecture hall, was full of criminal justice majors, all with crewcuts and baseball caps, chewing gum in the corners of their mouths like tobacco. I watched them covertly and wondered for a moment why they were there, at this lecture by a visiting professor who was talking about lesbians and violence in film. They must be fulfilling some class requirement. The students snickered over clips from *Basic Instinct*, nudged one another all through the scenes from *Thelma and Louise*, while the speaker talked about lesbian subtext. When she was finished, Joe Dyer, one of the criminal justice professors, stood up. "I just want to say that Louise was grieved at seeing her boyfriend leave." He paused to clear his throat, then glanced around the room. "I think this shows she was a normal," he hesitated, as if catching himself, then added delicately, "if I may still use that term, woman."

I could feel something click inside me, like a gun cocking. My heart began to beat faster and faster, as if it were gathering momentum and might take off at any moment. I didn't hear the speaker's answer. I knew the lecture was over only when the criminal justice majors around me picked up their notebooks and began to leave. Dyer stood between me and the door, expounding on his theory to a group of faculty.

"By 'normal,' " Deborah was asking carefully as I approached them, "do you mean heterosexual women?"

Dyer glanced at her, his brow furrowed in annoyance. "Yes," he said.

I heard myself talking before I could even think about it. "I object to the use of the term *normal* to apply to heterosexuals," I said thinly. My heart shook in my chest like a leaf. What was I doing?

"Oh, you're just arguing semantics here," Dyer said. He turned his back to me, waving his hand in dismissal. His back blocked my view. He was taller than I was. His voice was louder than mine. I could feel something growing taut inside me. He wasn't just Joe Dyer anymore, an innocuous criminal justice professor; he was my brooding German father, turning his back on me just one too many times.

"Hey!" I said. I went to put my hand on his arm, but before I knew what I was doing, I had a fistful of his coat in my hand. I swung him around to face me. "I am a lesbian," I said. His face grew pale in alarm. A roaring filled my head. I wasn't even in my body anymore. I had become a fine white light, surrounded by a group of disembodied faces, all staring at me in awe. I tightened my grip on his coat and looked him right in the eye. "And I am a normal woman."

He stared at me. Everyone was absolutely silent. We all stared at my hand, as if wondering what it might do next. I unclenched my fingers and pulled them away. For a moment I thought his coat might come away too, like the skin of a burn victim.

"Just a minute," Dyer said, but I had already turned away. His voice followed me to the door, but I had ceased to hear him. Inside me all that anger that had flared up so suddenly was gone, just like blowing out a match. I walked back to my office with my hands in my pockets, feeling the rain against my face. There was still an hour before my gay and lesbian literature class. If I hurried, I could get some work done on that tenure application, dig up some proof of my service to the community, mine my past six years for evidence of why the campus needed me.

If There's a Blue Line in the Large Window . . .

The night before the next insemination I dreamed that Dr. Gordon was inseminating me and that when it was done he lay down next to me and put his arms around me, and I lay with my eyes closed while he stroked my face and hair, and it felt wonderful. I awoke next to Connie, the room still dark, my cat a solid lump at my feet. I was still full of my dream, full of Dr. Gordon's arms around me. It felt like those all-consuming crushes I used to have on men when I was younger, when it seemed like just touching the other person, or being touched by him, was like coming into the presence of God. I remembered a moment of first touching a lover's face, someone I had longed to touch for months, and feeling that it was all I'd ever lived for, the only purpose my life would ever have. I could have spent my life serving him, thankful just to be in his presence.

Connie shifted in her sleep, pressed the length of her body against mine, and sighed. I had never felt like that with Connie, never felt that sense of adulation. When we first touched, it was two people coming together, two full grown and fully developed bodies coming into contact with each other. I ran my hand along her skin and felt its warmth against my palm. I used to worry that it meant I didn't really love her, not in the way that I had loved those men whose touch I craved. Lying in bed now I suspected that it meant that Connie was a real person to me, a human being, full of flesh and blood and flaws, and that I wanted to be with all of her, as opposed to those past lovers, whom I saw as gods at whose altars I might be fortunate enough to worship. They were like dreams I prayed would overtake me. Connie was so real. Lying next to her, I felt that I could get my hands on every part of her, sink my teeth into her, feel her flesh beneath my fingers, firm and solid. I knew that she breathed and shit and drank and smiled and was angry and made love like no one I had ever known. I pressed my face into her back and inhaled her warmth. I wasn't dreaming. I would never have to worry about waking up one day and seeing that the mist had faded, the god had disappeared—folded up his altar like a camp stool and fled into the night, leaving me alone with my illusions, asleep with my dreams.

Connie stirred beneath my touch and turned to face me, her face still soft in sleep. I kissed her eyelids, brushed her lips with my mouth. "Wake up," I whispered. "The morning is at hand."

She opened her eyes and looked up at me. Her skin was so soft, her mouth so perfect. "Are you ready?" she asked.

"I will be in a minute," I said, sliding my lips along her neck, deep into the hollow at the base of her throat. "Just hold on." I buried my head between her breasts, pressed my lips against her skin. "Just give me a little more time."

Connie stroked my hair, sighed, and settled back into the blankets. "Take all the time you need," she said. "We've got all the time in the world."

It was Halloween. A dry wind blew up the leaves and carried with it the scent of apples and pine. The world seemed full of ghosts. In a wild way I felt close to death. I felt intensely mortal, susceptible to decay. My body no longer felt like a sacred temple. It felt like what it was—a collection of flesh and blood and bones, subject to malfunction at any time. I felt human. Like the piles of dead leaves in the streets, I too would recombine with the earth some day.

By the time we presented ourselves at the doctor's office for insemination, I didn't even care anymore. I lay on my back, let him open me up and squirt the semen into my vagina, held Connie's hand, and looked into her eyes. It was all old hat by now—no mystery was left. It was just twenty million motile sperm going off on their run, salmonlike, toward an unpredictable future. It was nature, it was happening over and over and over, in the wild and in the houses up and down our street.

When Dr. Gordon withdrew his syringe, my cervix bled. It was as if my body were saying, "Enough." I brought my knees together and lay there for the required thirty minutes, holding Connie's hand. I suddenly felt liberated, sprung as if from a jail cell. I had just been inseminated, and I couldn't care less. If it happened, it happened.

We handed candy out that night to a stream of children dressed in masks and cloaks. They ran up and down our steps for hours while our dog barked frantically, begging to make friends. If some children didn't cross the street to our house, if their parents clung to them too tightly and steered them past our door before they could complain, I decided not to notice. I began to eat the leftover candy, cramming it into my mouth and feeling the chocolate slide down my throat. It felt powerful, as if I were swallowing blood. Who cared if it was full of calories? I was human now, as ready to die as I was to live. The wind whipped up outside the door and rattled the wind chimes. I could feel something in me stirring, whispering through my body. My whole being tingled. I bolted the door with satisfaction and turned to Connie. "Let's go to bed," I said. My body rippled like a wave. I turned off the porch light. Connie's eyes seemed to glow in the dark. I took a step closer to her. The air was alive with our breathing, electric with the smell of our beings.

"Let's do it here," she whispered, her lips barely brushing my ear. A thrill ran through me. "Come on," she said and pulled me down to the floor.

Kids in masks knocked on the door the whole time.

Three days after the insemination we went to the hospital for a blood test to determine my HCG level, which I now knew stood for human chorionic gonadotropin, a common way to test for pregnancy. I had wrangled the order for it from Dr. Gordon by using my feminine wiles, since I suspected he wouldn't want to do it. I waited till we were all ready to leave the office and then I leaned toward him. "Doctor Gordon," I said, making my voice deep and slightly husky.

"Yes?" he said, taking a step toward me. He put a hand on my arm.

"Could we possibly get a blood test?" I asked him. I could feel my voice rippling from me, like it was covered with fur. "You know," I said. My tone was like a caress. "So we won't have to wait."

He nodded at once. "Certainly. Just wait until the fourth day," he cautioned, "to make sure that the hormone levels have had a chance to change."

By late in the afternoon of the third day we were sitting around the kitchen table, fixated on the piece of prescription paper on which Dr. Gordon had scrawled his order for the test. Connie looked at me. I looked back at the paper. The cats lay around us on the table, nestled deep into the folds of our napkins. "Well," Connie said. "What do you think?"

I pushed my seat back. "I don't think I can stand much more of this." I felt like I might faint. "Don't you think enough time has passed?"

Connie studied the piece of paper again, as if the directive might have changed. "He didn't date it," she said slowly. We looked at each other again.

"Let's go," I said.

The halls of the hospital were narrow and dark. We waited in a line of people. My veins itched. I could hardly breathe. "Relax," Connie whispered. I glared at her. What did she think we were doing here? Waiting for a movie to start? When they called my name, I looked back at her. "You'll be OK," she said, squeezing my hand. I squeezed back. I felt as if I were drowning. The white-coated nurse waited with a pronounced lack of patience. I stood up. My legs shook. I glanced back at Connie, then stepped through the door.

"I'm sorry," the nurse told me over the phone later that night.

I hung up the phone numbly. Connie was out for the night. I was home alone. The night sky gave me a reflection of my face in the glass every time I turned around. I wasn't pregnant. My heart felt as if it were bleeding inside me, or maybe as if it had stopped bleeding and was instead wrung dry, a shriveled raisin in the center of my chest. I wasn't pregnant. I could see my womb, barren, a wide endless desert with a harsh wind sweeping across it. I wasn't pregnant. My ovaries, my uterus—it was all unnecessary equipment. I would never be pregnant. I stopped before the window in my office. My face stared back at me, ghostlike in the night. I wasn't made to have children. I took a deep breath. I wasn't meant to have children. I would never feel life inside me. I sat down at my desk and wrote for hours. I wrote poem after poem, the images seeming to come from deep within the soil of my being. My candlelight flickered, the incense burned. Its smell wafted through the air and spiraled around my head like cigarette smoke. When I was finished, I blew out the light and sat there for a moment in the darkness. My heart felt dark with blood, tight with sorrow. I was still sad. I still felt the emptiness. I was still not pregnant.

The days were filled with work. My copyedited manuscript arrived from the publisher with marks on every line of every page. My heart sank as I looked at it. They gave me three weeks to get it back. I couldn't even look at it without my stomach turning. I saw pencil marks when I closed my eyes. The publisher asked me for the names of writers who might be willing to provide promotional quotes for the book. I needed to write everyone I knew and ask permission to release their names. Two sets of student papers lay on my desk waiting to be read. If that weren't enough, the rains suddenly stopped and the sun came out, as if the afternoons were fairly begging to be played with. I felt an edge of bitchiness inside that I found annoying. Connie and I began to fight with startling regularity. I felt paralyzed with an inability to start anything. The elections came and went, leaving Republicans in power everywhere. I felt like I was weeping all the time. A chill permeated my bones, seeming to come from my heart. I wondered where my life was taking me and why. At night I dreamed about the manuscript awaiting my perusal. I dreamed that somebody was on the phone, asking whether I wanted to know what my mother thought about the book. "No!" I said. "Of course not!"

"She thinks it's slow," the caller said. "She thinks it's too slow, wouldn't you say?"

When I went to the bathroom, I found blood on my underwear, as if my body were having a private joke. "Here's your period!" it might have been saying. "A week early!" When friends called and asked us to join them at the bar of the local hotel that Friday night, we needed no urging. We got there an hour early. The bar was filled with locals. I felt a sense of unease. "I don't know," I whispered to Connie. It just didn't feel like a place where we belonged, like so many places in this town. This was one of the local bastions; walking in here was like walking into the town diner, located in an old railroad car in the center of town, where the county commissioners gathered to swill down coffee with the town fathers. A few heads turned toward us. Several conversations stopped midsentence. I felt like I'd walked into a bar in an old western, as if in a moment I'd have to pull out my gun and show them all that we belonged here, even if we had to shoot our way in.

Connie swallowed. I could hear it move along her throat. "Come on," she said, her voice cracking only slightly. "Let's sit down."

We chose a seat in the middle of the room. There might as well have been a spotlight on us. It seemed that everyone was watching us take our seats. In the moment before we sat down I wondered whether it would be easier just to leave, leave the bar, the town, my job, just leave it all behind us. I thought of my colleagues who had stayed here because there were no other jobs for them to take. What was I doing here? As I pulled back my chair, I wondered how long I'd been instinctively choosing a seat with my back against the wall. "Let's have Courvoisier," Connie said when the waitress came around to us. "To celebrate."

"What are we celebrating?" I asked her.

"Your book," she said. Her gaze caught mine. Toast with me, her eyes said. Don't look away. The liquor burned all the way down to my stomach. We ordered another round. Our friends joined us, and the pianist began to play. Somebody began to sing some old Irish drinking song, and one by one the townspeople around us joined in, singing at the top of their lungs. I stole a glance at Connie. They seemed to have forgotten us. I settled back in my chair. I could feel something in me start to lift. Maybe life wasn't so bad after all. I had a novel coming out. I took another sip of my Courvoisier. It slipped into my stomach, curled up there like a cat, and purred contentedly. For the first time in days I didn't feel cold. I felt for Connie's hand beneath the table. She smiled at me. Her eyes shone. I sat back in my seat holding her hand against my thigh, while around us the voices of the townspeople rose in song.

Another Courvoisier and I could almost shake the sense that I was back in a bar in Pittsburgh that I used to frequent during my organizing days, where immigrants from the city's Irish and German neighborhoods used to gather around the piano and sing, downing round after round of beer, occasionally culminating in an enthusiastic rendition of *Deutschland Uber Alles* that used to resound against the oak walls of the bar, mingling with the warm applause that used to spread through the room like cigarette smoke, the chill that ran down the back of my neck, the instinctive way I made myself as small and quiet as possible, in the hope that no one would notice me.

―――※―――

My period stopped abruptly. It seemed I had only been spotting. First it was one day late, then two. I couldn't be pregnant—I'd had a blood test. All those shots of Courvoisier that night . . . A list formed in my mind, as stark as a billboard, of everything I'd had to drink in the past two weeks, all the medication I'd taken. My palms began to sweat. I went back to the bathroom and checked again. Still no period. My stomach felt tight and hard to the touch. It had to be stress. It was the semester from hell. Stress could delay a period. Besides—I'd had blood work done. I *knew* I wasn't pregnant.

Connie and I went to the store to get some things, and I found myself in front of the pregnancy tests. Connie looked at me. "You're not pregnant," she said. Her tone was final. "You don't need a pregnancy test."

I kept staring at them. It was just like the ovulation kits. All I had to do was piss on a stick. Before I knew what I was doing, I had one in my hand. "I'm getting it," I told Connie, clutching it to me as if I thought she might try to take it away. My fingers were hanging on so hard I thought I might be incapable of setting it down when we got to the register.

Connie shook her head. "Fine," she said, turning away. "But I'm not having any part of this."

When we got home, I put the test in the bathroom. I wouldn't do anything until the next morning. Maybe I would get my period in the night.

I woke at 4 A.M., my heart beating wildly. For a moment I wondered whether I was having a stroke. Beside me, Connie slept, impervious. I went to the bathroom and checked the toilet paper. No period. I opened the medicine cabinet and looked inside. The pregnancy test was waiting on the shelf. I took a deep breath and took it down. It seemed to glow in my hand, as if lit with a light all its own. I read the instructions again and again. A blue line in the large window meant I was pregnant. It didn't matter how faint it was. I pushed the bathroom window open and sat back down on the toilet. Outside, the air was still. A snap of cold filled the bathroom. It was two hours before I had the nerve to try the test. I made myself some coffee, tried to write in my journal, lit a candle in my office, sat still at my desk, and tried to connect with myself, tried to reach deep down and find my soul, but my hands kept coming up empty. At six I went back upstairs and pissed on the stick. It felt like old times. I left the test to sit for the required time on the sink, forced myself to leave the room and set the timer, forced myself not to look at it until the time had passed. When the timer rang, I took a deep breath and went back into the bathroom, picked up the test stick and checked the window.

The line was so faint that I could barely see it. For a moment I thought I might be imagining it. I looked again. It was there, but it was the faintest blue line possible. It must be a mistake. I took a breath. Then another. The cold air stung my lungs. I closed the window and held the test stick up to the light. Was that really a line? It couldn't be a line. Surely, if I were pregnant, the line would be dark and bold, the same way my LH line had been. More of a pronouncement. I glanced at the clock. Six o'clock. I took the stick in my hand and pushed open the door of the bedroom. Connie and I had joked that we'd never have the experience of the straight couples in the commercials, where the wife says coyly to the husband: "Honey, I have some news."

"We'll never be able to do that," I'd told Connie, "because you'll know at the same time I do." But here I was, lightly kissing her face in the darkness to wake her. "Honey," I whispered into her ear. But I couldn't do the coy announcement. Instead I said, so quickly my words stumbled over themselves, leaving my lips, "I did the pregnancy test, but the line's so faint, it can't possibly mean I'm pregnant, I mean—"

Connie sat up in bed. She took the stick from my hand and turned on the light. Her fingers shook. We both stared at it. "There's a line," she said. We looked at each other. I could feel something in me start to shake, as if my heart had become a tree and someone had both hands around its trunk, trying to bring down its fruit. "There's definitely a line," she said. We looked at each other. "You're pregnant," she said. She sat bolt upright in bed. "Oh, my god—you're pregnant!"

I shook my head. "I can't be." I took the test stick back from her. "You can barely see the line!" I stared at it. Surely, this moment should be more conclusive. I should know if I was pregnant.

"I think you're pregnant," Connie said. Her voice shook. She seized my hand. "We're pregnant!"

"But what about the blood test?" I asked her. "We know I'm not pregnant."

Connie frowned. "You'd better call the doctor," she said, "and go in for a pregnancy test." She looked at me. "In the meantime," she said, "we can't tell anybody."

We met at the doctor's office that afternoon. We held hands in the waiting room, waiting for the nurses to call my name. "I told Deborah," I whispered to her.

Connie glanced at me. "I told *everybody*," she whispered back.

When my name was called, the nurse ushered me into the bathroom. I closed my eyes as I filled the little cup and gave it back to her. Was this it? Were we finally pregnant? Connie and I sat together in the examination room, waiting for Dr. Gordon. Neither of us spoke. When he opened the door, I could tell the answer from his face. "You're pregnant!" he said. I threw my arms around his neck. I could feel my eyes grow wet, but at the same time a part of me was standing back, its arms folded across its chest. None of it felt real. This felt like a part I'd been rehearsing for so long the lines had become rote. I couldn't really be pregnant. How could I be? Meanwhile, Dr. Gordon was calculating something over by my chart. "July twenty-second," he said. "That's your due date."

I looked at Connie. July 22. I had a due date. "Congratulations," Dr. Gordon said, hugging us both again before he left the room. I could hear his voice through the wall, greeting some other patient, moving on to somebody else's life. Connie and I left the office and walked back out to the car. The air was cold, the sky gray. I didn't know what to say. I suddenly didn't feel ready. I hadn't had enough time to prepare. Connie felt for my hand and held it in hers. Her palm was warm, her fingers strong. "Congratulations," she whispered. I took a deep breath. We were pregnant. I didn't know what would happen next. All I knew was that we were in this together. We were lesbians in Tioga County, and we were going to have a baby.

Well, Just Be Careful . . .

For a few days everything was different. I awoke full of energy and appetite. I ate vegetables and drank milk. I went to the gym every day. I gazed at my body in the mirror as I ran on the treadmill. Every muscle was toned. My stomach was flat and hard. My legs flashed as I stepped up the speed. I threw my head back. I was pregnant. There was nothing I couldn't do. I ran mile after mile, clocking my times. I was unstoppable. My reflection shone in the mirror, radiant with life. I was going to do it. I was going to have a baby. I was going to be strong. I would be a suit of armor for this baby. The blood surged through my body, flooded my head with a dizzying clarity. I was pregnant. Nothing was going to stop me now.

The truck pulled out in front of us without looking and slowed immediately to a crawl. It backfired and exhaust filled our car. Connie grimaced and closed the outside air vent. "What about the Pennsylvania inspection laws?" I said. "That's what I want to know. Aren't they supposed to be strict?"

Connie snorted and shifted down yet another gear. "Who knows?" she said. "Who the hell knows?" We were driving back from the mall, making our way up Route 414 from Liberty. Pennsylvania towns must have been named in a burst of great optimism, back when the pioneers were streaming through, en route to the territories: Liberty, Bethlehem, New Jerusalem, Promised Land, Prosperity. Any number of saints. Except for the one a couple towns over from us: Job's Corner. It's hard to maintain a lot of optimism in the face of so little light.

The road was narrow, lined on either side by a thick spray of trees, the remaining leaves dark gold in the half light from the setting sun. The truck in front of us was a dilapidated old white American truck driven by a dilapidated old white American man. We reached a hill and he slowed even more. As we watched, he cranked his window down and hacked a hunk of chew out into the road. "Yech!" we said in unison.

Passing was impossible. The road was so narrow and winding that you never knew if another car might be coming around the bend. People died on these roads every year, usually while trying to get around some driver just like this one. I'd learned a long time ago that it was better just to allow a lot of time and settle in to wait. However annoying the drivers around here were, they weren't worth dying to avoid.

The truck sputtered as the driver downshifted. I wondered if he'd even make it up this hill. How did people drive these junkers in a place like this, where every road crested a mountain at some point? The driver lit a cigarette and swerved into the other lane. Then I noticed his bumper sticker: "Elect David Duke." Without even thinking about it, I cupped my belly in my hands, as if to keep it safe. "Do you see that?" I asked Connie.

Her face paled slightly. She shook her head. "Well, this is militia country," she said, looking around uneasily. I drew closer to her. The trees around us were black and cold in the draining light. I imagined militia men riding out of them, clad in buckskin and brandishing rifles, surrounding our car. Then I remembered that somebody's house had been stormed by the FBI not too long ago; the officers had found dozens of weapons stockpiled in the living room. It wouldn't be rifles. It would be assault weapons. I locked my door. "It's clear up ahead," Connie said, pressing the accelerator. "I'm going to pass."

We sped around him, picking up speed as we went. I stole a glance through his window as we passed. He stared straight ahead, both hands knotted around the top of his steering wheel, his cigarette dangling from the corner of his mouth. There was a whiteness around his lips, as if he were used to pursing them hard. Connie and I were silent the rest of the way home. I cradled my stomach in my hands. Somewhere deep inside a life was forming. I wondered what I thought I was doing, bringing it into a world like this one.

I dreamed that night that I was running through a ghetto neighborhood just like the ones I used to organize, past housing projects and decaying buildings, and that people were staring at me. I tried to run faster, but my feet grew heavier and heavier, until I could barely lift them. I heard shouts behind me and saw a man running as fast as he could. "Thief! Murderer!" shouted the people chasing him. I was so relieved that they were chasing someone else that, as he passed me, I too began to yell, "Thief! Murderer!" But then he disappeared from view, and when I looked behind me all the people in the mob had faces, and they were all chasing me, all screaming at me.

I woke up without opening my eyes. Nausea rolled through me

like a tide, leaving me breathless and gasping for air, clutching at the sides of the bed as if at a ship's rails. My head ached. I lay motionless, my eyes closed. Here I'd been congratulating myself for not having morning sickness. I knew I wouldn't be one of those women who succumbed. I'd been confident my body could handle pregnancy. One of my pregnancy books suggested that the type of woman who suffered from morning sickness had been found to be hypnotizable, easily suggestible. That wasn't the kind of person I was. I'd been planning to go to the gym all the way up till I went into labor. I was going to do everything right. I'd watched my pregnant neighbors pushing their strollers up the street, pulling their dogs along behind, their stomachs huge and proud, their faces flushed with the exertion. I was going to exercise regularly, eat vegetables every day, drink four glasses of milk. I was going to read the information in the pregnancy books as religiously as if I were combing the Bible, searching for the answers to my life. I was going to be educated. I was going to be fit. I was going to be invincible, bringing my child into the world like an Amazon. Somewhere deep inside I was arming myself, just in case the hospital wouldn't take me, just in case the nurses wouldn't deliver me, just in case my doctor was shot dead trying to help me. I wanted to be strong enough to deliver my baby myself, if need be, squatting in a field and pulling my child from me with both hands. I wanted to be able to do it by myself. So what if I was a pregnant dyke in God's Country. I didn't need laws to protect me. I didn't need acceptance. I could do this on my own. No matter what.

At the moment, however, I couldn't imagine sitting up, let alone getting out of bed. "You've got to eat something," Connie said, setting a plate of soda crackers on my nightstand. I shook my head. I couldn't remember when I'd last eaten; just the thought made my stomach lurch. I wondered what I'd gotten myself into, how I'd ever finish what I'd started.

———— ⚬⚬⚬ ————

"Don't do it," Connie said, watching my hand hover above the telephone. "Don't call your mother and tell her you're pregnant."

I paused and looked at her, my fingers poised to punch out the numbers that I had known so well my entire life. "What do you mean?" I asked halfheartedly. I knew what she meant.

"Don't call her," Connie said. "Send her a card. Give her time to digest."

She was right. Deep down I knew she was right. I looked at the receiver longingly. I just wanted to call her so much, wanted to hear her voice on the phone, resonant with warmth, wishing me the best in my life. Never mind that I couldn't remember her ever actually having done that.

"You're making a mistake," Connie said, and even as I listened to the familiar electronic rhythm of the buttons I had pushed, I knew she was right. But I had to tell her. I waited longingly for her to pick up and when she did I almost hung up. "Mom?" I said. I shifted the receiver from one hand to the other and wiped my palm on my thigh. My hand shook. "I'm pregnant," I said. I closed my eyes. The enormity of it overwhelmed me. I had finally done it. I was pregnant. I was pregnant with her grandchild. I was pregnant with my child, just as she had been pregnant with me. I was finally a real adult. Falling in love with Connie hadn't done it, our pretend marriage hadn't done it, but surely this would. This would be the thing that would bring me real recognition, transform me in my mother's eyes from child to voting, taxpaying, mortgage-holding adult. My eyes closed. I imagined her joy, the delight she'd take in the news. I imagined her hand extending across the divide that separated us, to help me over to her side. Moments passed and there was no response. "Mom?" I said, opening my eyes.

I could hear her on the other end, inhaling with slow and careful precision. "Well," she responded. "Just be careful." Her tone was level, cold as frost.

"What do you mean?" I asked slowly.

"Well, your sister said that once too!" my mother said.

I could feel the excitement leaving my body like a bird. "What do you mean?" I said again, enunciating carefully. My tongue felt wooden, my body empty, its rooms left open, doors swinging on their hinges, sprung of the life that had filled them only moments before.

"Well, she *lost* it," my mother said.

⸻∘⸻

"You've lost five pounds," Dr. Gordon said sternly, flipping through his chart. "Have you been eating at all?"

I mumbled something and looked away. I couldn't eat. How could I eat? Thanksgiving had come and gone without even a glass of wine to mark its passing. The turkey carcass sat on the table, grease collecting beneath it. Our guests sat together on the couch watching the football game, while Connie washed the dishes. The house was filled with warmth and cheer. Normally, I loved Thanksgiving, the one holiday without any real family baggage. Granted, it was a celebration of a nation's genocide, but it was a happy one. Squanto had shared his maize with us. For a long time I thought that was all there was—we'd moved in, and the Indians had moved over, pleased to teach us how to survive in this new land and then politely disappear while we found our footing. My third-grade teachers had never mentioned the smallpox-infected blankets as we colored in our construction paper pumpkins and wove our multicolored potholders to give our mothers. Now the day seemed bleak and stormy, the skies swelling with withheld snow and the wind wild for revenge. I pulled my sweater more tightly around me and watched our friends curled happily on our couch, until I just had to go to bed and suffer through another night.

"She's not eating at all," Connie informed Dr. Gordon, as if I weren't even there. I glared at her when his back was turned. Traitor.

"How important is nutrition right now?" I asked him.

"Not important at all," he responded, "for the first fourteen weeks." He made another mark in his chart. What was he always writing down in there? "Are you tolerating the prenatal vitamin?"

Oh, that evil horse pill that got stuck every morning halfway down my throat. "No," I said a little petulantly.

"You can discontinue it until week fourteen," he said. Behind his back I threw Connie as victorious a look as I could muster. "In the meantime," he said, washing his hands in the sink, "eat whatever you can."

―∞―

My department chair ducked his head in the door of my office. I was sitting at my desk staring down a pile of soda crackers. Just one bite. I thought I could chance one bite. The crackers lay there, innocuous, as if they would not immediately turn to lead once I actually swallowed them. "Hi, Roland," I said, looking up at him. I tentatively nibbled a corner of soda cracker, as if making an offering. Who knew whether it would be accepted? "How are you?"

Roland stayed in the doorway. "I was just wondering," he said, "how you're planning to take off next fall semester?"

I had enough sick days saved up to cover a semester of maternity leave. I'd told Roland about it as soon as I found out I was pregnant. I almost told him about it before I told him I was pregnant. I didn't know which I was more excited about—having a baby or taking a semester off from work. The baby was due in July. Taking off the fall semester would give me the first six months at home. I imagined them longingly from time to time, as I watched the neighborhood women strolling the streets with their children, looking at the leaves. But something about Roland's tone was ominous. "What do you mean?" I said, the cracker leaden the minute it hit my saliva.

"You can't use your sick leave for maternity leave," Roland said. I stared at him, my mouth open slightly. I could feel the crumbs clinging to my lips.

"What are you talking about?" I said.

"Child-care leave is unpaid," Roland said. His face was pinched with worry.

I stared at him. Nausea roiled up in me like a flash flood. "But I read the contract, Roland," I said. "I can use all the sick leave I've accumulated with a note from my doctor."

"I don't think so," he said, drawing himself back until his feet were barely inside the door. My heart began to beat. Waves of nausea rose to my head. I could feel myself growing faint. I imagined giving birth in July, then reporting for the first day of classes barely four weeks later. And that was if the baby was on time. What if it was late?

"But I'll check with the provost about it," he said, ducking back out of my office. I sat there for a moment, staring after him. In my mouth was the taste of ashes.

"They have to let you use your sick leave for maternity leave," Dr. Gordon informed me cheerfully. "It's the law. I'll be glad to write a letter," he added, patting my knee. The office was warm, one wall papered with posters showing the stages of development. I studied the embryo's early stages. At first glance the baby looked more like a salamander than a human being, its little hands up by its face, its eyes huge in the side-view drawing. But what was that? I looked a little closer. An ear. A baby's ear. We were just beginning month two. I gazed at the picture in fascination. There were eyelids, a nose, lips, a tongue. It weighed one third of an ounce; it was about an inch long. And it already had fingers and toes—tiny hands and feet. A studious gaze. I pictured it looking up at me, its little lips half open. Well? it might have been saying. Here I am. What are you going to do about it?

I left the office with Dr. Gordon's letter in my hand. A cold wind blew, invasive as a knife blade. "We'll sue them if we have to," Connie said. I fingered the letter in my hand and thought about the baby in my womb. Dead leaves matted beneath my feet, sodden with rain. The mountains hunkered down around us, violet with the lack of sun. I took a deep breath. Crisp November air filled my lungs. The wind stung my face, making me gasp from its bite. We had conceived this baby in a wind like this. I closed my eyes and imagined our baby hurtling into my body, thrown there on a breath of wind, taking root like a seed.

I took another breath and drew the air as deep into my lungs as possible. My waistband felt snug. My stomach was expanding. I felt a swell of love for it. I could see it now, rooted deep within me, a stubborn little horseshoe crab clutching my uterus with its claws for dear life, embedded for good. My mother's words washed away and with them Roland's words as well. I wasn't powerless. I wasn't going to lose this baby. I was full of its life, immersed in it. I was going to carry to term, I was going to give birth, and I was staying home for the first six months, even if I had to sue the hell out of the university. I slid one hand around Connie's waist and reached covertly beneath my sweater with the other and undid the button of my pants. I was big, walking through the parking lot of Dr. Gordon's office. I was big and huge and I took up space. I was going to have a baby. I took a deep breath and felt that new life flood my body. I was a writer, I was Connie's partner, and before too long I was going to be a mother. I could do it. I could do it all. Nobody could stop me.

The next day I woke up without morning sickness for the first time. Maybe it was gone for good. I went into my office and wrote in my journal for an hour. My manuscript lay on one corner of my desk, waiting for my touch. I could almost hear it calling me. I put down my pen and gingerly opened it to the first page and began to read through the editor's pencil marks. They didn't seem as bad as they had at first. Maybe she had a point. Maybe the sentence did read a little more smoothly that way. And that correction—I didn't buy it, but maybe if I did this instead. I picked up my pen and touched it to the page. What about this?

It took me a week to make the changes. Most of the editor's remarks I agreed with, some I didn't. I added my own marks to hers, crossed out her suggestions and substituted my own changes, and made notes on a separate piece of paper to include in the letter I would write to accompany the new manuscript. There was something exhilarating about it, this reexamination of my work, something energizing about defending the words that I had written. When I mailed it off, I felt like I'd been given new life. *Amnesty* was done. The book was written. Now it was in someone else's hands. I could turn to something new.

The Precocious Child of an Eccentric Writer

I stood in front of the mirror examining my silhouette. We were just beginning the third month. The baby was supposed to be only four inches long and weigh no more than an ounce. How could my stomach already be bulging? I pulled on a pair of stirrup pants, then quickly took them off. The waistband felt like it was squeezing me in half. I hunted through my drawer for something looser. If only I could wear sweatpants to work. Finally, my fingers settled on a pair of oversized elastic-waisted canvas pants. I pulled them on grimly and turned to face my reflection. They fit. And if I wore an oversized sweater, nobody would see that I seemed to be showing already. I turned slowly before the mirror, inspecting the finished product. Nobody could tell I was pregnant. I took a deep breath. My belly was hidden. I met my eyes in the mirror. I wondered why, after trying so hard to be pregnant, I suddenly felt so compelled to hide it.

The stained glass windows of the Second Presbyterian Church loomed around me like the distant windows of prison cells. I could feel claustrophobia setting in. Around me the pews filled with townspeople, and a few of my students, to whom I'd offered extra credit for attending. It was World AIDS Day, and for the first time Wellsboro was hosting an AIDS benefit. A young mother squeezed into the seat beside me, dragging along a baby stuffed into a snowsuit and securely fastened in a car seat. I could barely see its face. The woman smiled at me briefly as she settled a bag bulging with diapers and god knows what else onto the pew, freed the baby from the car-seat straps, and then went to work unstuffing the baby from its suit. Unease gripped my stomach. She pulled the baby free and cradled it in her arms, taking a bottle from the bag between us and slipping it between the baby's lips. The baby began to suck contentedly. I watched fixedly. I couldn't seem to look away. The mother settled back in her seat, surrounded by baby paraphernalia, and glanced at the program balanced on her thigh. How did she know what to bring with her? Look at all that stuff—she took up half the pew. The baby burped, and milk ran down its chin. She pulled a rag from her bag and deftly wiped its face. The baby settled back into her, reaching for the bottle with both hands. How did she know what to do? Panic rose in my stomach, closed my throat. I had no idea what to do. I glanced at Connie, sitting on my other side scanning her program. Did she know what to do? How would I learn, how would I ever figure it out? Maybe it was something you were born with, like an aptitude for math. Maybe it wasn't something you could learn; maybe if you didn't come by it naturally, you could never pick it up. Maybe it was a knowledge handed down from mother to daughter, and mine had been too busy conditioning me to expect the worst from life to give me any tools to actually get through it. My baby would be born and I'd never step foot outside the house again, for lack of knowing how.

I sighed and turned my attention to the podium. Our neighbor, Maude, was at the podium, preparing to greet her audience. "Welcome to our benefit for World AIDS Day," she said warmly, her voice distorted by the microphone. I winced as it pierced the air. The baby let out a thin cry of protest. Maude frowned. "If you have children," she said, glancing over in our direction, "I'd ask you to remove them from the sanctuary so they don't disturb the program." The woman next to me quickly bent her head to gather up her volumes of equipment, but not before I saw the color staining her cheeks. The baby screamed in protest as she bundled it back into its car seat. At the front of the church Maude paused. The woman quickly squeezed her way out of the pew, the car seat in one hand and the diaper bag in the other, whispering apologies to people as she climbed over them, disappearing quickly down the aisle. She had paid for her ticket, I thought. She had made her donation, and now she was relegated to some back room with her baby till the program was over. I glanced back at Maude, who was welcoming the pastor to the podium. I wondered how my life would change, once the baby that was in my womb was in my arms instead. I thought suddenly of the anti-abortion people. It seemed that the people in this country loved children until they were actually born. Then we mothers were on our own. All they cared about was that we keep them quiet, so everybody could pretend that they weren't there.

At the front of the church the pastor was providing us with some history of the AIDS epidemic, his voice somber. This benefit was a big deal in this town. The local Red Cross had organized candlelight walks before, but they'd always ended on the steps of some church with a handful of people listening to some well-meaning minister caution us that we had to take AIDS seriously because it affected more than just the homosexual population. Tonight the church was packed, and as I looked around me I marveled that so many people had actually left their homes on a cold December night for a cause like this one. The pastor delivered some statistics on the numbers of people dying from the disease. Despite myself, I found my mind wandering. I wondered how Patrick was and if he'd ever been to an AIDS benefit like this one. I wondered if he'd ever been to any. Who would be with him when he died?

I wondered where that woman had gone, whether she was walking her baby around some cold and empty room somewhere all alone, or if she'd already left to go back home. Maude stepped back to the microphone and welcomed Art and John, who would be entertaining us with piano and organ duets.

Time passed. Connie nudged my shoulder and pointed at her watch. Art and John had been playing for thirty minutes. I glanced around me. Everyone's eyes were riveted on the front of the sanctuary. Everybody was still. There was absolute silence. We'd been warned, after all. The babies had already been exiled. Nobody wanted to be next.

At the front of the church Art and John paused, then launched into a rousing rendition of "Glowworm." To my horror I felt a giggle rising in my throat. They played and played and then paused. Thinking they were done, the people around us began to clap, only to have them plunge into another verse. I could feel the laughter bubbling up inside me. I pressed my hands over my mouth and tried to disappear behind Connie. They paused again, and the audience again began to clap, but the pastor had returned to the microphone. In a somber steady voice he gave us the latest statistics on deaths in Africa from AIDS, and then Art and John recommenced with another verse of "Glowworm." I could feel my shoulders shaking. Connie pressed her elbow into my side. "Stop it," she hissed. At the podium I could see Maude scanning the audience, looking for the source of the disturbance. Art and John paused again, the audience began to clap, and the pastor gave us another set of grim statistics. I couldn't help myself. The laughter rolled out of me. Connie took one look at me and began to laugh too. People all around us began to snicker into their handkerchiefs. Tears streamed from my eyes. The woman in the pew behind me patted me on the back. I laughed until I could barely breathe. Art and John played for fifty minutes. When they finished, Maude called an intermission. When she found me in the hall, her face was grim. She bore down on me, purposeful as a train. I felt myself quail; simultaneously, I could feel the laugher rising in me again, wild as a flash flood. Maude only had one word for me, though. "Hush," she said and turned and went back into the sanctuary.

"Now it's highly unlikely that we'll hear a heartbeat today," Dr. Gordon cautioned, rubbing jelly on my stomach. "Eight weeks and three days is much too early in the pregnancy." He frowned and pressed his monitor deep into my stomach. The jelly was cold against my skin. I looked out the window. Everything was covered in snow and ice, a grim and uninviting landscape. This winter was no huge bed of fluffy snow to fall into—it was a thin sheet of ice to trip you up. Connie squeezed my hand. Together we listened to the sounds of my intestines rumbling. Dr. Gordon pressed a little harder on the monitor, then smiled. "There," he said. Connie and I looked at each other. What did he mean? Then we heard it, faint at first, then, as he turned up the volume, huge and rhythmic, resounding through the room. "That's about a hundred forty beats per minute," he said, nodding. I tightened my grip on Connie's hand. Our baby's heartbeat filled the room. I could feel my own heart increasing its pace, as if to keep up. I closed my eyes for a moment. I felt suddenly as if I might cry. Our baby was alive in there, its heart beating as if it had somewhere intensely important to go.

"I didn't think we'd hear it this early," Dr. Gordon said, sheathing the monitor and wiping off my stomach. He smiled at me. "Precocious child of an eccentric writer," he said, extending his hand to help me up.

My baby's internal organs had begun to function. I washed my hair and thought about it as I got dressed, prepared to face down my morning quotient of soda crackers. It meant that inside me my baby had begun to pee, something I was doing a lot of these days. Everyday it peed into the amniotic fluid. It had also begun to suck and swallow. I sat down, pulled on my shoes, and laced them up. I wondered briefly what it was sucking and swallowing.

"Time for breakfast," Connie called from downstairs. I could smell her coffee drifting up the stairs. It smelled like something that had died. I stopped back in the bathroom to pee again. I saw the blood as soon as I pulled down my underpants, dark and impenetrable, staining the crotch. My stomach lurched. I touched myself with toilet paper; it came away wet with blood. I could feel the color leave my face, like sucking all the juice from an orange, as if the blood that was leaving my body was coming not from my baby but from my skin, my heart, my brain, any place but from my womb. I tried to take a breath, but my throat no longer seemed to open. "Honey?" Connie called from downstairs. "Are you OK?"

I touched the paper to my vagina again. I was still bleeding. I felt as if my heart had stopped. My head pounded. "Honey?" Connie called again.

I leaned forward and clutched the rim of the sink. "Can you come up here?" I called back.

"It's perfectly normal," Dr. Gordon told me, over the phone. "We heard a good healthy heartbeat last week, so we shouldn't worry."

"He's right," Connie said that night. "We shouldn't worry."

We shouldn't worry, I thought dumbly. Inside I could feel worry coursing through my blood, mixing with the nausea. I couldn't imagine going through this again, enduring all these weeks of nausea only to start all over again. If I miscarry, I thought, it's over. I wasn't doing this again. I couldn't.

"You're not going to miscarry," Connie said. "Don't worry."

Don't worry. It felt like a directive I couldn't carry out. Worrying would only make it worse, but if not worrying was the only thing that could save my baby, I wasn't sure I was up to the mission. How could I not worry? It was like being told not to breathe. In fact, it was easier not to breathe. Meanwhile, Connie moved around the house as if it weren't even affecting her. Was I the only one who was worried and, if so, why?

Deborah called four days before Christmas. "Louise," she said, and I could tell by her voice that something was wrong. "I found a lump in my breast." Her voice shook. "I've got an appointment for an ultrasound in Williamsport."

"Oh, Deborah," I said. "Do you want me to go with you?"

"Yes," she said. "I do."

We met at our local department store before we headed down to Williamsport, and we went up to the lingerie floor. We both confessed to a secret predilection for this place; it was set up like the department stores of our childhoods: creaky floors and wooden railings and a little place to get sandwiches between Men's Clothes and Shoes. Deborah was looking for a pretty bra to wear, a bra, she said, that would show she was serious about her breasts. "What about this one?" she asked me, holding up one that was covered with huge red roses.

"Perfect," I said.

It was a long drive down to Williamsport, down that same stretch of road where we'd seen the guy who wanted David Duke elected to Congress. The ground was hard and parched by frost, empty of snow. I wanted it to snow for Christmas. I wanted some semblance of normality. If I couldn't drink eggnog, at least we could have a good snowstorm. We were only blocks from the hospital after all, and I couldn't think of any other place we'd have any urgent need to go. I tried not to think about the bleeding. "If you're going to miscarry," the obstetrics nurse had informed me irritably when I called again to talk to Dr. Gordon, "there's nothing we can do to stop it."

"Well, here we are," Deborah said, as I pulled into the parking lot of the Women's Health Center. We sat there for a moment, neither of us saying anything. I reached across the seat and took her hand. There didn't seem to be anything else that I could do.

While I waited for her to get the ultrasound, I stopped in the bathroom. I was still spotting. We sat side by side in the waiting room when she was done, waiting for the doctor to interpret the results. It felt almost like we were a couple. I wondered what it would be like if we were, what it would be like to be sitting here waiting for Connie's ultrasound results. Or mine. "Wayne couldn't come with you?" I asked her.

Deborah studied the line of her skirt, tracing it with her finger. "Wayne isn't very good when there's something wrong," she said. "He always acts like everything will be OK."

I thought about Connie telling me not to worry. I thought it must be hard to be the other person, the one not directly affected by the crisis. There just weren't any rules on how to be supportive. I thought someone should develop them, hand them out with marriage licenses. Of course, that still wouldn't help us.

When the doctor came out, he shook my hand as well as Deborah's. "Everything's fine," he said. "It's a cyst. There's nothing to worry about."

I could feel Deborah exhale. There was nothing to worry about. A sense of reprieve was in the air, electric as frost, as if the Christmas spirit had just danced its way down into her after hovering for a long, long time offstage. Suddenly I wanted to get back home, back to Connie.

That night I lay back on the couch and spread my labia and let Connie see the blood, pooling around my vagina, a bright and violent red, before I went into the bathroom to mop it up with toilet paper. When I came back, her eyes were red. "I'm so afraid you're going to lose the baby," she said. Her lips trembled. Tears spilled from her eyes. "I wanted to be strong," she said.

I put my arms around her. "You're being strong," I said.

She sobbed against my chest. I could feel her tears seeping through my sweater. "It's going to be all right," I said, and suddenly I felt as if it would be. As long as I could hold her and comfort her, everything would be all right.

We went back to Dr. Gordon the next day, after I'd been bleeding for seven days. "It's going to be fine," he said, rubbing the jelly on my stomach and positioning the monitor against the skin. "I just want you to hear the heartbeat to reassure you." He paused as he felt for the right place in my womb. "We never lose the baby once we've heard the heartbeat," he said, pressing the monitor deep into my flesh. Silence filled the room. I could feel my own heart seeming to stop of its own accord. Connie tightened her grip on my hand. Dr. Gordon frowned, pressing the monitor so deep into my stomach that it almost hurt, and then we heard it, all three of us at the same time, our baby's heart pounding like a freight train, filling the room with its presence till I almost thought that I could see it, diffusing the room with its own kind of light.

Connie and I held hands all the way back to the car. "Everything's OK," Connie said. Her voice rang through the crisp winter air. A cold wind swept through the parking lot. I closed my eyes as she unlocked the doors. We were going to have a baby. I shook my head to clear it. I couldn't believe it. When I opened my eyes, I could almost see the cold covering the branches of the trees like frozen rain. We were going to have a baby. It didn't seem possible. It just didn't seem possible.

When we got in the car, I looked over at Connie. "You don't have to be the strong one, you know," I said. She took my hand, tears filling her eyes. "We're in this together," I said. We pulled out of the parking lot, the wind around us whipping the trees into a frenzy.

I dreamed that night that I was playing basketball and that my head was filled with complicated strategies, maps of game plans, and then it occurred to me that all I had to do was catch whatever ball was thrown to me.

Nothing had ever seemed so simple.

Why Don't I Run Down to the Liquor Store?

With the new year came the takeover of the House and Senate by the Republicans. Anti-abortion fanatics killed two young women at family-planning clinics. "Justifiable homicide," someone called it in the papers. The Republicans' "Contract with America" advocated forcing women to establish paternity before being eligible for welfare or food stamps. Newt Gingrich, the new Speaker of the House, suggested that orphanages were a good way to raise children and recommended that Hillary Clinton watch the movie *Boys' Town* if she disagreed.

"Doesn't that star Mickey Rooney?" Connie asked, looking up from the paper and taking a sip of coffee.

"Orphanages!" I said. I shook my head. "What are they thinking?" My grandmother had been raised in an orphanage after her father had shot her mother to death and abandoned the children. I remembered her telling me that if they drank water from the river, the authorities locked them in the attic alone for three days to see if they developed typhus. It was the only story she had ever told me about her childhood. I put the paper down. I hadn't even made it past the first page.

I glanced around the kitchen. The morning light danced on the copper tiles around the stove. I was actually hungry this morning, actually thinking of shoveling in some food. I had awakened so hungry that I'd thought I would faint before I got down to the kitchen. I had dreamed about food all night. Now, as I helped myself to some cereal, picked up a banana, and began to slice it into my bowl, I could feel a mild nausea starting up in me again. "Whatever happened to family values?" I asked.

Connie snorted, setting down her cup of coffee, smoothing out the paper, and turning it over to the next page. "This is family values," she said. "Republican-style."

The new year also brought me the proofs of my novel from the publisher, with a directive to proofread it for errors. I tore it from the envelope eagerly, then nearly dropped it on the table. I was shocked by how thin it was, how small and vulnerable it looked. I feared for it suddenly, out on its own in the world. As I leafed through its pages, I was taken by the beauty of the writing. Simultaneously, I was afraid that it didn't hang together as a novel. I worried that the critics would jump all over it, flatten it, stomp it into dust along the edges of the road.

I feared that no one would pay any attention to it at all.

A string of 60-degree days heralded the start of the new semester. I convinced Deborah to leave the president's opening address an hour early so we could go for a walk on the bike path. As we left, the president was announcing that personnel costs were rising to 80 percent of the budget. "And I will not permit that," he informed us sternly, as if it were somehow our fault. He didn't elaborate on how he might prevent it. For a moment I imagined my tenure application as it sat on someone's desk somewhere, an easy line cut for any budget. I could lose my job, I thought, as I squeezed as inconspicuously as possible past someone's knees on my way out into the aisle. I could be denied tenure! A flush of exhilaration flooded me as we pushed open the back door and slipped out into the sudden spring. I could be fired! The warm air greeted me like an arm around my shoulders. For a moment I imagined a sparkling future of unemployment and long, long days in which all I had to do was write and be pregnant. Maybe it wouldn't be so bad. I inhaled deeply as we walked down the path, away from the campus. The bare branches sparkled in the sun. The sudden warm weather reminded me how much I loved the seasons, how it took some cold weather to be able to feel like this. Otherwise, I might not be able to recognize the smell of promise in the air.

The morning of the first day of the semester was warm and soft. I pulled my best dress out of the closet and pulled it on, slipped on a pair of hose. I glanced at my reflection in the mirror. I looked great—my hair lay perfectly, its cowlicks miraculously subdued. My skin glowed. Only the faintest roundness around my stomach gave me away. I felt wonderful. Hunting for a pair of earrings, I remembered the black crushed velvet dress that Connie had given me at Christmastime and how my spirits had dropped when I saw it. I thought I would never feel like dressing up again. Now I suddenly felt like the most beautiful woman in the world. It was like having a second lease on life.

When I got to school, a senior male colleague stepped into my office. "Oh, my," he said, seemingly startled when he saw me. "You look very nice." A touch of worry creased his brow. "May I say that?" he asked, licking his upper lip. "Am I still—ah—*permitted* to say that?"

Why, I wanted to retort, are you suddenly afraid of being a sexist asshole? But I felt too good to be angry. I smiled magnanimously. "Sure," I said. "You can say it." I felt full of queenly dignity, fully able to drop dispensation wherever I went. I had no need of petty likes and dislikes. I was a new woman now, preparing to leave my first trimester and enter with dignity into my second. It was nice to have months to mark off like this, each day taking me to a more mean-ingful level in my existence. It was like that first year with Connie, when we celebrated the tenth of each month in honor of our blos-soming commitment, both silently ticking off the years until we'd each outlasted our longest previous relationship.

I glanced at my watch. It was time for my first class. I rose to my feet, adjusted my dress, and ran a hand through my hair. It was the closest I ever got to combing it during the day. I took a deep breath and picked up my books. I was ready to meet my new army, ready to break in a set of new recruits.

The students perked up when I walked into the room. "Wow," said one woman, whom I'd had in class the previous semester. "You look awesome!" I introduced myself and took a few minutes to describe the class. I felt flushed with enthusiasm, charged with new energy. This was my favorite creative writing class. I'd designed it the year before to teach students the freedom of freewriting, to give them a chance to learn to write without worrying about the consequences of grammar. I faced the class, smiling warmly. I felt a little like Gandhi, taking writing to the masses, giving them the tools with which to liberate themselves.

"So," I said, clasping my hands. "Let's go around the room and introduce yourselves and tell us why you're taking the class." I turned to the student nearest to me in the circle. "Let's start with you."

The student looked at me and then rubbed his head, as if I'd already asked him to do too much for the first day of class. "My name is Ed," he said, looking around the room. "I'm just taking this course to fulfill a writing requirement." To his credit he did sound mildly apologetic.

I was not to be floored. "That's OK," I said. "How do you feel about writing?"

Ed looked at me. His face bore a look of slight confusion. "Well, I don't like it much," he said.

"Next," I said quickly. Maybe I could move this along, get to the students who were waiting for this class the way somebody else might be waiting for religion. Or the way Ed might be waiting for me to bring the class to a close.

"I'm a criminal justice major," the next student confessed, as if he might have been admitting to ax murder. "I've never really had to write anything."

"I don't mind writing," the next student said brightly, as if I'd asked her how she felt about cleaning the house. "It's OK."

I sighed. Surely, Gandhi hadn't had to deal with people shrugging their shoulders and saying, Well, I don't really care if we ever get our freedom. The same thing happened every semester. I started the first class feeling like Jesus and ended it feeling like Mary Magdalene—still, when all was said and done, a whore.

I smiled as compassionately as possible at them and moved on to the next part of the class the way I always did, even though I felt like screaming. I wondered what would happen if, instead of writing the rules of freewriting up on the board, I threw my chalk on the floor and yelled, "If you don't like writing, then get out of this class!" It probably wouldn't do much for my tenure application. I should probably feel grateful to the criminal justice majors. Their quest for an easy writing class was paying my salary. I wondered what it would be like to teach creative writing to students who actually wanted to write creatively. I shook my head to clear it. I doubted I would ever know.

By the second week of school the parade of students in and out of my office was as constant as the rain that had replaced our respite of warm sun. It felt more like November out there than January. Between students, I sat at my desk and looked out the window and remembered my childhood in the snowbelt of northeastern Ohio, how winter regularly deposited three to four feet of snow throughout the county. For a moment it seemed positively blissful, cross-country skiing through the fields of my youth, a rough wind reddening my cheeks, my father at home tending the fire, and my mother in the kitchen canning apples. I shook my head. Whose childhood was that? Sometimes it was like Ted Turner had occupied my brain, colorizing my memories. They surely didn't have anything to do with real life.

I shook my head and leaned back at my desk. I felt so tired. It wasn't the fatigue that would balloon in my head like a mushroom cloud throughout the first trimester. It was a plain regular tiredness, one that weighed down my eyelids and put pressure on my neck and shoulders. All I wanted to do was put my head down and close my eyes. I was only days from the second trimester. Surely, it would be all downhill from there. I massaged the back of my neck, trying to work out the kinks. How much lousier could I feel? If this was what it was like, why would any woman ever get pregnant more than once? Who in their right mind would go through this again?

A student coughed politely from the doorway of my office. "Do you have a few minutes?"

I rubbed my eyes and tried to look awake. If only I could still drink coffee. No, I debated saying. Or, rather, yes, but they're *mine*. Instead I made myself smile. "Sure," I said. "Come in and have a seat."

The student sat down, nervously folding and refolding his hands. I waited, folding my own hands across my belly, checking its dimensions as I did routinely these days. "The counseling service sent me to see you," he said, clearing his throat with vigor. "I don't know if they called you." He looked up at me. His eyes were beseeching, like those of the deer that not too long ago the hunters had chased through the hillsides in their own private genocide, eager to stock their freezers with bodies that they'd killed themselves. "I'm gay," the student said, and I nodded, waiting for the rest, waiting to hear his story, the same way I heard all the stories, of all the students that the counseling service forwarded to me, as if by virtue of being gay I could also double as a therapist.

"So what year are you?" I asked him, gently, settling myself back into my chair.

"I'm a freshman," he said, his lower lip trembling. "My dad thinks I'm going to meet a girl up here."

I just sat there and let him talk, thinking about this place where we lived, the people sequestered in those hills just beyond my window, grateful not for the first time to the deer who took our bullets for us, who distracted the townspeople from what could have been their real target, thinking about the father who hoped this place would make a man of his son, who might never understand how thoroughly it really could.

───◈───

"I *need* to have sex." Connie's voice shook, trembling like the branches of our forsythia in the wind. I could see it out there in the yard, feeble and alone, looking for all the world like it had already died, succumbed to the winter that had only just begun to rage around us. The rain outside had turned to a light snow, drifting down through the light of the streetlamp and dusting the street like soap powder. I reluctantly tore my eyes away from it. For not the first time, I thought it looked warmer and more inviting outside on the street than it did in our own living room. Connie stood between me and the front door, almost as if to keep me in. "All I want is for you to make love to me," she said. Her eyes flashed with anger.

I sighed and glanced at the clock above the kitchen sink. Eleven o'clock. I'd wanted to be in bed by nine. I shifted my weight and leaned against the door frame. All I really wanted was to go to sleep. It was all I'd really wanted to do since breakfast. Connie and I had been fighting about sex continuously for weeks, always late at night and always, it seemed, with me standing in a doorway, as if trapped in some limbo between worlds. This was just one in a long succession of fights in which I felt that everything terrible that I'd ever done got dredged up and flung in my face. The problem with having a long-term commitment, I thought wearily, trying to prepare myself to mirror her, was that you could never escape your past. You could never grow up enough to leave behind who you used to be. It was like getting together with parents and siblings, who remembered only the worst aspects of your past and dragged them out at every family gathering.

"I need you to make love to me," Connie said. Her face was tight with fury, like the sky just before a storm. Oh, god, I thought, closing my eyes and leaning against the door frame, can't you just make love with someone else? I could barely get up the energy to brush my teeth, let alone bring someone to orgasm. I imagined Connie making love with someone else. It seemed like that would work, didn't it? I was sure it would bother me in principle, but at the moment it seemed like the best solution possible. "I need you to initiate sex," Connie said.

I looked at her helplessly. Nausea and fatigue dogged my every step. The second trimester had arrived with no relief. My fetus was developing either uterus and ovaries or ducts to convey sperm. It occurred to me that my baby at this point had more of a sex life than I did. At least it had potential. My own sex organs felt about as developed as a block of wood. "I don't know what to say," I said. "I just can't do it."

Connie looked at me, her lips as tight as if they had been stitched together. "Fine," she said.

We went to bed barely speaking to each other. I wanted to make up but didn't know how. My mother had raised me never to go to sleep on my anger. I liked that idea, but resolving the argument seemed to be more than I could handle at the moment. Leg cramps kept me from sleeping. Every time I shifted position, Connie sighed through her teeth. She hated having her sleep disturbed. How would she deal with the baby? I wondered. How would she deal with any of this? Everything was going to change—our sex life had already changed and not for the better, obviously. We were having trouble now—what would happen after the baby was born? My forehead itched. I tried to ignore it, tried to stay as still as I could on my side of the bed. I wondered if Connie would leave me, unable to deal with my escalating hormones. The bedroom took on a sudden chill. I remembered a coworker from years before whose husband had left her in her eighth month of pregnancy and moved in with his girlfriend. My coworker had cried all day at work; her eyes were always red-rimmed and watery. She was befriended by another woman at work, who had come home one day after nineteen years of marriage to find the house empty, a note on the bed from her husband. I wondered what had happened to the pregnant one. I'd helped her write a résumé; I liked to think she did OK. Now I wondered whether she had. I pulled the comforter up to my chin. Something in me expected Connie to act the same way as those deserting husbands. Why wouldn't she? I wasn't much fun to be around. I was tired all the time. My head ached. I was continuously nauseous. Another cramp gripped my calf. I rested my toes against the foot of the bed and pushed my heel down, trying to straighten it out. Connie had sworn she wouldn't leave me. I brought my knees back up to my chest and curled into as small a ball as possible. Maybe she should leave me. Maybe we were finished. I tried to breathe evenly. We would have to be careful, I thought, that we didn't fall into the trap of staying together just for the sake of the children.

Connie nuzzled me from behind. "Hey," she said softly.

My heart opened up like a flower. I could feel it in there, warm and pulsing with my blood. "Hey," I said.

She wrapped her arms around me. "I love you, you know," she said.

I closed my eyes and pressed myself into her breasts. "I know," I said and waited for the sleep to settle in.

The start of February brought a sparse gray snow, just enough to

require shoveling so it could sit along the sides of the road and col-
lect exhaust. I felt as if I would be pregnant forever, this baby sucking all the life out of me, just like the passing trucks robbed the
snow of its true color. In the kitchen I could hear Connie setting
the table, getting ready for our friends, Cheryl and Sam, to come
over for dinner. Beset with a sudden desire to create, I'd spent the
day cooking up a pot of bean soup. Smelling it now, I could hardly
imagine eating it. I walked into the kitchen, dragging my body
along like a set of chains, and dropped into my chair at the table.
Once I'd had a vision of myself sprinting through my pregnancy. I
saw it again, wavering briefly before me like an apparition, before
I closed my eyes and let it go. Fuck it. "What time are Cheryl and
Sam coming?" I asked Connie.

She took the saltshaker over to the counter to fill it. "About ten
minutes or so, I think," she said. She took down the box of salt. I
could see her weighing it in her hand, wondering if we had enough.
"We don't have any wine," she said, glancing at me. "Do you think
that's a problem?"

I shrugged. "Not for me," I said. "I'd prefer it if there wasn't
any—do you think that's OK?"

"I guess," Connie said, filling the shaker and holding it up to the
light in an attempt to see its contents. She looked at me. "I talked
to the Weight Watchers leader about your diet," she said. "She said
you should really try to eat green vegetables."

"Really?" I said. "You told the Weight Watchers woman about
me?" I could feel a lift in my chest. Connie had been going to
Weight Watchers for several years now, and to my knowledge she'd
never mentioned me. Now she had talked about me in a meeting
full of all the old girls from the area. I felt a flush of pride. I'd been
claimed.

"I told her I had a friend who was pregnant," Connie said,
replacing the saltshaker on the table. "How's the soup doing?"

A fuzz filled my brain. "A friend?" I said slowly. "You said I was a
friend?" I shook my head. "You're kidding."

Connie looked at me. Her brow furrowed. "What's the big deal?"
she said. "You know I'm not out at Weight Watchers."

I stared at her. Who was this woman standing in our kitchen, the
woman who had held my hand through every insemination, this
woman who was going to raise this child with me, be its mother just
as I was? "You said I was a friend?" I repeated. Tears rose to my eyes,
stinging the lids till I had to close them. "I'm not just a friend," I

said softly. My throat closed on the words. I wasn't even sure she had heard them. All I knew was that I couldn't speak, couldn't think of anything else to say. We both heard the knock at the front door at the same time.

"I'll get it," Connie said, leaving the kitchen like casting off an old shirt. I stared after her stupidly. What had just happened, and was I the only one to feel it?

Cheryl and Sam swept into the room, bringing with them the vague scent of incense and candles and long exotic dinners. "We don't have any wine," Connie said apologetically.

Cheryl stopped halfway through taking off her coat. "Really?" she said, glancing at Sam, who had collapsed into a chair beside me. She looked at her watch. "Why don't I run down to the liquor store and pick up a couple bottles?" she said.

"I'll go with you," Connie said, grabbing her coat.

The door slammed behind them, signaling their departure. Sam looked at me idly, one finger playing with the napkin at his place. "I really feel like drinking tonight," he said.

I stared at him under cover of an interested, listening look. We both just sat there, waiting for the wine to arrive.

The bean soup was a success, with the liberal addition of horseradish and cayenne. I played with my spoon, unable to eat. I could barely contribute to the conversation. My throat felt as if it had closed up on itself, leaving a raw and gaping wound. Connie refilled her glass from the second bottle of wine. "It doesn't even matter that it's Louise that's pregnant," she said, her voice energetic with alcohol. "I feel completely bonded to this baby." Cheryl and Sam nodded, sipping from their glasses.

"That's wonderful," Cheryl said, her voice suffused with warmth. Their cheeks glowed with a sense of shared community. I sat with my bean soup, now cold in my dish, my glass of water untouched. Oh, really, I thought. I could feel myself begin to shake. You feel bonded to this baby? I stole a glance at Connie, her voice full of excitement in the middle of some story about her life. If you feel so bonded to this baby, why did you pretend in public that it didn't belong to you? I stirred the soup in my bowl so vigorously my spoon clanked against the edge. Nobody noticed. A heat spread through me. Connie felt bonded to the baby. I glanced down at my stomach, a soft round lump in my lap. What baby? I just felt like I was getting fat. What did she find to bond with? It was just something that got in the way of our sex life, that caused fight after fight. So far it had done nothing but drive us apart. What the hell was she bonding with?

I picked up my glass of water and drained it, carried my dish to the sink, and deposited it there with a crash that stopped all conversation. "I'm tired," I informed them pointedly. "I think I need to go to bed."

"Of course," Sam said, draining the last of his glass of wine. Cheryl wrapped me in a warm hug. "You take care," she said. I bit my lip not to cry. What had I done? What had I gotten myself into?

I dreamed that night that I gave birth, and it was just a pan of tissue and blood. Sam brought it in, pointed to a lump of flesh, and said, "I think this one might develop into a baby." I took it home, but then I realized that something was wrong, that Margie and Julie had brought home an actual baby. It occurred to me that I must have miscarried, and I went to the doctors, but they weren't there. My colleague Roger met me at the door and pushed me back on the table and pulled out a huge pair of shears, and when I felt their blades inside me I realized suddenly that I was nine months pregnant, and I began to scream "No!" When I woke up, my heart was beating and my mouth was dry. Connie was fast asleep on her side of the bed, and no matter how hard I tried, I couldn't get back to sleep, could find no comfort anywhere, no safe place to be.

Zoe = Life

What about Audre?" Connie asked, looking up from her pencil and paper. "For Audre Lorde?"

I took a sip of tea and rubbed my eyes. "Or Adrienne," I said. "For Adrienne Rich."

Connie consulted the *Baby Name Book.* "Adrienne means dark one," she said. We looked at each other dubiously. Did we really want to curse this baby with a name like that? "What about boys' names?" she asked.

We were both silent for a moment. Boys' names. I shifted in my chair uneasily. I knew we needed to think of boys' names. There was always Max, our original choice, but it no longer seemed right to name the baby after a store in the mall. There was Sam, and Gabe, names I'd always liked. But now they sounded like good names for a blues bar, not for a baby. There was Noah, but did we really want to name our baby after one of the most patriarchal guys in the Old Testament? What about Sampson, whose power was stolen by a woman? Would that be any better? I closed my eyes. Deep inside myself, I knew I wanted this baby to be a girl, but I tried to deny it. I even had a name for her—Zoe, the Greek word for life, but it wasn't a name we had discussed. I'd had it in my mind for days. Zoe, I called her in my mind. My little Zoe. That was when I didn't call her La Niña, for the warm fall winds that had brought her to my womb. My tiny Niña. I shook my head. It didn't matter if it was a boy or a girl. What I really wanted was for it to be healthy, right? Besides, we'd read that most insemination babies were boys. Margie and Julie had had a boy. There was something about female sperm living longer but male sperm being faster, or something like that. It sounded about right. I played with the cereal in my bowl. It was mid-February, and as soon as we finished our breakfast, we were heading up to Elmira for the amniocentesis. My appetite was gone. It was snowing out, the air so cold that the wind chill had closed schools all over the Twin Tiers. Amniocentesis could uncover any of hundreds of fetal abnormalities. Surely, the gender of the baby was the least of our concerns. I tried to swallow around the lump that was growing in my throat. I was afraid of the amniocentesis, afraid of the procedure, afraid of the

163

results, afraid of my reason for doing it in the first place. What if something was wrong? What would we do then? We'd spent long hours discussing the possibilities. Connie had spent years working with the developmentally disabled. We had already resolved not to bring a child into the world with that kind of disability. I shifted in my seat, felt for my belly. It was warm beneath my hand, warm and full of life. I'd thought I knew what I wanted, I'd marched in Pro-Choice rallies, had counseled my students who considered abortions, but I hadn't counted on how I would feel once this baby was in my womb, contentedly sucking its life from my bones.

Connie drained the last of her coffee and reached for my hand. Her fingers were cold. "It's time," she said. My lungs felt as if they couldn't expand another inch, as if they had frozen in place with just that quantity of air inside and I would never be able to inhale again.

Connie squeezed my hand. "Come on," she said softly. Her eyes sought mine, a soft warm green in the thin winter light that filtered in through the window above the sink. Her hand held mine as if she would never let it go. Her touch gave me life. We had made love four times in the last four days, a deep, warm, wonderful love, full of soft flesh and warm skin, beating hearts. It was week sixteen, and I was beginning to feel like a human being again, like a woman, oiling my body with cocoa butter after my shower in the morning to combat the stretch marks, stretching out my limbs in the afternoon to my *Jane Fonda Pregnancy Workout* tape. It had felt so good to make love, to use my body for its pleasure, to remember that I was a woman, and to forget for a time about this baby that I carried inside my body. I could allow myself just to fill with love for Connie, to feel safe inside her touch, protected by her skin. It reminded me that we had come first, before this baby that took up so much time, before it was even fully in our lives.

The snow fell the whole way up to Elmira, piling up along the road as if to keep us on the path and prevent us from turning back. I sat in the passenger seat with my hands on my belly, feeling its swell with my palms, feeling the pulse of my fingers against my skin. The snow swirled and danced, swept up by the wind. Inside my belly a separate heart beat, a separate life took shape. I closed my eyes and imagined my daughter curled up inside me, small and as fully formed as my hand. I could see her there, clear as the snow that danced about the sides of the road, doing her own dance, deep in my womb. Suddenly, she seemed as vulnerable and susceptible as I was. She even looked like me, fine brown hair and dark eyes. Her look was accusing. How could you have brought me here? To what kind of life have you summoned me? I closed my eyes. Who was I to bring a child into the world? Somehow, it had been so much easier to imagine a son, rough and wild, tumbling from my womb like a wolf cub, already able to outrun me, attend to his own needs, survive in the wild. He would be strong, just because he was a man. The world, after all, was made for him.

I rested my head against the window, felt the cold of the glass against my face. To picture a daughter broke my heart. She would be just like me, alone in her life, stepping through her journey with careful feet. She would suffer and question. This world would not be her birthright. She would ache to express herself. She would shout to be heard. She would ask me why I brought her here. And I would not know the answer.

Connie squeezed my hand. We were almost in Elmira. The snow did a ghostly dance around our tires, pushing us on. We were going to meet our child. I watched her, alone in my womb, full of her own life. I had imagined a boy with strong legs who would throw balls and fix cars and be an alien to me. He would be all right. His body would carry him through his life. I had never imagined a daughter, standing tall and straight and alone, looking at me with that silent accusation in her eyes: You knew what this world was like, yet you brought me here anyway.

I turned my eyes to the window. It almost seemed as if I could see her out there, standing on the side of the road thumbing a ride. I watched her stand there, flagging us down. She looked so much like me it made my throat ache. I knew how much was out there that could destroy her. I knew how many pitfalls lay in wait along her journey. She shook her head as we neared her, tossed back her hair, and turned away from me. I ached to follow her, to grab her hand, to open our doors and usher her in, give her her ride. Yes, I did it anyway. I lay back and opened my legs and summoned you up from your private depths. I called you here against your will. And now I could choose to send you back.

Connie turned to me. "Well," she said. "This is it."

I took her hand. Her fingers shook. I looked into her eyes, soft and deep and as frightened as my own. "This is it," I said. We sat there for a moment surrounded by the snow, watching it churn across the surface of our windshield, skate across the glass. We were doing what we needed to do. I thought of my daughter, still standing on the side of the road, the wind chill numbing her cheeks, waiting for her ride. "Let's go," I said, and together we left the car.

"Well, it's hard to say for sure about the sex," the doctor said, pressing the ultrasound deep into the cold gel that covered my stomach. On the screen in front of us, our child wavered, coming in and out of view as the doctor pointed out her body parts, first a head, then an arm, then a part of a foot, all of it a swirl that bore more resemblance to the snow outside than it did to a human form. The doctor moved his probe around my stomach as if he were steering the prow of a ship, a frown of concentration on his face. "I can't find a penis," he said, pressing the probe deeper into my stomach. I watched our baby's image dancing on the screen. So early we are defined by what we lack. The doctor shrugged. "I can't seem to get between its legs," he said apologetically, "but I'd say, seventy-thirty, it's a girl."

I could feel my heart swell. Connie squeezed my hand, but I hardly felt it. I knew. I knew at that moment, absolutely, that not only was she a daughter but she was my daughter, guarding her privacy, preserving her essence. She was there, she was inside me, and she was coming out one day, full of her own fire.

"Hold on a second," the doctor said, prodding my belly, "and I'll get you a picture." I stared at the image on screen. My heart raced. My daughter was alive. She was already alive. She wasn't out there on the highway, shuddering with the cold. She was right here with me, going about her life, regardless of what I did. If I didn't drink enough milk, she would take her calcium from my bones and teeth. Already she was taking what she needed from me, accepting what I had to give. I stared at the ultrasound, at the pulsing throbbing heart. She was there. She would be born despite my fear. She would suffer despite my joys. She would triumph despite my agonizing.

The computer whirred and ejected the photograph like an offering into the doctor's hand. We all bent forward at the same moment, staring at the image. It looked like an Edvard Munch painting, trapped midscream. Her head was just a skull, her cranium massive, her face gaunt.

"Gee, I'm sorry," the doctor said, staring at the picture. "That's not a really good shot. Do you want me to try to get another one?"

I stared at the photograph, stared into my daughter's eyes. She looked like death in there, like she hadn't quite made the passage over, hadn't quite completed her return. She looked just like the ghost I knew she was. My Niña. My warm and violent autumn wind. My Zoe. My vivid little open mouth, poised to scream her way into the world. "No," I said. "It's perfect."

The rest of the procedure lasted less than two minutes. Connie held my hand. I kept my eyes on hers as the needle entered my abdomen. I felt its pinch as the doctor withdrew the fluid, and then it was over. Connie squeezed my hand. "There it is," the doctor said, holding up the syringe like a prize. I stared at it in awe. Its contents were startlingly yellow, somehow familiar.

"It looks like urine," Connie said.

The doctor nodded, his hands already busy tapping off the syringe. "It is urine," he said. His tone was matter-of-fact. "Amniotic fluid is made from urination." I surveyed it with wonder. There it was, my first tangible contact with my daughter—her pee.

Connie and I held hands all the way out of the doctor's office. "We don't know for sure if she's a girl," Connie cautioned. "We can't let ourselves get too excited."

"No," I agreed. We pushed the button at the elevator. Somehow I didn't even think about abnormalities. It was as if we'd done the whole procedure for the sole purpose of determining her gender. I glanced at Connie. "There's a name I've been thinking of," I said cautiously. "It's not on our list."

Connie looked at me. "Me too," she said. "There's a name I've been thinking of."

For a moment neither of us said anything. The elevator doors opened and we stepped in. "It's Zoe," I said. "It means life."

Connie stared at me. "Yes," she said. "That's the name I was thinking of."

We watched the light above our heads tick off the floors. Zoe Sullivan-Blum, I thought. I dug in my pocket for her ultrasound shot and held it up. Connie slipped her arm around my shoulder, and we both stared at it. This was the child I carried in my womb. I could hardly breathe. When we walked back out into the parking lot, the falling snow was gone. The air was clear and cold, the snow on the ground sparkling in the sunlight. "Our Zoe," I whispered.

"Our Zoe," Connie said, and we walked out hand in hand, back to our car.

The phone call from the doctor's office came in less than a week. "Everything's fine," the nurse informed me. Her voice was full of warmth. "Do you want to know the sex?"

"Yes," I said. My heart pounded. My mouth went dry. This was it. This was our moment.

"It's a girl," she said. "Congratulations!"

I hung up the phone. The air around me seemed suddenly thinner. I took a deep breath, trying to get it into my lungs. My hands shook. I sat down, my head spinning. It was a girl. Everything was fine, and we were having a girl. I closed my eyes. "Oh, thank you," I whispered to our goddess, our god, to anyone who might be listening. "Thank you so much." I pushed my chair back and looked at the ultrasound picture that sat on my desk. "Hello," I whispered. "Hello, little Zoe."

There Is Something Out There Known as Mother Nature

The air was cold and the gas tank nearly empty as I got ready to leave for work. The snow sparkled like dew in the early sunlight. I took a deep breath, filling my lungs with the chill, feeling it all the way down to the roundness in my belly, the tiny life that bubbled away in there, like a pot about to boil. Just the day before I'd been in the department store to get a new maternity bra for my burgeoning breasts. The saleswoman had eyed me as I combed through the rack for a new style. "So you're how far along?" she asked.

"Four months," I told her confidently. I pushed my coat back a little, brushed a hand through my hair. I was in the second trimester. I was officially pregnant. No danger of miscarriage. No false hope. No fear of something being wrong. I'd had amniocentesis. I'd seen my baby on the screen. I had a picture of her on my desk. We existed, she and I. We were a team, preparing to face down the world. She was snuggled down deep inside me, weaving her nest from the stuff of my womb. I was four months pregnant. I reached for a new bra, a new size, herald of a new chapter of my new and ever newer life.

"Really?" the saleswoman asked. "Four months?" Her eyebrows lifted in appraisal. She glanced at my belly pointedly. "Four months and you're showing already?"

My hand fumbled, missed the bra, and came down on nothing. I fought for my balance. I was showing already. I thought back on this month's drawing in my pregnancy book. Why was I showing already? The baby was only eight inches long. What was the matter with me? I glanced around me at the racks full of maternity clothes that looked like they'd hung there for thirty years. Where was I going to find clothes that wouldn't make me look like a huge six year old?

The saleswoman smiled at me, full of new warmth. "Can I help you find anything?" she asked. Her smile slid across her face like a snake.

"No," I said, backing up slowly, feeling my way through the racks of bras and half slips. I could feel myself, huge and bloated, growing more ungainly with each passing step toward the stairs. "That's

OK," I said, feeling the cold comfort of the stair rail beneath my hand. "I'll just come back another time."

———— ⚭ ————

It was Friday, and I sat back in my office, making myself a snack of crackers and peanut butter from the stash I kept in the file cabinet. I was brewing a cup of decaf tea. I was done with classes for the day, looking forward to sitting back with that day's copy of the student newspaper, checking out the campus situation. My mouth full of crackers, I leafed idly through it page by page, looking for the editorials. Then it hit me. "Reader Speaks Out on Gay Morality," the headline read. I sat up. The peanut butter turned to glue in my mouth. One of my colleagues had apparently written an editorial the previous week about the removal of *Heather Has Two Mommies* from the public schools, likening it to the Holocaust and other instances of oppression. Where had I been? That amniocentesis must have taken up all my thoughts. I must have forgotten for a moment where I lived, thinking I could just sit back and relax and gestate my baby from within the haze of my hormonal peace. I was on the campus of Mansfield University, after all, deep in the confines of Tioga County, right in the middle of real America.

"Gay literature is nothing more than a moral issue," read this week's letter, by the president of the Student Government Association, and shouldn't be coupled with the Holocaust or other events of "historical significance." I sighed. "If we can't teach morals through prayer in schools," the student wrote, "then how can you justify teaching morals through deviate literature? There is something out there known as mother nature." I put the paper down. I raised a hand to my head. My hormones must be in an uproar. I couldn't get out of my head the image of that margarine commercial from my childhood, the one in which the big powerful woman rises up from the woods in a fury, proclaiming: "It's not nice to fool Mother Nature!" I forced my attention back to the page. He didn't even have his language right. *Deviant*, we were *deviant*—not *deviate*. Lesbian parents alter Mother Nature, the letter continued, and "if wc try to play God the results are bad." Oh, that's a strong sentence, I thought sarcastically. "We shouldn't allow gays and lesbians to have children," the letter concluded. "Children have enough obstacles to overcome today."

I put the paper down, pushed away my peanut butter crackers.

My appetite was gone. With one hand I felt for my stomach. It was still there. My Zoe was still with me, taking up space inside me, her whole being a contented heartbeat sounding its private song within the confines of my womb. The words were already forming in my brain. "As a Lesbian pregnant by alternative insemination, I feel compelled to respond to this letter." I turned on my computer and turned my chair to its screen. "I was stunned by the writer's ignorance," I wrote, "of the connection between gay rights and the Holocaust, as well as his several invocations of `mother nature,' a phrase which he never clarified, but which rings too closely for comfort to Hitler's obsession with the natural order." I went on typing, feeling a flush of heat rising through me. "Many groups were included among those deemed inferior and thus targeted for extermination by the Nazis," I wrote, going on to detail the different colored triangles for the different groups of people. My fingers flew across the keyboard, dashing off my arguments. Who does he think he is? Should not be allowed? "Is he suggesting I not be 'allowed' to have a child because I am a Lesbian?" I wrote. "The implications of what other groups such logic might extend to are chilling. Who else in our society might be deemed unworthy of having children, and how would they be prevented from doing so? It is hard to shake the image of the Holocaust when someone starts talking about reserving something as basic as reproduction for certain privileged groups of people." Take that, I thought, hurling the words at the keyboard. "Children do indeed face many obstacles," I concluded. "It seems to me that to 'allow' children to grow up in a loving household with a parent or parents who really want them is perhaps the greatest gift that we can give them."

I whipped the letter from the printer and signed my name with a flourish. There, I thought, folding it neatly and sliding it into the envelope. I got up and put on my coat, buttoning it securely around my stomach. I would take it over at once, deliver it to the student newspaper office. That would take care of that. I marched across the campus, the snow crunching beneath my feet like shots of gunfire. Let them just try to mess with me. I threw my head back, let the cold wind whip the color back into my cheeks. Inside me, my baby slumbered, safe and warm and snug in her sack of amniotic fluid, sheltered from the winter that raged all around us. I wondered for a moment how easy it would be to protect her once she was outside my body, exposed to the elements, vulnerable to each passing wind.

My stomach churned uneasily. This was just the first attack. How many were there yet to come?

—⚬⚬⚬—

Connie hung up the phone, her eyes bright with that flash that signals fury. "What is it?" I asked her, ladling our soup into our bowls and carrying them to the table.

"Oh, it's my sister," she said, shaking her head. "They're just so stupid!"

I waited, pouring myself a wine glass full of juice. One of Connie's aunts had died, and her mother had called her about the funeral, the first contact in two years. When Connie told her mother that she loved her, her mother had hung up on her. Now she had just spent an hour on the phone with her older sister, trying to decide whether she should go to the funeral. "What happened?"

Connie poured herself a glass of seltzer and pushed back her chair. "Oh, she said she talked to my mother, and my mother said she just hoped I wouldn't bring *Louise*, because it might upset my uncle." She took a sip of water and stared glumly at it, as if hoping it might turn to wine before her eyes. I took a sip of juice, privately imagining myself showing up at the funeral in one of those big T-shirts with the word **BABY** emblazoned on it, an arrow pointing down. I remembered one of their family baby showers, back when we were still in contact, which I attended in one of my old activist T-shirts that read **Contra-ceptives, not Contra aid.** I'd thought it was funny. After two hours of frozen silence from Connie's Catholic family, I'd begun to suspect that going topless would have been a better idea. Connie slammed her glass down so hard the water sloshed onto the table. "And then my sister said she didn't have a way to get there with her kids, and when I said we might be able to give her a ride in our car, she said her husband didn't want his kids in the car with us."

I stared at her. "Really?"

Connie shook her head. "He thinks we might molest them."

"Really?" I thought of the student's letter in the newspaper, my own impassioned response. Where were we, anyway? What did people really think we were?

"I don't want to go," she said. She stared down at the water on the table. "I just can't deal with this right now."

I nodded. I silently agreed. We'd just gotten another of Connie's mother's letters in which she urged Connie to leave me and come back to the church. "The Sisters put you up on the altar when you were a baby," she wrote. "Well," I'd said. "No wonder you're a lesbian." I couldn't imagine seeing her mother face to face, least of all at a funeral. I'd had visions of running into her at the mall or somewhere public, telling her what I thought of her mothering. But what could you really do at a funeral?

"I'm telling them we're not coming," Connie said. Her tone was one of defeat. Thank god, I thought. One less battle to fight this week.

Month five merited the shortest chapter in my pregnancy book. "Your fetus is taking a rest," the book proclaimed. Most of the changes that were taking place were happening in the skin. Oil glands were appearing, hair follicles. If she'd wanted to, my baby could now raise an eyebrow, much like the bra lady at the department store. I pictured her in there, kicking back, floating around her amniotic fluid like a guest at a pool party, a vodka tonic in her hand. What are you getting all worked up about? she'd call to me where I stood, wringing my hands beside the water. Relax! Come take a dip. Get comfortable.

I longed to join her, but rest just didn't seem to be in the cards. I was a mass of tension. The next issue of the student newspaper had been full of letters to the editor from students and faculty, all defending gay and lesbian parents. People all over campus stopped me to congratulate me on the coming baby. "I had no idea you were pregnant!" they said over and over, "till I read it in the paper!" It was late February, and the semester was still in full swing. I was already counting down the days till May, or at least April, when my novel was scheduled to be released. On the national front the Republicans had cut Clinton's AmeriCorps, his program to have college kids do public service work and get money for tuition in return. "So much for education," I told Connie over breakfast, as I leafed through the newspaper.

"So much for anything Clinton wanted to do," she said, stirring artificial sweetener into her coffee. Just the smell of it made me want to gag. She glanced up at me. "Is that meeting still on for tonight?"

I nodded as I gathered my things together for class. A group of students had resolved to start a gay and lesbian support group on campus. One brave student, Gina, a senior and the English Department's outstanding major, had put up signs all around the campus: "Want to form a gay support group? Call Gina," followed by her phone number. Their first meeting was that night. I slipped my hand beneath my sweater to feel my stomach in a gesture that had almost become subconscious, checking to see what new shape my baby might have taken. I wondered how the meeting would go.

That night, Gina called us to order. "OK," she said. "I've done up a tentative agenda and I'm interested in your input." I looked around the circle. A dozen or so anxious-looking college students squirmed in their chairs, avoiding eye contact. Some I recognized from classes. I recognized the woman with the long hair and the hidden face from my gay and lesbian lit class the previous semester. The counseling center had referred others to me. Still others I'd never seen before. Gina led them through the agenda with careful skill, electing officers and identifying new agenda items. When the business items were taken care of, everyone began to relax, sending cautious glances around the circle.

"I never thought there were this many gay people here," said one, a nervous-looking young man with a sweep of blonde hair and wire-rimmed glasses.

"Neither did I," a young woman added, looking around.

"Well, if the ten percent rule holds," Gina said, "there should be three hundred of us on this campus."

"Wow," the first guy said. I could see them all looking around, stronger suddenly with the sheer weight of the statistics on their side. "There aren't that many people in my whole town," he said.

"Mine either," somebody else said. "My town's so small it doesn't even have a stoplight."

"Mine has fourteen churches," a timid-looking young man with short brown hair offered, "and no bars."

I watched them, talking to each other, beginning to make eye contact, beginning to loosen up. Sometimes I got so wrapped up in the provincialism of this town that I forgot how rural the hometowns of these kids could be, that Mansfield, with its stoplight and its brand new Wal-Mart, could take on a nearly cosmopolitan air.

"Our town burned a cross on the lawn of a mixed-race couple after they moved in," another woman volunteered. "The woman was pregnant," she added, glancing at me. I could feel the now familiar cold begin at the back of my neck and seep along my spine. Connie took my hand.

"How about two weeks from today for the next meeting?" Gina asked. "This time and place work for everybody?" They nodded and began to get their coats and move toward the door, then stopped to exchange names and phone numbers. I watched them go, a group of suddenly hopeful kids, full of energy and ideas for their futures. As Connie helped me on with my coat, I wondered what that future would bring. A cold wind was blowing as we left the parking lot. I wrapped my coat more tightly around me and hoped it bore us no ill will.

This Is Your Conscience Speaking

At first I thought the queasiness deep in the pit of my stomach was the morning sickness coming back. I fought to finish teaching my classes for the day, but the nausea kept rising like a tide, threatening to overtake me. By the time I got home, I had a raging fever and chills. Diarrhea and vomiting kept me moving between the bed and the bathroom. Sustaining a fever for even a day can cause harm to your developing fetus, my pregnancy book admonished. Connie called the doctor.

"You've got to get liquids in," Connie reported, brandishing a bowl of ice chips, "or they're going to put you in the hospital with an IV."

I looked at her wearily, then took a mouthful of ice chips and threw them up immediately. Connie sat beside me all night, rubbing me down with cool cloths until I was able to swallow a few pieces of ice. The phone rang, but we ignored it. A freezing rain fell all night, covering the world in a cloak of ice. When morning came, I crawled out of bed and crept downstairs. I felt like a small animal, leaving its lair only out of necessity.

"How are you feeling?" Connie asked me as I dragged myself into the kitchen. I shrugged and opened the refrigerator, searching for Jello. Connie didn't look much better than I did after a night of sitting at my bedside and eating chocolate chip cookies for comfort. Deep circles rimmed her eyes. Her hair was tousled. She looked like hell. I wondered what I looked like. Connie poured her coffee, and I turned away instinctively, as if the thick black liquid would suddenly rise up and force itself down my throat.

"Let's see who called," she said, turning on the machine.

I sat down at the table and put a spoonful of Jello in my mouth. It felt like it had its own life in there. I tried to swallow, but my throat refused to cooperate. Exhaustion overcame me; even my bones ached. Where was this glowing second trimester? It must be a myth, invented to keep us getting pregnant, generation after generation. The answering machine buzzed and clicked, then discharged its message.

"Louise Blum," the voice said. Something trembled in my belly. I looked at Connie. The sound quality had been altered somehow, as

181

if the voice were coming to us through a tunnel. "This is your conscience speaking," it said, echoing through the room. "Artificial insemination is wrong, wrong, wrong, wrong, wrong." The voice dissolved into the faint sound of laughter. A sharp pain gripped my stomach like a claw. I rushed back into the bathroom just in time. My head pounded, as if all the contents of my brain had just slid to one side, piled there like rocks. When I emerged from the bathroom, clutching the door frame for balance, Connie was replaying the message.

"Little shits," she said. "How dare they think they can tell us what's right and wrong?" Her cheeks were pink with anger. I leaned against the doorway and felt for my stomach with one hand. Where was my anger? Surely, there was no real threat here, just a group of guys sitting around drinking and playing with their speaker phone. But all I felt was fear, coiled in my stomach, as real as this flu, filling me with an icy wind. I went back upstairs to our bed and crawled beneath the covers and pulled them up around me. I could feel myself shaking. I touched my stomach with both hands, trying to feel the life inside. Artificial insemination was wrong. Our baby, our Zoe, this tiny being forming deep inside me, was wrong.

I stroked my belly, as flat now as it had been five months earlier, all the excess liquid sucked out by the diarrhea and vomiting. I wished I could feel her move. I wished I had some sign, some physical sensation that she was still in my body. I imagined a group of guys passing around a bottle and dialing our number. I wondered what kept them from getting in their car and driving over here, doing physical damage to the house or the cars. Or to us. I rolled over on my side and curled my body up as tightly as I could. I was afraid to bring this child into the world. I was afraid to let her go, expose her to the elements, to the society that waited for her like wolves, hungry for her blood. I was afraid of so much. I was afraid of the letters to the editor, afraid of the obscene phone calls, afraid of the people who stared at us in restaurants, afraid of the boys who yelled at us that night to go away. I was afraid of the intensity with which Connie's family had turned its back on her for loving me. I thought of Zoe, preparing to leave my body, about to become our daughter. I was afraid of how easy it seemed to have been for Connie's mother to relinquish her, to tell her her relationship with me was repulsive and sick. I was afraid of the way she had shut the door on Connie, as if this daughter were not the greatest gift that she would ever have. I was afraid of the people who prayed for us to change.

I felt my belly, tried to imagine Zoe cuddled there, untouched by my illness and my fear, unconscious of this world I was about to bring her into. Please keep her safe, I prayed, please, please take care of her. My own life had never felt so precious somehow, nor so tenuous. I had a constant pain deep in my throat, as if something was growing there, seeking to block my voice till my words could only come directly from my heart, spilling out from my chest like blood. It seemed the February cold would hang on forever in the darkened snow that clung to our lawn, in the cinders that covered the road out front, in the ice that weighted down the branches. I felt as if the freezing rain had worked its way into my bloodstream and curled up around my heart. I feared it would freeze me out, turn my body to ice, immobilize me in place as Lot's wife had been immobilized. I closed my eyes, felt for my stomach, and tried to imagine my Zoe, floating deep inside. Please keep this baby safe, I prayed, please let her live.

That night I dreamed that a young white boy in his early twenties drove up to our house and hurled a cannonball up into the air. I saw his muscles flex. His jaw was rigid; his baseball cap hid his eyes. There was no way to tell who he was. I ran up to the attic to hide, but just as I reached the top of the stairs, the cannonball crashed through the ceiling directly over my head. I didn't move. If it's meant to hit me, I thought, it will.

It didn't.

I spent the next night on the couch, pillowed by Connie's body, comforted by her arms holding me close. That afternoon I had managed to eat some Jello, and now I was actually sipping some broth. I could feel myself growing stronger, my body returning to itself with that incredible power we have to regenerate ourselves, even when we think that all is lost.

Behind me, Connie stroked my hair and laid her cheek against my head. "I'm sorry," she said.

I closed my eyes, snuggled deeper into her arms. "For what?" I asked her.

She tightened her grip. I could feel her lips against my hair. "For not claiming you," she said. "For not claiming our baby, at Weight Watchers, or anywhere else." She kissed my head. "This is my baby," she said. "I'm not going to let my fear stop me from making her mine."

I sighed. "Thank you," I said. I took a sip of my broth. Inside, I felt strong and solid, as if I had just stepped from the deck of a boat to firm soil. I was safe. I was here, I was in my home, I was in my lover's arms, Zoe was securely inside my belly, held there by Connie's hands. I was absolutely safe, absolutely taken care of. I snuggled back against her and took another sip of broth. I reached for the television remote and turned on the set. A tiger cub pounced on a bug in some distant jungle, while its mother brought down a deer and savaged its guts. Her cubs came running. I watched despite myself, the cup of broth warm in my hands. Blood ran down the mother's teeth, soaked her gums. Her babies fell over themselves to eat the same way she did, laying into the carcass with their tiny teeth. I imagined feeding my baby the way that mother fed hers, with flesh I'd torn from the bones of my victims with my own sharpened teeth. What would it be like, I wondered, to feel like the predator, instead of like the prey? I watched the deer's body, still twitching, still probably conscious, feeling its life leave it with every mouthful. The tiger cubs began to play, falling over each other, their bellies full. I closed my eyes for a moment and took a deep breath. I'll keep you safe, I promised, I'll never let you starve. Connie slipped her hands beneath my waistband and cupped my stomach in her palms. We both felt it at the same time. "Oh my god," Connie said. "Was that—?"

"I don't know," I said, but there it was again—a tiny fluttery thump, as if a little soccer player was in there using the walls of my womb as her goalposts. Zoe's first kick. We had both felt it at the same time, Connie from the outside, me from the inside. "That's her," I said. My heart began to pound. "She kicked! She kicked!"

∞

A burst of spring-like weather brought with it the spring catalogue from Alyson Publications. The cover featured *Amnesty* and its advance promotional blurbs. I felt a flush of warmth just seeing them. The book looked so serious and important. The blurbs curled themselves up in my mind like happy cats. That's right, I thought, I'm a writer!

"Yes," Connie said. "More than just a pod." I ignored her and studied my blurbs. Some people liked my book. Some people thought it was good.

"Where should we put everything?" Connie asked. We were supposed to be cleaning the house. Several months earlier a lesbian friend had approached us about building some sort of community.

"There's nothing going on here," she'd said. "No political activism. Everyone thinks they're all alone." We'd decided to start with a lesbian potluck, making up dozens of bold purple fliers and sending stacks to every lesbian we knew. "Come to a lesbian potluck!" the fliers said. We'd volunteered to host the first one. The day had come, and we had no idea how many women would show up.

I had no idea where to put anything. Our kitchen counter was covered with piles of newspapers and junk mail that we hadn't managed to sort through yet. Our life together was full of piles—piles of paper, piles of sweaters, piles of magazines, piles of laundry waiting to be separated into lights and darks. There was no keeping up with them. Everywhere I looked we had piles of something, some undisturbed since we'd moved into this house. Every few months we'd pick up a stack of old mail and just throw it all away, the same way I deleted messages from my voice mail halfway through from people who talked too slowly. I didn't have time in my life for these details. Before either of us could move, the phone rang. Just the sound of it made my heart leap. Every time it rang, I had to stop for a minute, prepare myself to answer it, gather up my resources, just in case. I closed my eyes for a moment after I said hello, waiting to hear the other voice.

"Hi," it said. "This is Brenda." I relaxed and let out the breath I hadn't even realized I'd been holding. Brenda was a lesbian in her midtwenties, a coach at a nearby high school who had just moved to the area. Like several other lesbians from the surrounding towns, she'd called us after the newspaper article came out. We'd made a lot of contacts from that article. Brenda had already spent hours on the phone with us, talking about what it was like to live here. We weren't supposed to leave any messages about the potluck on her answering machine, even though she lived alone. She kept her lesbian-themed books locked up in a safe in her bedroom. I felt a surge of impatience now; there was only so much time to get ready. "I can't come today," Brenda said. Her voice was deep, almost a mumble.

"Oh, that's too bad," I said almost mechanically, glancing at my watch. "Why not?"

I could hear her take a breath. "Well," she said, "what if I ran into one of these women from the potluck on the street some time?" She paused. "Well, what then?"

I waited for a moment, wondering whether this was some kind of riddle. "You'd say hi?" I asked tentatively.

Brenda exhaled, a sharp final sound that came through the

receiver like a punctuation mark. "I can't risk that," she said. "I can't come." Neither of us said anything for a moment. "Maybe I'll call you later," she said.

"What is with these lesbians?" I said to Connie, hanging up the phone. "What are they so afraid of?" I pushed a pile of old advertising circulars to one side. "She might have to say hi, and then everyone would know." Annoyance rolled through me like a wave. "She'll talk to us for hours on the phone, and then when she gets the opportunity to actually meet some other lesbians, she stays home." I sat down in my chair and glared at the kitchen. Piles of things lay everywhere, surrounding us like quicksand, threatening to suck us in, smother us with our own junk. "She'll call us later," I said, glaring at a pile of slick gay magazines that we'd originally subscribed to for news and later found included only gossip about celebrities who *might* be gay or lesbian or at least hung around with gay and lesbian people. I dumped the whole stack in the trash. The surface of the counter gleamed up at me, startlingly white. Satisfaction flooded through me. Connie was laying out new piles of plastic cutlery and paper napkins.

"Well," she said, "What do you think?"

I sighed and shook my head. "I don't know," I said. "I guess we'll just have to wait and see."

Thirty-one women filled the house and spilled out onto the front porch; their cars flooded the street. Inside, women bustled about with casseroles and soda; outside, they smoked a covert cigarette or two in full view of the neighbors. I wondered what our neighbors, Effie and Leon, would think of this. I felt positively regal, swaggering through the crowd in my stretchy black maternity jumper and bright purple turtleneck, showing at last, a fully pregnant woman. Women smiled at me from every corner of the room.

"How are you doing?" Maude asked, stopping on her way to the kitchen to pat my stomach. "How's the baby?"

"She's fine," I said, leaning back a little to show off my blossoming belly. I liked showing, looking like I was pregnant. I liked the surrender of it, just saying, OK, here I am—pregnant as can be. And it was nice to have some body for a change.

"You're looking good," Maude said. She glanced around. "Good turnout." She leaned in a little closer. "You know, Sue and Becky won't come," she said confidingly of two women who lived nearby. "They're afraid they might see somebody."

Irritation pecked at my brain. I tried to shrug it off.

"Well," Maude said. Her tone was level, as if she were smoothing out some quarrel. "Becky has family in the area."

I glanced at Connie over by the kitchen door, deep in some story. Her eyes were glowing. I thought of her parents and her brothers and sisters and their spouses and children, all living well within the confines of the "area." After the article had come out, one of her sisters-in-law had sent us a letter. "Don't you ever do this to my children again," she'd said. Becky was in her forties. I wondered if she was still afraid of what her parents thought. She had teenage children living with her. She didn't plan to tell them. I wondered who they thought Sue was, this woman who shared their mother's life. Did she share her bedroom as well? I shuddered and wondered about this lesbian world I'd become a part of, about all the fear that shrouded it.

I glanced around the room, at all the women in our house. I wasn't even sure I liked lesbians. Why were they all so scared all the time? Get over it, I wanted to say. Get real! Connie and I had come out. We'd survived. Nothing bad had happened to us, and we'd come out like nobody I'd ever heard of, slapping ourselves across the front pages of the newspaper like a beacon. Somehow I'd thought everybody would just come out after us, as if we'd dug a trail out from underground and liberated the burrow in which we'd all been hiding. I'd thought everybody would be glad to see some light. I touched my belly possessively. Pride flooded through me like a rising temperature, staining my cheeks with its heat. I didn't even have tenure yet. Sue and Becky were cowards, I thought, hiding in their little house. I looked at all the women who swarmed our house. Did they really think that anyone didn't know? I shook my head. My belly was firm against my palms, round and hard as a huge nut. I felt invincible. Nobody could keep me down. That obscene phone call might never even have happened, for all it really mattered in my life. I was over that fear. Outside, the temperatures were wavering, as if at any moment they might begin to rise and bring us out of our hibernation. Soon it would be spring. I was deep into the fifth month of my pregnancy. Next month my novel would come out. I took a deep breath and felt it flood my body like a wave. Deep inside, Zoe kicked her fluttery kick. I was ready to go, ready to tear up the world.

"Here she is!" somebody said, clapping me on the back so hard I nearly fell over. "How you doing, kiddo?" Lee asked me, her arm so tight around my shoulders I had to fight for a moment just to breathe again. She patted my stomach and looked around the room. "Isn't this just great?" she asked the women around us. "I mean, look at her!" She coughed into her hand, a ragged smoker's cough. Lee was in her late fifties, her face lined with wrinkles and her voice as deep as a man's. She and her partner, Ginger, had called us the day the article came out, excited to make a contact. They lived in a tiny town in upstate New York, a couple of hours away. "Anyway," Lee said, continuing some story to the rest of the room, "everything was fine in our town till a new minister came and started preaching about us." She glanced around to be sure she had our full attention. "Our neighbors next door put up signs in their yard, aimed right at us: 'Repent or be damned!' " The women listening all shook their heads. "They blamed us for the shooting at that welfare office," Lee said. The year before, a man whose paychecks had been confiscated for child-support delinquency had opened fire at the welfare office in Watkins Glen. Four caseworkers had died. "The preacher said we brought immorality to the area," Lee said, her voice deep with satisfaction.

"We'd been living there for fifteen years," Ginger chimed in, her hand on Lee's arm. "He was the one who was new." Everybody laughed.

"Then they went after my day-care center!" Lee said. Her voice cracked, and she stopped to clear her throat again. I looked away. Ginger and Lee had been together far longer than we had. Ginger taught home ec in a high school and Lee ran a day-care center. What power did they have? They had to look at signs every day that damned them to hell. My skin itched uncomfortably. I looked at Connie, still over by the door holding forth to her own group of women. We weren't the only ones who were out. I shook my head. Women were out all over the place in their own ways. So what if Sue and Becky didn't want to live the way we did? Who was I to judge? I patted Lee's hand and made my way across the room to Connie and tucked myself beneath her arm. We were all in this together. Did I really think we were something special?

———

The birds began to sing at the end of February, their songs mingling and filling the air as if they had forgotten where they were, still trapped deep in the throes of winter, their feet still frozen in the ice. I brewed myself a cup of tea and put on some Bach and aimed the tape player at my stomach, hoping that it would sink in and calm the baby. I'd read about that in one of my books. Unfortunately, I'd been too busy to really do it. As I hit the play button now, I couldn't help wondering if I'd missed my opportunity. Maybe I was just too late. I'd wasted a whole month of perhaps contributing to her fetal development. She was probably way behind by now. I got up and opened the kitchen window a little to let in some fresh air and stopped. A robin trilled merrily, filling the air with its song. The street was full of happy pregnant women. I watched them, mesmerized. I had never seen them before. Where had they come from? The woman from up the street was virtually running up the hill, pushing a stroller filled with toddlers and leading a string of dogs behind her. Her stomach filled the air in front of her. Her energy seemed boundless. Where had she gotten it from? I could barely get myself to work. Her face was flushed with exertion; her cheeks glowed with health. I stared at her. What did she know that I didn't, and from what source had this wisdom been imparted to her? I had trouble making my way up that hill when I wasn't pregnant. I shut the window quickly and turned back to the kitchen. Strains of Bach rose glumly through the air, faintly funereal, as if highlighting how futile this effort really was. I glanced back out the window. The woman was still out there, bouncing around like all the pregnant women did on that horrible Jane Fonda workout video that I sometimes made a pretense of doing, their hair perfectly in place and their thighs full of muscle. I felt my own thighs covertly, once so muscular, now as soft as jelly. I wasn't exercising. I wasn't talking to my baby. How could she recognize my voice if I never said anything to her? Tears stung my eyes. I was failing. Five months into my pregnancy and already I was doing it all wrong. From the street I could hear the shouts of happy children basking in the glow of their mothers' attention. I took a deep breath. Things had to change. I had to get a grip on myself. There was still time. I could still do this thing. There was still the hope that I could get it right. I looked at the clock above the sink. Anyway—I had to get to work.

Gina was waiting for me when I got to my office. "Look at this," she said, handing me one of the fliers for the gay support group meeting. "Fucking Cocksuckers," it said, the words scrawled in an angry black magic marker. "It's our first defacement," she said. I studied her carefully. She didn't seem afraid. Her voice was proud. Maybe I was the only one who still felt fear.

"I want to talk to you about my stuff," Gina said, kicking her foot into the jamb of my door. She pulled a sheaf of papers from her pocket. The students were having a reading that night in honor of the student literary magazine, which had finally come out again after a hiatus of several years. I was the adviser, though my involvement was nominal, consisting mainly of pep talks and a lot of listening and nodding. The students were getting this together, all on their own. "I want to read my poems," Gina said. She scowled. "But I don't know." She looked up at me. "Do you think I should?"

I took off my coat and sat down, settling Zoe as gently on my thighs as if she were actually there in the flesh, which, of course, she was. "Why wouldn't you?" I asked her.

Gina glared at me, got up, and paced around the room a couple of times. "Oh, I don't know," she said. Then she turned to me. "Are they any good?"

I settled back into my chair. "I don't know," I said seriously. "Why don't you read them to me now?"

The auditorium was packed that night. Students lined the walls, holding sheets of paper in their hands, some reverently, some with shaking hands, a few almost angrily, their hands balled up into fists as if someone might try to take their writing from them. Against the far wall a few musicians tuned their guitars. Connie and I found a seat and settled in. A band warmed up at the microphone. There was an air of seriousness in the room. Gina took the mike with her head down and her cheeks flushed with color. Her voice rose, strong and trembling. "I'm glad I'm a fat dyke," she read to the roomful of students. My cheeks flushed with pride as I watched her read. I felt almost as if I'd created her. There was a press of students on either side of me. When she finished, they gave her a standing ovation. I took a deep breath. I felt like a tree in the middle of a forest, surrounded by the company of other oaks. Connie took my hand and I squeezed her fingers. We weren't the only ones. We were surrounded by community everywhere we turned.

A student from the gay support group touched my belly shyly as we left after the reading. "You give me so much hope," he said, his dark eyes shining. "Maybe some day I can have a child too."

That night I woke at 2:30. The room was full of darkness, flushed with our sleep. Connie's arms enfolded me, her lips covered the back of my neck with kisses. "What are you doing? I asked her sleepily.

She tightened her arms around me. "I just saw you, and I loved you," she said, and I drifted back to sleep to the feel of her mouth against my skin.

Hell—We're All Sinners!

March came in like a lion, giving us morning after morning of wet and wild energy. I felt as if I'd lived through a thousand years of days just like that. Zoe kicked like she was dancing back and forth across the ballroom of my womb. It was like the whole world was open for me, waiting for my words to paint a picture of it, pin it down. Everything was out there, waiting, poised at the edge of spring. In a matter of weeks my novel would be out, in the stores, and maybe people would buy it and read it and like it. Maybe they would talk about it. Maybe someday I would get on a bus somewhere and see somebody reading my book. I was full of power, full of love for Connie. We unloaded the car and unlocked the front door, pulling the mail out of the box. We both saw the letter at the same time, at the bottom of the stack, the return address immediately familiar.

Connie picked it up gingerly, holding it out as if she didn't really want to touch it. "It's from my mother," she said.

I nodded. We both looked at it for a moment, and then Connie took a deep breath and tore it open. I could feel all the wildness of March going flat inside me, like a bottle of seltzer when you leave it out on the counter. Connie sat down at the kitchen table, one hand holding the letter, the other propping up her head. I sat down next to her and waited, playing with one of the piles of junk mail. Finally Connie sighed and looked up. We looked at each other for a few minutes.

"Well?" I said.

Connie shook her head. "She says that Satan has a hold on me, that it's wrong for me to have this baby."

I felt a flash of irritation, quickly complicated by the old familiar shiftings of fear inside my stomach. Connie's father had said in his last letter that I was Connie's "enticing ticket to Hell." I'd felt kind of complimented—did that mean he thought I was attractive, that he had watched me move across the room, admired the sway in my hips, the wiry thinness of my body? At the same time, however, I'd felt uneasy. It was ludicrous enough to laugh about, the idea that they would truly believe that Satan had a hold on us, but this was her family after all; they had conceived her, birthed her, raised her.

Their tentacles extended still, locked deep into some obscure recess of her soul, as if at any moment they could tighten their grip and retract, suck her back into their womb, tuck her in and pat her down and hide her away from me forever.

The next week brought a torrent of rain, slicking down the pavement and turning the grass a deep and vibrant green. Robins appeared spontaneously at every corner of the lawn and hopped about the ground, pecking at the pine needles beneath the trees. Birds sang from every direction. I lay in bed next to Connie, listening to the tires slide on the wetness. There was a light outside that came from spring, as if the sky were lit from within. I felt a slow stirring, deep in the pit of me. My belly was full and round and hard as a ball. Connie lay beside me, a tumble of dark hair and amber skin. The room was soft, ripe with our smell, dark and damp and tinged with musk. Inside me Zoe rippled from side to side as if she were swimming laps. I could almost make her out beneath my skin, bubbling just beneath the surface of my stomach like volcanic rock. Satisfaction filled me like a quiet rain.

Connie sighed with pleasure and turned toward me in her sleep as I touched her earlobe with my tongue. Yesterday I had canceled my classes and she'd called in sick and we'd stayed in bed all day and just made love. Saturday night we had made love even though it was late and I was tired. Friday we made love before meeting friends for dinner. My body felt eminently sexual. All I wanted to do was to hold and be held, to feel Connie's fingers exploring my clitoris, slipping into my vagina, making me come. All I wanted was her fingers everywhere, touching my back, stroking my sides, cupping my ass, sliding down my thighs. All I wanted was the feel of my breasts against hers, my whole body pressed up against hers, my arms around her and my mouth against hers, sucking her lips as if for water. I couldn't get enough of her smell, her taste, the warmth and texture of her skin, the color of it in the morning light. Outside the air was damp and heavy, as if the whole neighborhood were a moist vagina, waiting for entry, longing to be touched. I pulled Connie toward me, buried my face against her throat, plunged my fingers deep into the hair between her legs, while all around us the rain-slicked road, the deep green grass pressed flat by the rain, the moist, heavy air, the dampness of the light, enveloped us in their soft velvet walls, lulling us with their smell, my fingers so deep inside her it seemed they could pulse with the beat of her heart, till there was nothing else except the movement of our bodies, in the quiet wild wetness of the spring.

I spotted the plain manila envelope in my mailbox as soon as I got to work. Only my name was on it. No routing slip, no return address. My fingers hesitated above the seal for a moment, and then I tore it open and reached inside. When I pulled it out, I nearly dropped it on the floor. It was the "lesbian issue" of *Playboy* magazine. Who would put this in my box? Almost instinctually I glanced around. I was alone in the mail room. Gingerly I flipped the pages. I didn't have a problem with pornography. Did I? I was cool about this kind of thing. There was nothing too spectacular in what I was looking at, nothing too disturbing. I took a deep breath. I could handle this. Then I turned to a full page spread of two very un-lesbian looking women engaged in oral sex. Their long blond hair cascaded across their backs; their pubic areas were shaved and glistening, exposed, there for everyone to view. Zoe stirred in my belly and I snapped the magazine shut. My heart was pounding. I fought down a wave of nausea. I stuffed the magazine back in the envelope and threw it in the trash, then just as quickly pulled it out again. It had my name on it; what if someone found it and thought it was mine? I slipped it into my briefcase and snapped it shut. My cheeks burned with shame. I would take it home and throw it out where it was safe; no one would find it there. All that mattered, I thought, was that no one think it was mine.

The spring weather dissolved at the beginning of April. Frost covered the ground like scattered ashes and filled the air with mourning. "It's like an April Fool's joke," Connie said, peering out through the window that overlooked the kitchen sink. A cold breeze slipped in through the glass like a thief. I squeezed my tea bag out and tossed it into the trash. Fuck April, I thought, lifting my cup to my lips. Zoe kicked me so suddenly I nearly choked. Connie brought her coffee over to the table. It smelled like rot.

"So," she said brightly. "You ready for that discussion group tonight?"

I sipped my tea and glared at her. Had she always been so cheerful? I glanced at her coffee with a sudden longing. When would I ever have caffeine again? No wonder I was always tired. So much was going on. I had forgotten we were doing another discussion group. For a moment I felt almost cheered. A church in a nearby city was attempting to educate its membership about homosexuality, hosting a round of discussion sessions in people's living rooms with gay and lesbian volunteers from the area. It was part of a process to address the spiritual needs of gay and lesbian congregants. This particular church had been active in the abolitionist movement, breaking from its parent church in order to state its opposition to slavery. The first discussion group we'd done had gone well, with the congregants seriously interested in what we had to say. People had brought a lot of desserts and many well-considered questions. Afterward a member had asked us whether we might have Zoe baptized there.

"I don't know," I'd said, looking at Connie helplessly. The question startled me. It had never occurred to me to baptize Zoe anywhere. But I felt so warm and welcome and full of chocolate cake that it suddenly seemed like a great idea. This particular church was liberal in the best sense, ready to denounce our oppression just as they had denounced that of African Americans a hundred years before. So what if a couple hundred years before that they'd been burning witches at the stake? We could have our own church, a built-in community that would automatically support us in exchange for our embracing the tenets of their faith. True, I hadn't been in a Protestant church since my childhood, when my brother's dodging the draft during the Vietnam War had exiled us from the congregation. But here was the church again, back in my life, seeking me out this time instead of pushing me away. Who said small towns were narrow-minded?

I took another sip of tea and savored the warmth as it traveled down my throat. Another discussion group. I kind of enjoyed these things, being the center of attention, getting to talk about myself and my personal struggle with spirituality. Besides, who knew what dessert they'd have this time?

"So," said Alice, the group leader of the evening, happily looking around the circle. "We have Connie and Louise with us tonight, ready to talk about their experiences. I'd like to just start with a little history of the process."

"Just a minute," a man said, getting to his feet. "I just want to check the score." He lumbered into the other room. I dumbly watched him go. Harvey was an active church member, but he appeared more interested in the game on television than in the issues concerning his fellow congregants. "Fred, you want a beer while I'm up?" he asked. Fred looked up eagerly and nodded. I felt a trickle of dread easing down my spine like a reluctant rock climber.

Trixie, the hostess, jumped up. "Anybody want another drink?" she asked. All the women in the room raised their empty glasses. Connie and I exchanged a glance. In the next room Harvey turned up the volume on the set. The announcer's voice filtered into the room, only mildly softer than Alice's. I looked around. The coffee table was bare. Where was the dessert? I could feel Zoe moving restively inside me. I checked my watch, wondering how long I could go without food before she would revolt, sending my blood sugar plummeting.

An hour later there was still no food. "Listen," Fred said, leaning forward and slurring only slightly. "I've been meeting with a lot of people who don't like the direction this church has been going." Heads nodded around the circle. Trixie got up to freshen everyone's drinks.

"What's the score in there?" somebody asked.

"Thirty-eight—sixteen," a man called back. Everybody groaned.

"What sport is it?" I whispered to Connie. She shrugged. Her look was mildly alarmed.

Fred took another sip of beer. "It's the pastor," he said. He knocked back the rest of his beer and crushed the can in his hands. "The sermons used to be so nice," he said. "Now they're all full of social issues."

Heads nodded around the room. Irritation flooded through me. Social issues. Wasn't that what Jesus was all about?

Beside me, Harvey nodded succinctly and settled back on the couch. "There was all that civil rights stuff in the sixties," Fred said, shaking his head. "And what good did that do? There's still discrimination!"

"Of course, there's still discrimination," I said before I could stop myself. "But it's illegal now." I looked around the room, hoping to get their attention. Nobody looked at me. A few men were turned toward the other room, where the television was. One woman had her fingers deep into her glass, trying to retrieve her slice of lemon. "It's not illegal to discriminate against gay and lesbian people," I said vainly. Across the room Alice, the discussion leader, sat still, as silent as if she'd suddenly lost her voice. Come back, I implored her, wordlessly. Take control of the meeting!

"There will always be discrimination and prejudice," I said, looking back at Fred. "That doesn't mean we shouldn't fight against it."

"Oh, I'm not saying we shouldn't," Fred said quickly. "I don't have any problems with gay people." He looked around the room. "I mean, hell," he said, his voice flushed with feeling. "We're all sinners!"

Not me, I thought. My whole body felt hot, as if the thermostat in the room had gone out of control.

Harvey nodded sagely from his spot on the couch, his chin sunk deep into his chest. "I always think of my dear old great-aunt," he said suddenly. "She was truly Godlike," he mused, gazing off past our heads as if she might be in the room, floating around behind us. "She walked with God in a whole different way than I do." He paused. We all waited as he studied the wall above our heads. "She was Italian Catholic," he said. "Dear old Concetta." I could feel another surge of irritation flooding through me. I was starting to hate the woman. "She wouldn't agree with what I'm doing," Harvey said, "but I'm just trying to walk with God." He stared off into the next room. I waited to see if he would say something else, but apparently he was no longer with us. Maybe he was communing with Aunt Concetta.

"This issue is just causing too much divisiveness," Fred said.

A woman from across the circle nodded. "You can't even say anything about gay people anymore without someone accusing you of being homophobic!"

Connie leaned forward. "You're going to have a schism anyway," she said. "You already have it." She paused. I could feel her take a breath. "All you can do is act in your integrity." She looked around the room. Everyone avoided her gaze. "I mean, the division in the church is too deep to repair."

I looked at the others. Some men were concentrating on the television in the other room. Harvey was still staring vacantly at the wall. Fred shook his head. "I just wish we didn't keep talking about schisms," he said. He sent a beseeching look around the room. "I mean, what about the old people?" he asked. "All I care about is old Bill Somes, eighty years old and a member of this church all his life. He should have a safe place to die."

"My mother's eighty years old," I said, "and she's been working through her feelings about my being gay." I could feel a hot flush working its way up my face. "And I think she'll die a wiser woman because of it." Nobody paid any attention to me. The meeting was breaking up all around us. The men were spilling out into the other room to catch the end of the game. Trixie and the gang were heading for the kitchen, their drinks in their hands. "I've got a great recipe I wanted to show you," Trixie was saying. I glanced at my watch. 9:30. I could feel the blood rising to my head. I was dizzy from lack of food.

"You look great," Harvey was saying next to me as I pulled myself to my feet. "Pregnant women are so beautiful," he announced, fumbling for my belly.

I dodged his hands and headed for the door, pulling Connie along with me. "I hope you'll consider baptizing Zoe with us," Alice said softly as we neared the door. In your dreams, I thought, looking down at her. In your fucking dreams. I pushed open the door and breathed in the crisp wintry air on my way to the car.

"Idiots," Connie said, opening the door for me.

"Morons," I said, pulling the door shut behind me. Morons, I repeated, to myself. I felt furious with them for not taking us seriously and furious with myself for ever thinking I could find a place with them.

Your Silence Will Not Protect You

Frost covered the windows, etching delicate patterns onto the glass. The air was cold and brittle, as if it might crack in my lungs. It seemed like winter would never end. Just an hour south of us flowers were probably blooming by now. A mourning dove called from the roof, its voice deep with grief. I pulled a comb through my hair and studied my body in the mirror. I felt full of grief too. Zoe was right there, in full view of everyone. How could I ever protect her? She had no privacy and neither did I. Everybody who looked at me knew that I was carrying a baby. Everyone felt free to comment on her, to touch my belly, to ask her name. How could I ever keep her safe?

The phone rang as I was looking for my purse, and for a moment I considered not answering it. I glanced at the clock on the wall, then picked up the receiver. I was already late. What did a few more minutes matter? Deborah's voice was slow and solemn. "I just wanted to warn you," she said. "I didn't want you to just see it in your box."

"See what?" I asked. I felt a little impatient. I just wanted to get going, shake this sense of sadness. Was this from that church discussion group? I didn't need those people. We had our own community, right here where we lived.

"Somebody made up a mock newspaper," Deborah said, "and distributed it in people's boxes." She hesitated. "It's called the *Phaglight*."

I wondered for a moment if I'd heard her right. "What?" I said stupidly.

"They make some comments about me and my feminism," Deborah said, "and they said some things about you."

"About me?" I repeated. My brain seemed full of some kind of fog. I shook my head to clear it.

"Yours is much worse than mine," Deborah said. She paused for a moment. "Much, much worse."

I didn't say anything. I just couldn't seem to get it somehow. What was she talking about?

"I wondered when you're coming in," Deborah said carefully. "Because I want to be with you when you see this."

When I got to campus, I pulled the car into a parking space as carefully as if I were maneuvering a plane onto the runway. The frost sparked in the sunlight as I made my way through the parking lot. I scanned the faces of the people I passed, as if they might be able to tell me what was happening, but no one seemed to notice me. Maybe it was nothing. Maybe nothing was going on, and this was just one of Deborah's things she got upset about. I took a deep breath and pulled open the door of the English building.

Deborah and another colleague, the professor who had taken issue with the Einstein quote on my door a few months before, were waiting for me beside the mailboxes. I could see it in there, a flat sheet of paper, lying innocuously inside my box, still as a snake, just waiting for my touch.

"I just want to apologize to you," my colleague said, his cup of coffee quivering in his hand, "for what you're about to read in there."

I looked at him dumbly. What was he talking about?

"My advice to you is to take it somewhere private before you read it," he said.

"Let's go upstairs to my office," Deborah said. Her eyes were soft. She took my arm. I let her lead me up the stairs and close the door behind us. I looked at the piece of paper in my hands, tried to make out what it said. I still didn't get it. I didn't get it even when I read it. "Lesbian Loses Mutant Alien Baby," the headline read. The sperm had been replaced with instant coffee crystals, the article said, causing the mutation. I was a bull dyke who had gone against the "natural order" and resisted men, and I'd gotten what I deserved. My partner had been unavailable for comment, the article concluded, because she was at a "Fattydyke Weightloss Clinic."

At first the words had no impact on me. I stared at the paper for a moment. I didn't want to look up. I could feel my cheeks growing hot with embarrassment. Instant coffee crystals. I thought of the insemination, that vial of yellow, egglike liquid. What if it hadn't been sperm? What if it had been something else? I squeezed the paper between my fingers as if it were flesh, something tangible, something I could really touch. I felt exposed, vulnerable. They'd written about my insemination as if it were public property. They'd made a joke of it. How many people had seen this? I wanted to go downstairs to my office, hide myself away. I wanted to pretend this hadn't happened, that this stupid piece of paper didn't exist, didn't even matter in my life. I looked at Deborah. "I'm OK," I said.

She looked dubious. "Are you sure?"

I nodded. I looked back at the paper in my hands.

"Do you want me to throw it away?" she asked.

I held it for a moment. I was seized with the impulse to save it, to file it away the same way I had filed all those letters to the editor, to close it up in my file drawer. I shook my head. Why would I save this? It was nothing. Just trash. I wanted to forget it. I handed it to Deborah. "Yes," I said. "Throw it away." My voice sounded mechanical to me, like someone else was sounding out the words.

"Are you sure you're OK?" Deborah asked.

I nodded. "I'm going down to my office," I said. All I wanted to do was get away. I went back downstairs. Gina stopped in to check on me.

"I'm sorry about the hate sheet," she said.

I shrugged. "It's OK," I said, but inside I could feel myself beginning to tremble. Hate sheet. Was that what this was? Could you call something that talked about instant coffee crystals a hate sheet?

I did paperwork in my office the rest of the day and drove back home beneath a steady gathering of clouds. I peered at the sky uneasily through the windshield. Where was the sun? It was as if the mountains had conspired against it, seizing it by the throat and sucking out its light like blood. I pulled into the driveway and turned off the engine. Our yellow house stood there calmly, its fraying freedom flag barely visible in the darkness, just a collection of boards and nails, easily disassembled, eviscerated, and reduced to rubble. I pulled my keys from the ignition and hurried into the house, clutching my coat around me tightly. Inside, our house was full of light and color; spider plants and geraniums graced our windows, paintings glowed on the walls. Annie Lennox wailed joyously on the stereo. In the kitchen something simmered on the stove; I could hear it bubbling in the pot as if at any moment it might explode. I looked around me. This was our house. This was our life. Inside me Zoe was quiet and still. Before I knew it, I was shaking, and then I was crying, and I thought that I might never stop, that something inside me had been hurt so deeply that I might never heal, that this might have been the final time. I might not come back from this one.

I didn't go in to work the next day. I couldn't imagine it, walking back into that building. My sister's words from long ago rang in my ears: "You did choose an alternate lifestyle that people were going to have problems with, after all." Those words had stayed with me all this time, a tiny whisper in the back of my consciousness. I had asked for this, hadn't I? What did I expect? What could I ever expect? Despair rose in me like a huge wave, pinning me down, threatening to stop my breath. I fought to breathe against it.

"But Deborah was also slandered," Connie pointed out, "and what was her crime? She has a husband. She's straight."

But her words had no effect on me. I lay on the couch with a blanket around me. Inside me was only a cold, deep blackness that permeated every contour of my body. Deborah called to tell me that several colleagues had gone to the president and that he had dismissed it as an April's Fool joke. "Nothing to get upset about," he'd said. Someone told me that the walls of the student union had been plastered with the paper.

Snow fell throughout the day, hiding the grass, covering up the car's tailpipe, whitewashing the street. I sat on my couch covered with my blanket and watched the snow. Nothing mattered anymore. There was a hole so deep in my soul I feared I might slip through it, just drift out to sea on my tears, leaving the shore far behind with nothing around me but the quiet rocking of the waves and the blackness of the water and the calming certainty of drowning. I could swim until I died. I could tread water and watch the shore recede and disappear until there was only the water joining hands above my head.

They had written about me as if I weren't even a human being. Outside the snow fell like the stupid punch line to a joke that had gone on much too long. I was so alone. I would always be alone. It would always be just me and Connie, alone against the world. I watched the snow fall, thought about the lesbian potluck. Even other gay people couldn't understand it, unless they were also out, unless they had felt it themselves, this wound, this emptiness, the nothingness that expanded and spread through me like an invincible gas, killing me in silence. There was no one I could talk to. I sat there till the sunlight began to ebb, teasing me, appearing and disappearing like a child playing hide-and-seek. It would not give me any place that I could count on. I sat on my couch and watched the darkness fall. There was no support for us, no one to soothe our suffering. I was so off balance, so open to attack, so pregnant. Steps and sidewalks were treacherous. I dropped things when I picked them up. I couldn't pass cars on the highway anymore; the oncoming traffic was too frightening. It was too much to protect myself. I couldn't do it.

I tried to go in to work the next day, but the closer the signs for Mansfield became, the harder I cried, until I could barely see the road for my tears. I kept reaching in the back for tissues, until I began to find them on the passenger seat beside me, as if someone were laying them out for me. I turned around and went back home. I tried to tell myself that it was probably only a handful of people, at most, but it didn't matter. The obscene phone calls, the letters to the editor, the town meeting, the church fiasco, my relationship with my family. Nothing had touched me the way this had. There was nothing I could do that would let me out from under this sorrow that crushed me like the snow. Nothing would set me free. I could not go in to work. I couldn't imagine ever going back again. I could not stop crying, as if my heart had been cleaved in two and left to rot inside my body. I was supposed to give a reading from my novel on campus at the end of the week. I couldn't imagine doing it. I couldn't imagine ever going back, teaching another class, going to another meeting, talking to another student.

I thought of the letters to the editor that had followed our story in the newspaper, the anger I'd felt in response. I wanted that anger back. I wanted it to fill my body, give me power, fuel my rage. I didn't want to be this powerless, quivering, fearful being, unable to stand up for myself. I tried to call that anger up, and all I could find inside myself was a quivering mass of jelly, limp and flaccid, falling from my hands like flesh from a bone.

I made myself another cup of tea and carried it back to my desk, safe in the comfort of my home. I wanted to write in my journal. I wanted to do something. I wanted to go in to work; the women students were having an open mike poetry reading, and Gina was reading. I needed to be there. I needed to go see the president, talk to him about the importance of making a statement. Above my desk hung my Audre Lorde quote, slightly yellowed with age: "Your silence will not protect you." I stirred my tea. I couldn't go in. I was afraid that if I did, people might see me cry. I couldn't let that happen. I couldn't let anyone know how deeply this had hurt me. I wanted to be strong. How could I have allowed something so stupid to have such an effect? I took a sip of tea. It warmed me like whiskey. Your silence will not protect you. I remembered reading those words at our wedding, remembered crying as I read my vows, crying as we entered into our life together, unable to see where the path might lead. I wondered if I could afford to wait until I was not afraid to go in to work. Wasn't that like waiting to live my life until the fear had gone away? I had done that long enough, lived whole years of my life in silence, waiting to find the courage that would let me speak. I thought of Gina, of all the gay and lesbian students. Was it fair to only allow my strength to be visible, to have this calculated vulnerability in what I chose to allow my students to hear and read? How could I not be a whole person, as full of fear as I was of anger, as susceptible to gay bashing as anyone else?

I took another sip of tea and held the cup in my hand, feeling its warmth against my palm. Inside me, Zoe slept, still as the day, waiting to see where it might take us. I was a whole person, I thought. I was strong. I could act despite my fear. I took a long, deep breath, felt it fill my lungs. Zoe stirred, a movement as vague as a brush stroke.

I got my coat.

The miles ticked by like markers on a race. The sun shone dubiously, casting a hesitant light on the frost that tinged the road. Every mile that took me farther than I'd been able to drive the day before felt like a victory. But at the same time the grief welled up regularly, threatening to crush my lungs. Each time I struggled for breath, fought for it as if for life. I am a whole person. I am powerful. I repeated it over and over again, till I could feel the air enter my lungs, feel the grief recede like a tide. Pulling into the parking lot was like reaching land. I did it, I thought. I sat for a moment, breathing deeply. I had gotten here. It felt like all I needed to do.

So many people were at the women's open mike that all the seats were taken. Posters for an upcoming forum, "Everything You Ever Wanted to Know About Homosexuality," hung in every hallway, my name dark and deliberate, listed as the moderator. My stomach dropped, like taking a dip on a roller coaster.

When I saw Deborah, I made my way over to her. Her jaw was tense. "I spent all morning arranging security for this and for your reading," she said between gritted teeth. "I talked with everybody about it at the Women's Commission, and I'm sick of talking about this issue!" Her eyes flashed. "I can't spend any more time on it," she said. "When I came to school and saw the posters for the forum on homosexuality I thought: I cannot spend another minute on this issue!" She exhaled so sharply I could almost see the air leaving her lungs like smoke. "So I hope you don't mind that I don't come to the forum."

I backed away from her and looked for a seat. When I sat down, I felt a fury rising up in me, more than anger, more than anything that I had ever felt before. How dare Deborah call my life, my world, what I lived with every single day, an "issue," as if my life were a cause she could just pick up and then discard when it no longer fit her schedule? Rage filled me like a bull, its hooves striking at my chest, cutting through the flesh. I took a long deep breath and then another. I knew Deborah was stressed, but I didn't care. This was a stress that I was forced to live with every day. I made myself pay attention to the women who took the microphone and read their poetry to the world, to anyone who would listen.

⸙

The president leaned back behind his desk, surveying me as if I were some kind of animal with which he was not entirely familiar.

"I just wanted to talk with you about the hate sheet," I said. I made my voice as strong as possible. I kept that anger with me, nourished it like a flame. Thank god I *had* the anger. I made myself say the words. It was a hate sheet. Anything that could make me feel like this was about hatred and nothing less. "I want you to make a statement of support for the gays and lesbians on this campus," I said, "in the next issue of the newspaper."

The president brought the tips of his fingers together and frowned at them. He was a former football coach who regularly walked the campus and greeted students by name. He had made his reputation by being moderate; an all-around nice man, everyone agreed. "Well, I don't know if I should mention homosexuals specifically," he said, giving me a sincere scowl. "I could just say 'minorities.' "

I took a deep breath. "I think you have to mention us," I told him. "Because every other group, every other minority, is included by default, except for us." The president looked confused. I could feel a part of me throwing up its hands, throwing in the towel. "We're not included in civil rights legislation," I said pointedly.

He looked at me. His eyes narrowed. "Do you mean I could fire you for being a lesbian?" he asked.

My heart skipped a beat. I thought fleetingly about my application for tenure and promotion that was slowly but surely making its way toward the president's desk. I pictured his hand moving in slow motion toward my cover page, about to stamp **DENIED** in permanent ink. I tried to swallow, but my mouth was dry. "Yes," I said. "There are no laws protecting me." I fought to take a breath before my lungs collapsed. I made myself look him in the eye. "But

I'd sue you," I added, almost mumbling, one hand covering my mouth. My voice sounded thin, a tiny birdsong lost in the wind of a huge and storm-ridden forest.

The president sat back in his chair. "I'll certainly think about it," he said, nodding his head reflectively. "I'll give it some thought." He opened the door for me, thanked me for coming in. We shook hands politely. "You take care of that baby now," he said and closed the door behind me.

The morning of my reading, I felt as if the morning sickness had returned. I couldn't eat. A nervous diarrhea drained my body. "I don't want to go in," I told Connie, throwing my clothes on the bed. "I'm sick of performing for Mansfield." I wrapped my bathrobe more tightly around me. I thought about Deborah, tired of the issue of my life. "I don't give a shit about that place," I said.

"It's not for them," Connie said. "It's for you. It's to celebrate your publication."

I pulled on my clothes. My publication. My heart felt cold as ice. Who the hell cared about my publication? I couldn't give the reading. I couldn't imagine being able to do it. Mansfield felt like a prison cell, just waiting at the other end of the highway for me to serve my sentence. All I wanted was to get it over with, get all of it over with, get on with my life.

Campus police lined the stairs that led to the room where my reading was scheduled. Their arms were folded across their chests, their faces impassive. I moved through them as circumspectly as possible. I knew that Deborah had arranged for their presence, but somewhere deep down I still feared they might really be there for me, that at any moment they would close their ranks around me, snap their cuffs around my wrists, and lead me away. My rib cage felt as if it were closing in on my heart. My legs shook. I shrank behind Connie. When I reached the door, I couldn't go in. People flooded the room, filled the chairs, and spilled out along the back, where they leaned against the wall. "I've got to go to the bathroom," I told Connie. "I'll be right back."

When I emerged from the stall, I clung to the sink and stared at myself in the mirror. You can do it, I told myself. I took a deep breath. I am whole, I repeated, silently. I am a whole person. I closed my eyes. All I wanted was to get out of there, disappear into the world, leave no traces behind. I opened my eyes. I was still there, standing in this bathroom. I had to go back in.

Upstairs, people poured into the room. The police stood on either side of the door, motionless. My heart pounded. How could I do this? Who knew who might be in that audience? The student who wrote the letter, the obscene phone callers, whoever was behind that hate sheet. I scanned the faces of the people in the room. How would I ever know which expressions concealed hatred, whose coat might hide a gun?

Connie slipped her hand into mine. "You can do this," she whispered. "See? There's Gina." I followed her eyes and made out the faces in the room. I recognized students from the Gay Support Group, several women from the potluck, the elderly gay man who lived in the center of a nearby town with his partner of nearly forty years. The room was filled with friends, with gay and lesbian people. I didn't see an unfamiliar face in the crowd.

I took the podium and glanced out across the sea of faces. I can do it, I thought. I can give this reading. I opened my copy of the galleys, looked at my audience, and began to read. As I read, my voice soared. The nervousness fell away, and there was nothing but the beauty of my words. This was my novel, and all that mattered was the story that I had already told, that needed only my voice to give it life. I was reading to people who understood what I felt, who understood what this all meant. I avoided Deborah's eyes. I read to my community, to the lesbians and gay men who peopled my world. When I finished, the applause was deafening. I grasped the podium, suddenly weak. People squeezed my arm, hugged me, patted my back. I felt like Jesus, everyone clamoring to get a piece of my hem. I was dizzy with it. I reached for Connie to steady myself. The room shimmered around me. A mild cramping seized my belly. I took a deep breath to still it. I had done it. I had given my reading. I was a whole person, and I was filled with power. I left the room on Connie's arm, heading for the nearest bathroom, to deal with the last of my nervousness.

We went out with Ginger and Lee and several others to a local bar, where we took up an entire table, and I sipped a club soda and lime and tried not to inhale too much cigarette smoke. The cramping continued, slight but constant, the way it used to at the beginning of my period. I massaged my belly covertly beneath the table. This was my night. I wanted to celebrate it. Ginger had recently had heart surgery after nearly dying, and Lee was telling the story. "Oh, go on," Ginger said, when she was through. "It wasn't exactly like that."

Lee patted her arm and shot a knowing glance at the rest of us. "Ever since she got that new heart she's been so ornery!" she said.

I sat back and breathed deeply. I was at home. I was with the people I belonged to. I hadn't invited Deborah to come. Why would she want to? My stomach clenched and I closed my eyes. "I need to go," I told Connie regretfully, and we rose to make our good-byes.

Lee enveloped me in a hug that smelled of whiskey. She smelled like my father. I felt a sudden homesickness overtake me. I'd hardly spoken to my family throughout this pregnancy. I didn't know if my father even knew. I wondered what he would think when he saw my novel, which was largely about him. A pain shot through my stomach, though whether it was a cramp or a bolt of fear I wasn't sure. "You take care, kid," Lee said.

The next night, at the planning meeting for the forum on homosexuality, I sat in a soft chair trying to breathe through the cramps. I wondered whether something was wrong. I must need more sleep; it had been a long and difficult week. We went to bed that night at 9, but by 3 A.M. the cramps were fierce enough to wake me. "Let's go down and have some tea," Connie said. By 5 A.M. I could hardly breathe for the pain.

"I think I need to call the doctor," I said. Connie nodded. Her eyes were dark with worry.

We met Dr. Gordon at the emergency room. "You're probably dehydrated," he said, frowning with concentration as he connected me to a fetal monitor and checked my cervix. "The lowered fluid level probably stimulated the oxytocin [hormone] level," he said, "which stimulated the contractions of the uterus." He looked at Connie. "Has anything been going on?"

When we got home, Connie tucked me into bed. "I'm going into my room to pray," she said. Her voice shook. The contractions continued into the early evening, getting steadily worse. I knelt on the bed, folding both hands across my belly, forcing myself to breathe. I'd refused Dr. Gordon's intravenous line, promising to drink a lot of fluids instead, but now I wondered whether I would have been better off letting someone else rehydrate me. Pain tore at my uterus in regular waves. I choked down glass after glass of Gatorade. It was evening before the contractions began to recede. I lay back in the bed, struggling to breathe. I wasn't even sure I could sit up. Dr. Gordon had instructed me to stay in bed that day, but what about the next night, when we had scheduled the forum?

Connie shook her head. "You can't do it," she said. "It's too much." She scowled at me. "I'm not letting you."

I closed my eyes. Relief rolled through me like a calming wave. If I let it, it could take me right out to sea, where I could float forever, sustained by my belly, instead of the other way around. Thank god, I thought. I didn't want to moderate that forum. I never wanted to get out of bed again. "We can get somebody else to moderate," Connie said. She glared at me. "It's not such a bad thing to have something happening about gay issues on campus that doesn't center around you."

I nodded. I knew she was right; I didn't want to do it, but deep down I had a nagging feeling of regret. Our big forum on homosexuality, and I wouldn't be there to oversee it. I thought about the students in the Gay Support Group. Was I letting them down? Who would give them their pep talk? Who could do it, if it wasn't me? Could anyone else moderate as well as I could? I thought about the students who had put together the hate sheet. I wondered if they would think that they had won, when they saw I wasn't there.

More than a hundred people attended the forum, including the president. According to Gina, it went well. People had asked questions; discussion was active. I wondered what it meant, if it meant that this was over now, that we had won. The president had been there; that had to be a good sign. When the next issue of the student newspaper came out, I rifled through its pages tentatively, looking for the president's statement condemning the hate sheet and supporting his gay and lesbian faculty, students, and staff.

It wasn't there.

I put the paper down and looked out through my window. Everything was quiet, still. Even the wind was absent. It was as if we were all waiting for something, hanging on the edge of spring, waiting for something to happen.

It's Just So Hard to *Get* to Brooklyn

A month after my novel came out, the press was sold. "We've all been fired," my editor told me flatly.

"You have?" I said dumbly. "That's terrible." I chased the concept around in my mind for a while, like chasing dust mice in a breeze. The press had been sold. But what did that mean? What about my book, my contract, my next-book clause? Never mind that all those nice young women were losing their jobs. What about *me*? "Who bought it?" I asked.

Karen paused. "The guys who run the *Advocate*," she snarled. Her tone dripped venom. She might as well have been telling me it had been purchased by right-wing fundamentalists as by the owners of the largest commercial gay men's magazine in the country.

"Oh," I said. I cleared my throat as delicately as possible. "What about *Amnesty*?" I asked. "You know—coming out in paperback and all?" My voice shook despite myself.

"Forget it," Karen snapped. "Those guys don't care about you."

After I hung up the phone, I sat there for a moment, staring at the receiver. Just a few moments before I'd been so happy, so full of hope for my future. Now the skies had clouded over again, threatening to dump more rain all over my head. Alyson Publications had been sold. I pictured my novel gracing the shelves of bookstores everywhere, and the long tentacles of the *Advocate* guys reaching out to pull them all back. I shook my head. What was this, anyway? My press had been sold, my editors fired, my job stuck in limbo somewhere in the tenure review process. When would I have some measure of success that I could just enjoy, instead of having to worry every moment that it might be snatched away from me? Inside me, Zoe kicked as if on cue. I touched my belly, softly, tenderly. At least this was still happening, at least one aspect of my life was still going on, untouched by the bureaucratic comings and goings of the business world.

Birds chirped merrily, impervious to the sinking feeling in my chest. A robin pecked beneath the window, its beak full of grass and straw, gathering materials for its nest. It paused for a moment and looked right at me, its beady little eyes on mine. We watched each other for a moment. I wondered if it was male or female. The

217

bird flapped its wings, gazing at me as if it had some questions of its own. I wondered where birds went to sleep, if they had nests only for their young. I pictured her eggs cuddled together deep in the nest this bird was building, gestating silently until the first beak came forth, pecking its way through the fine shell of its outer atmosphere, opening its mouth for food. It would know exactly what to do in a way that my baby never would. From what I'd read, Zoe wouldn't even know how to latch onto my breasts in the beginning. I ran my hand across my stomach, waiting for her kick. We were born without instincts, forced to learn everything from scratch. If left to our own, alone, there was no point at which we wouldn't die. The robin blinked, lifted its wings, and flew away, the straw trailing from its beak. I watched it go, one hand on my stomach, watched it fly off to a life where certain things were guaranteed, like the sure and present knowledge of how to stay alive, a guarantee that we would never have, at any moment in our time on earth.

"I don't know what to do about your reading," my sister said, calling me from Yonkers the day before Mother's Day, the last Mother's Day that I wouldn't be celebrating. I was scheduled to read in Brooklyn the next week, in a lesbian bookstore called A Room of Our Own.

"What about it?" I asked. I was surprised she'd called at all. We talked to each other only every couple of years and even then only out of some obligation to remember that we had, after all, sprung from the same gene pool. I still harbored the secret conviction that I'd been adopted somehow, that surely I had a more exotic set of parents somewhere else, people whose lifestyles and philosophies would instantly make sense of me, clarify my existence in the world in a way that my supposed family never seemed able to.

"Well, Mom's coming that weekend, and I don't know whether we should both come, or I should just come, or neither of us should come," my sister said.

I didn't say anything. My mouth had gone dry from the mere possibility of their coming.

"It's in *Brooklyn*, after all," my sister said, as if I had asked her to travel to the Persian Gulf.

"Well," I mumbled noncommittally.

"Mom read some of your book," my sister said.

"Oh?" I said, swallowing with difficulty. Something sharp and rough seemed to be growing in my throat, sending its roots deep into the flesh.

"She was horrified by the descriptions of Dad," Nancy said.

But it isn't *Dad*, I wanted to say, it's a *novel*, he's a *character*, but the words just wouldn't come. My larynx had been immobilized. Besides, of course it was Dad. Nobody who knew the man could deny it.

"It's just so hard to *get* to Brooklyn," my sister said. Her tone was severe, the implication that it was somehow my fault that Brooklyn lay so far away, several subway trains from where she lived.

After I hung up, I could feel an emptiness deep inside me, a hollow place where my family should have been. Why did I care? What gave them such power, this group of people who ultimately had so little to do with me? And yet they did matter. I wondered how much of my life had been spent chasing after them, tugging at their hems and sleeves, fighting for their notice.

My mother's voice on the phone was bright and cheery. "Do you want to get together before or after the reading?" she asked.

My heart stopped. She was coming? I thought they weren't coming. "I thought you weren't coming," I said faintly.

"Don't you want me to come?" she asked.

I closed my eyes, pictured her face, that line between her eyes that always seemed to be there when she looked at me, as if I were some foreign image she couldn't quite make out, couldn't begin to understand.

"I won't come if it will make you nervous," she said.

I opened my eyes. The sun streamed through the window, illuminating the room, our profusion of spider plants, the yellow paint on the walls. She was already reading the book. I had no more secrets. She would know everything there was to know about me. She knew what she was getting into. The worst was already happening. "It won't make me nervous," I said. And in that moment I felt absolutely sure.

"It won't make you nervous?" Connie asked me, her eyes narrowed in disbelief. We sat at the kitchen table, poring over the map of New York City we'd gotten from AAA, so dense with streets their names were indiscernible.

I shrugged. Inside me something flipped. I suspected it was my stomach knotting in fear, not Zoe ambling around the confines of my womb, checking out what was for dinner.

"How are we going to find this place?" Connie asked, peering at the map.

I shook my head. I'd called the woman at whose apartment we were staying to see if she could tell us but had no luck.

"In a car?" the woman had said dubiously. I might have been asking her for the best place to land a private jet. "Gee, I don't know," she'd said. "I've never driven a car."

"We'll find it," I told Connie, wishing I felt more sure of myself. Everything about this trip was making me nervous. That moment of epiphany I'd experienced with my mother had dissolved like Alka Seltzer, without the accompanying sense of relief. The woman had sounded a little disorganized on the phone, but surely that didn't matter. I didn't care, as long as her apartment was clean. "Let's order a pizza," I said. I was starved and suddenly gaining much more weight than I was supposed to. I thought about my mother. Weight gain was the last thing I had to worry about. I looked at Connie. "Pepperoni and double cheese?" I asked.

"Nancy says there's a train we can take to Brooklyn," my mother informed me in a call later that night.

"A subway train," I said.

"Oh, no," my mother said. "I won't ride a subway. Nancy says there's a *train*."

"That's what she means," I said. "A subway."

There was a slight pause. I glanced at Connie and shrugged. My back ached. I'd had Dr. Gordon, who doubled, thank the lord, as an osteopath, crack it during my last prenatal, but it still ached. Every now and then I felt something akin to mild menstrual cramps. I tried to ignore the fact that both were listed as symptoms of premature labor in my ever pessimistic pregnancy book. "As many as 40 percent of all premature babies are born to women who were thought to be at 'low risk' for early labor," it scolded, presenting expectant mothers with a list of signs to watch for. I'd memorized it at first glance, in a way I'd never managed to memorize important facts before exams.

"Oh, I don't know," my mother said. "I don't know if we'll come or not."

"Well," I said, feeling a twinge of irritation, "whatever."

"Couldn't they take a taxi?" Connie asked when I'd hung up the phone.

I shrugged. Taking taxis just wasn't something my family did. It was akin to charging something on your credit card and then paying it off in monthly installments, a thing I, of course, did regularly and still hid from my mother. We'd practically charged the down payment on the house, had contemplated quietly taking $500 cash advances and squirreling them away in our savings account. This was not something I'd shared with my parents.

"They won't come," Connie said.

I nodded. She was right. They weren't going to come. As I got ready for bed, I tried to feel relieved, but all I felt was a mild regret, so faint that if I tried I could almost pretend it wasn't there.

All night I lay awake, trying to lie still, to keep from waking Connie. The small of my back ached, making every position uncomfortable. Zoe did so many back flips I thought she must have turned into a dolphin. I tried to breathe. It was hard enough for me to breathe normally when I was afraid, but now my lungs were so compressed by my swelling uterus that I was eternally short of breath.

My mother might come to my reading. My mother wanted to hear me read. The very prospect of it struck fear into my heart. I'd been writing all my life. My mother had never asked to see anything I'd written, though on occasion, beside myself with joy or doubt, I would show her things. She read them all with the same expression, the same quizzical line between her eyebrows. "I don't understand why you wrote this," she would say. I rolled over and tucked a pillow beneath my stomach, trying to ease its pull on my back.

I never knew how to explain. Why did I write? My mother was the one who'd started me off on telling stories. She used to hold me on her lap, and I would name three things for her to tell a story from. After a while she named the three things, and I told the story. I had written them down since the very first moment that I learned how to print in Mrs. Fisher's first-grade class, when the simple movement of the pencil on the page had brought the whole world into focus. My favorite place, other than the woods behind our house, had been the public library. I'd carried around two books at a time, so that I could start one the moment I finished the last. In all the time I'd lived with them, I didn't remember ever having seen anyone else in my family even pick up a book. My brother would stomp through the room where I sat curled in a chair reading. "I don't see where some people get all this time to sit around," he'd say on his way to cut down some tree, clear some trail in the woods. I used to sneak up to my room and do my reading and writing where nobody could see. My mother had never approved. "Don't you want to spend time with your family?" she would ask me.

The truth was, I never did.

My back ached. I readjusted my pillow and touched my belly, firm as a metal casing around my baby. Every morning she was a little bigger, stretching and growing through her seven months of life. According to the books, consciousness began now. If hypnotized, people could remember back to their seventh month in utero. She could make out light beyond the confines of my womb. She was a constant presence in the center of my belly, pulling me forward. If my mother came to hear me read, three generations of us would be in the room, three generations of women, from one whose history had already been written to one whose slate was still clean. I slid my palm across my stomach and caressed my daughter's home. I wondered whether she would be listening too.

My mother wanted to hear me read. Connie shifted in sleep, her face at rest, her features composed. Her breath was deep and even, her sleep a state I could never get to anymore. A thrill of excitement rippled through my body. My mother had never seen me in my element before, in front of a roomful of people, giving voice to my words. I pushed off the blankets and looked at my body in the quiet moonlight of the room. It was long and still and full of my baby. It resembled those snakes we used to study in school, boa constrictors who had swallowed an egg, whole.

Zoe stirred and shifted her weight the same way Connie did. A part of her protruded from one side of my abdomen, faintly visible in the moonlight that filtered through the blinds. A foot? A hand? The smooth curve of her rump as she snuggled into me? What would she do that I would not understand? What ways would I look at her that would strike terror into her heart, make her lose her voice in fear?

I took a deep breath and turned to my side, closed my eyes. The truth was I wanted my mother there. I wanted her to see me read. She was the one who'd started this, the one who'd turned me on to storytelling. I wanted her to see me, pregnant, take my place at the podium, open my book in my hands, and give my voice to the things that I had written. I wanted to read, to my mother and to my daughter, to let them in on who I was, the woman I had become.

"Where the hell are we?" Connie asked, peering through the windshield. "This can't be right."

I glanced uneasily out the passenger window. This part of Brooklyn looked like a war zone. Trash littered the streets; dog shit and broken bottles lined the sidewalks. Connie pulled the car over to the curb. We both studied the address on the building. This was it. We were in the right place. This was the apartment where they were putting us up. We looked at each other for a moment. "I don't know," I said, peering up at the building.

Connie turned off the engine. "Let's check it out," she said.

Climbing the four flights of stairs to the apartment, I could feel my courage waning. The stairwell smelled strongly of roach powder. I put one hand on my belly protectively. What had we been thinking of, bringing a baby to a place like this? I sorted through the keys we'd picked up from the woman at the bookstore and unlocked the door. The smell of oil-based paint hit me like a toxic explosion. Connie and I exchanged a look. The woman had said she was an artist. I remembered that now, belatedly. Canvases dotted the wall, splattered with what looked like a spray of noodles, painted brown and affixed with some kind of industrial strength glue. Plastic stars stuck to the ceiling above the bed. An array of dildos covered the wall, grimy with dust. Connie peeled back the bedspread, gingerly. "The sheets are dirty," she said. Her voice sounded thin, as if she were speaking from a high elevation. The fumes were stifling. From the street we could hear shouting, the sound of glass breaking.

"I wonder if that's our car," I said. I lacked the energy to go to the window and check.

Connie stepped into the kitchen. "I think there's an iguana on the refrigerator," she said.

I nodded. "She said it eats the roaches." We both looked away at the same moment, uneasily. I made a mental note not to open any cupboard doors too suddenly.

Connie glanced at her watch. "We have an hour before the reading," she said. "Do you want to shower?"

I glanced into the bathroom, lifted the shower curtain a little. Grime lined the tub. The grout was black. The toilet smelled. "I don't even want to pee in there," I said.

We looked at each other. The paint fumes were suffocating. I wondered if any were making their way through my uterus, into Zoe's little forming lungs. "Let's get out of here," I said.

The bookstore was empty when we got there. "Well, there's a softball game tonight," the woman at the register told me.

Oh, great, I thought, surveying the empty chairs. My first reading at a lesbian bookstore and I'm competing with a softball game? No self-respecting dyke was going to come hear *me*!

Fifteen people attended the reading. I took a deep breath to quell the nervousness and began to read. I knew these passages backward and forward. The words rolled off my tongue, all the right pauses, perfect delivery. I could have been reading to an auditorium. Despite myself, I kept watching the door. At any moment my mother might walk in, take her seat in the audience, and listen to what I had to say.

She never did. It was the best reading I'd given, and my mother never came to hear it. When I was done, I closed the book and took a sip of water, then talked to the women present for at least another hour. We talked about our families. We talked about our silent fathers. I tried not to watch the door. I imagined my mother coming in late, breathless with her haste, full of apologies for not having made it sooner, not having gotten there in time to hear her beloved daughter read aloud. I sighed and looked around for a chair, imagined going back to that dirty futon on the floor, leaving the light on to scare away the roaches. I wondered how long it would take me to finish paying the dues of being an unestablished writer.

Making Room for My Baby

Y̶ou can do it!" Jane Fonda called to me, leering from the television set as she rocked her skinny little body back and forth in a stretching exercise. Pregnant women surrounded her, all happy and glowing in their various trimesters, all rocking away. "Think of this as making room for your baby!" Jane called, chipper as a squirrel.

Oh, fuck you, Jane, I thought, shaking my head to get the hair out of my eyes. My back ached. I closed my eyes and tried to concentrate on the rhythm of Jane's tireless counting. I might as well make room for this baby, I thought, rocking dutifully. I wasn't writing anything. I had nothing else to say. My mother hadn't even called since the reading. My family hated me. What else was there but the baby?

"Round that back!" Jane called. Around her, beautiful women all rounded their backs, smiling as ecstatically as if they'd been sipping on Manhattans. I rounded my back as best I could over the bowling ball that had become my stomach. It grew bigger every day, threatening to topple me forward every time I stood up. It didn't seem like Zoe needed me to make room for her, I thought, stretching my back out carefully. She seemed to be doing a pretty good job taking up space on her own.

I took a deep breath and let it out slowly. The readings were over for now. All I had left to do between now and Zoe's birth was one trip to Chicago for the American Booksellers' Association Convention, where I would be doing a signing of *Amnesty*. That was it. Then I could just concentrate on my baby. I took another deep breath and tried to flow with the music of Jane's fourteen-year-old video. I opened one eye and glanced at her. There she was, bulimic and annoying as ever. Why didn't she bring this tape up to date and re-release it? Probably, she didn't want anyone to see how old she was getting.

I exhaled mightily. My sister had told me on the phone that she had done the Jane Fonda video every night of her pregnancy. I was lucky if I got to it once a week. On the screen Jane rocked back and forth, the cords on her neck standing out like ropes. I was entering my eighth month. Only a few weeks were left for me to make room

227

for anything—my writing, the baby, my relationship with Connie. Then I would be catapulted into motherhood, and everything would change.

I rolled my head gently, trying to ease the knotted muscles of my neck. I'd spent the morning cleaning every room, scrubbing out the corners as diligently as if I'd been cleaning out my head in preparation for a host of new ideas. Lately, all I wanted to do was work on the house, repaper the bedroom, tear up the carpet in the kitchen and lay down linoleum, and paint the bathroom. The only room I couldn't seem do anything about was Zoe's. Every time I tried to think about it, my body balked. I kept the door closed and walked wide circles around it. It was a mess—heaps of baby clothes that people had given us, several infant car seats, a bassinet a friend had loaned us. The floor was covered with a blue shag rug that must have been there since the '70s, sometimes doubling as a litter box for a cat we'd had to put to sleep. I knew I had to rip it up, but I just couldn't make myself go in there. The day before I had tried to sort through the baby clothes, but panic froze my fingers. What was going on with these sizes? What would she be wearing when? How would we know what to take with us to the hospital? My heart had begun to beat so hard I'd had to leave the room, close the door behind me as if shutting away monsters, and lean against it like I was making sure it wouldn't open again of its own accord, its contents spilling out to fill the house.

I stood up and turned the television off. I trundled down to the kitchen to make a cup of tea, one hand on my back just like every other pregnant woman I'd ever seen. It must be an instinctive thing, maybe the only instinctive thing about this whole process. A soft breeze drifted in across the sill, ruffling the curtains and filling the air with its scent. The lilacs that we'd planted the year before were blooming. The azalea that had masqueraded as dead all winter was in full bloom, and one of the rhododendrons was almost ready to open. I took a deep breath, inhaling their smell. Their growth amazed me. I hadn't really believed it would work. I couldn't imagine that we could just stick something in the ground and have it take root. "Like sperm," Connie had said.

I made myself a cup of tea and sat down on the couch, pillows wedged behind my back. I took a deep sip of tea and held the cup in my hands, feeling its warmth between my palms. I'd been sitting like this for hours lately, between my bouts of housecleaning, just reading and writing in my journal. I lay back against the pillows.

This was the only position I had found that didn't rack my back with pain. I glanced out the window. Robins pecked about the lawn, squirrels chased each other through the trees. I took another sip of tea. I was thirty-one and a half weeks pregnant now. Once we got to thirty-six weeks, we were home free—the baby would no longer be considered premature. Soon I would go into labor, give birth, and nothing would ever be the same again. She would enter our lives, whether we'd made room for her or not. I readjusted the pillow behind my back and reached for my book. The silence of the room was deeply satisfying, empty now of Jane's annoying voice. I settled into the pillows and opened the book. Maybe I'd try to make some more room for her tomorrow.

I awoke at 4 A.M., so hot I couldn't breathe. My shoulders ached; my stomach clenched with nausea. It was like morning sickness all over again. I turned on my side and reached down and wedged a pillow between my knees. My shoulder hurt. My upper arms ached as if I had been lifting weights. I rolled onto my back and stared up at the ceiling. The thought of my maternity leave loomed up at me, one long stretch of time. Fear shot through me, direct as a heart attack. I was afraid to be alone with the baby all fall semester, afraid for the baby. What did I know about taking care of her?

I rolled over to the other side. I wasn't supposed to be lying on my back this late in pregnancy. According to the pregnancy books, sleeping on your back put too much pressure on your inferior vena cava, a vein that carries blood back to the heart, causing all kinds of problems, from hemorrhoids to impaired circulation. Sleeping on my stomach, however, was about as comfortable as curling up atop a basketball. I felt as if I might throw up. Connie turned onto her side, her back to me, exhaling pointedly. I'd awakened her. I sighed. Now there would be hell to pay.

When the alarm rang, Connie sat up and shut it off as violently as if she were killing a fly. She glared at me. "I just don't see why you don't get up when you can't sleep," she said. "Why do you have to keep me awake too?"

I said nothing, just lay there dutifully on my left side, the way the pregnancy books said to.

She flung back the covers and got out of bed. The floor shook beneath her step. Above my head the dream catcher wavered slightly in the breeze. When she got to the door, she paused. "*I* have to go to work," she said pointedly.

Guilt shot through me like rifle fire. She was right. She did have to go to work. I, on the other hand, was just going to spend another day wasting my time at home. I wasn't writing. What the hell was I doing with my time? I should just go out and get a job, maybe third shift since I wasn't doing anything else with my nights. At least I'd be bringing in some money. I rolled over and pushed myself up to a sitting position. My belly must have swelled three times in the night. I looked down at it. The skin was stretched so tight I couldn't imagine how it could possibly stretch any more. I took a breath. My lungs barely had any room, they were so crowded by my stomach. I pushed off the mattress and staggered to my feet. I could hear the sound of the shower. Connie and her sacred sleep. Irritation rippled through me. How was she going to deal with it after the baby was born? I was afraid that taking care of the baby would be my primary responsibility because I would be the one home with her. I imagined the baby crying in the middle of the night and Connie saying: "Shut that kid up—I have to get up in the morning!"

I pulled on a robe and lumbered down the stairs to the kitchen. When Connie came down, we avoided each other. I took my tea back up to my office in silence. I sipped it silently, gazing out at the street, imagining going into labor in the middle of the night and not waking her up, just leaving a note that said: "Didn't want to wake you."

My tea was cold. I took my cup downstairs. Connie scowled at me when I entered the kitchen. "Are we not speaking to each other?" she asked.

I shrugged. "I don't know," I said. "Are you speaking to me?"

"Yeah, I'm speaking to you," she said. We glared at each other. "Are you speaking to me?"

I could feel my irritation raising its shaggy head, gruff as a bear. "Well," I said menacingly. "I answered you, didn't I?"

We looked at each other for another moment. A shadow of a smile played about the corners of her mouth. I could feel my anger melting inside me, much as I wanted to hang onto it, the way our dog hangs on to his pathetic tattered little bones.

"Yeah," Connie said. "You answered me," and then we both began to laugh. "I'm sorry," Connie said, pulling me toward her in a hug.

"I'm sorry too," I said, pushing my head against her face. Zoe's presence was as subtle as a Mack truck, keeping us from getting too close to each other. It was not the last time, I suspected, that she would get between us during a fight.

"I'll see you later," Connie said, kissing me on the cheek and leaving me alone with my pregnancy, alone to face the day.

I made myself another cup of tea, sat down on the couch, and pondered my list of things to do. Nausea racked my stomach. This was almost as bad as the first trimester. Around me the plants drooped, desperate for water. Our dog, Ned, panted beside his empty food bowl. I couldn't imagine getting up for anything. A little flame of hunger licked at my stomach, but the nausea quickly drove it back. I closed my eyes. Maybe I could just sleep a little here and wait until my energy came back. Zoe turned over and wedged herself up under my rib cage, as if to say I'd better make more room for her, before she kicked out a wall herself.

The tattered POW-MIA flags rippled in the wind up and down Wellsboro's Main Street. It was nearly July, and once again every lamppost was bound with an American flag. The announcement board in front of the Methodist church read: "Spaghetti Dinner Tuesday—Come Meet Jesus!" I stared at it for a while. Sometimes I just couldn't figure out what people around here were trying to say.

I pushed open the door of the car and hauled my body carefully out of the driver's seat and up over the curb. I felt like a huge duck, waddling my way down the sidewalk to the store. All along the street the catalpa trees wept lush white flowers that covered the sidewalks, their scent skimming the breeze. A few women smiled at me as I passed them; a man held the door open for me as I made my way up the steps to the office supply store. "Take care now," he said, when I thanked him.

I stood in line at the photocopier, waiting my turn. The woman at the cash register caught my eye and smiled. "When's your baby due?" she asked. Her tone was benevolent. Everywhere I went these days I felt blessed. Everything was so different now that I was pregnant. People treated me in a way they never had before. The first reaction to me had always been distrust; I could read it in faces everywhere—in stores, on the street. My short hair, my height, my clothes—everything called attention to the fact that I was somehow different. When I was younger people used to call me "sir" regularly when I waited in line at cash registers. No one ever smiled at me, even when I smiled at them first. That had been my experience every day of my life, and I'd never even realized it until now.

Now everyone smiled at me. They held doors open for me. They waved at me when I walked down the street. They asked when I was due. In New York a few men had given up their seat for me in the subway. The waitresses at diners asked me how I was, cautioned me to be careful, and called me "Hon" as I pulled open the door to leave. A woman in a bathroom had spontaneously touched my stomach with both hands, as if she couldn't help herself, as if she had been drawn to me like a magnet. It was as if the world had united to embrace me, as if I were passing through some initiation rite with people waiting on either side to help me. For the first time in my life I had a place.

When it was my turn, the cashier came around from behind the counter. "You want me to make those copies for you?" she asked, "so you won't have to stand in front of that Xerox machine?" She took them from my hands. "Have a seat," she said. "This will just take a minute."

My throat hurt suddenly. Tears stung my eyes. I thought I might cry. I hadn't realized how it felt to ease my guard, relax my control. I hadn't realized how hard it had been to live without this acceptance. My life would have been so different if people had smiled at me instead of frowning. It would have taken so much less energy to live, so much less courage just to enter a store or walk down a street, have any human contact of any kind.

This pregnancy had given me a place entirely on its own, a place my wedding ring and my home ownership had not, even though they were among the hallmarks of adulthood. It was true that my baby had no father, but neither did a lot of babies. The truth was that as far as my pregnancy went, a man had been involved somewhere in the process, and I suspected that was all it took.

The cashier turned to me. "Are these OK?" she asked, showing me the copies.

I nodded, reaching quickly into my purse for my wallet. "They're great," I said.

"Good luck," she called after me, as I pushed open the front door.

The summer breeze hit my face as I walked back into the street. The flags were clinging to the lampposts as if for dear life. Zoe rolled over, kicking a foot somewhere in the vicinity of my liver. Someone waved from a passing truck. This was my baby I was carrying. Unlike Connie, Zoe would have automatic rights guaranteed by law—the right to my health insurance, the right to my name, the right to be my heir, the right to have a relationship with me that was defined, unquestioned, and protected, even in the event of a custody hearing.

As I reached my car, I wondered how things would change once this baby was outside my womb, once my difference was back again, flagrant as that American flag rustling in the breeze.

Give Me the Stamps

O K, coaches!" Our Lamaze instructor clapped her hands to get our attention. "I want you to get behind your partner and massage her shoulders. This will be very helpful throughout the early stages of labor."

Connie stood behind me, her hands on my shoulders, her fingers touching me firmly, perfectly, just the way they always did. The expectant mothers sat in a row, like ducks, I thought grimly, while our instructor surveyed our ranks. I glanced up and down the line. Most of the other pregnant women, accompanied by their boyfriends, were young enough to be my daughters. Around us rose the musty smell of the instructor's basement. Connie and I were the only pair of women, which of course didn't surprise me. No one made any comment when we introduced ourselves as spouses, though as usual I could feel the tension in the air, tangible as glass between us and the rest of them.

"OK," the instructor said. "Let's talk about what's going to happen just before the baby's born." She sat down on her folding chair, and we formed a circle on the floor around her feet. "Your breasts are going to grow even larger in the days before childbirth," she said.

One of the teenage boyfriends nudged the boy beside him. "Oh, boy!" he whispered eagerly. "I can't wait for that!"

Connie scowled at him. "Oh, right," she said. "Believe me, they're going to be so sensitive she's not going to want *you* to touch them!" The boys stared at her, dismay evident in their faces.

The instructor cleared her throat. "At birth the baby is likely to be covered with a thin coating of vernix," she said, "the grease that protected the baby in utero."

"Yech!" said another one of the boyfriends, an auto mechanic in town. "I'm not touching it!" He glanced around for support. The other boys looked furtively at Connie and then at the floor, apparently afraid to meet his eyes.

"Let's take a break," the instructor said, looking at her watch. I glanced at it too. Another hour of this. Every week it was the same. We sat in a circle, and I felt huge and full of wrinkles, surrounded by the tight young bodies of seventeen-year-olds. It occurred to me that I was twice their age.

One woman headed outside for a cigarette break. I stared at her in horror. "I smoked all through my first pregnancy," she informed us proudly. "And it didn't make any difference with the baby."

The Lamaze instructor nodded in sympathy. "It *is* hard to quit," she said.

I shook my head. Waves of heat rose through my body, persistent as a hot flash. It was really getting warm in this room. I pulled my sweatshirt off over my head. The instructor started. "What are you doing?!" she exclaimed sharply, then recovered herself. "Oh, you have a T-shirt on," she said. Relief flooded her voice. I wondered if she'd been afraid I might be planning to flash my naked breasts to the room, do my Lamaze breathing topless. I could picture her saying to her friends: "You just never know what those lesbians are going to do!"

One of the teenaged girls looked at me. "You teach over at the university, right?" she said. "My dad was just talking about you down at the GTE plant."

I looked at her nervously. "What was he saying?" I wondered whether I really wanted to know.

"Oh, he was telling the guys that you two are in my Lamaze class," she said breathlessly. "He says you've really got balls!"

Well. "Thanks," I said dubiously. At least I had a fan at the GTE plant. It was better than nothing.

"All right," the instructor said, bringing the break to a close. "I want you all to lie down and do some deep breathing now." I lay down on my back, pillows beneath my knees, my head in Connie's lap. Above me I could see the exposed beams of the unfinished ceiling. "Now close your eyes and relax," the instructor intoned, her voice deep and even. "Breathe in. Hold it. Now release." I closed my eyes and drew in a deep breath. "Picture some place completely relaxing," the instructor said. I lay still, my eyes closed, Connie's lap the softest pillow in the world. Her fingers massaged my temples. Recorded womb sounds from the tape player filled the room, rhythmic and monotonous. Some place relaxing. I wondered where that was.

Connie brought her fingers down my face, massaging my cheekbones. I could feel my body letting go. The sound of the mother's heartbeat filled my head, causing my own heartbeat to slow in response. I breathed in and out and imagined swimming down the center of a nearby lake, submerged in the water, surrounded by the mountains that had become so familiar to me in the last six years. I opened my eyes and looked at Connie. She smiled at me, her eyes full of warmth. We were doing this. We were actually doing this. In no time at all we would have a baby. I shut my eyes, let the music from the mother's womb lull me with its rhythms, and listened to Connie count my breaths. Despite its shortcomings, Lamaze was a godsend. Finally, we had something concrete that we could do together to get ready.

Six weeks before my due date I awoke with contractions radiating down my stomach like lightning bolts. Braxton-Hicks, the pregnancy books called them. "Uncoordinated tightenings" that gave the uterus practice for "the real thing." I focused on the dream catcher above the bed and practiced my Lamaze breathing. The contractions alternated with waves of nausea. My thighs and lower back ached. Connie was gone; she'd taken to going downstairs to the couch as soon as I started twitching. I fought down a rising panic. The real thing. What the hell was that going to be like, if this was just a tightening?

As I stepped off the scale at the next prenatal visit to Dr. Gordon, the nurse smiled at me and handed me a plastic cup to take to the bathroom. On the toilet I hesitated. My stomach was so big I could hardly wipe myself anymore. It was getting harder and harder to position that cup in the right place to catch the flow of urine. Most of the time I ended up pissing all over my hand. I gave my cup back to the nurse and waddled into the exam room for Dr. Gordon to pull up my shirt and measure the distance from my pubic bone to the top of my uterus, now somewhere in the vicinity of my collarbone. Let's face it. There was just nothing dignified about this process.

He frowned at my chart again. "You've only gained another half a pound," he said. "Are you eating anything at all?"

"No," Connie answered. "She's not eating anything."

"I can't," I said. "Everything I eat makes me want to throw up." Nobody told me the last trimester would be just like the first trimester. I guessed that the glowing period the pregnancy books talked about had passed me by entirely. It was unlikely it was going to happen now.

"What about milk shakes?" he asked. "Could you drink a milk shake a day?"

Connie and I exchanged a glance. "Yes, we can," Connie said, as if we were both in this together, which, I supposed, we were.

A contraction woke me at 3:30 like a gunshot, followed by waves of cramps that kept me up for hours. I got up and went downstairs to where Connie was again sleeping on the couch. "Come back to bed," I whispered. When I fell asleep cradled in Connie's arms, I dreamed that we were both swimming in a pool along with an older woman. I drifted away from them, swimming long even strokes. When I looked back to find them, I saw a huge swell of wave coming toward me, rising far above my head. Panic rose, but then I saw Connie and the older woman standing on the side of the pool, cheering me on as the water bore down on me. I struggled to breathe, and opened my eyes, but there was nothing but the ticking of the clock and the darkness of the room, no sound but that of my heart, which was beating hard enough to wake the dead.

—— ∞∞ ——

"Can you tell the court why you wish to change your name?" Judge Anderson asked me.

I sat in the witness chair and looked out over the courtroom, empty except for the court reporter, our lawyer, and Connie, who sat in the front row smiling at me as if I were the most beautiful thing she'd ever seen. She was wearing the same dress she'd worn at our commitment ceremony; her wedding ring shone on her hand. I looked into her eyes for a moment, her soft, green, shining eyes that I had loved for such a long, long time now. "To show my commitment to Connie," I said. My voice shook. Tears stung my eyes. I closed them for a moment and took a deep breath. We were finally hyphenating our names, Sullivan-Blum, so that all three of us, Connie, Zoe, and I, would have the same last name.

"You may step down," Anderson said, smiling at me. He was a tall and courtly man in his forties. I knew him from the days when I used to work out at the gym, and we would run side by side on the treadmills in silent camaraderie. "The court now calls Connie Sullivan," he said.

I took my seat in the front row and watched Connie announce her commitment to me publicly, for the record, before the judge. This must be what it felt like to get married, I thought, to proclaim your love and get a document to prove it. Except that we weren't married and that our document, if it were issued to us at all, had cost us about $400 and brought us no closer to any real legal connection.

"The court grants the petitioners the right to change their names," the judge said, lowering his gavel. Connie threw her arms around me.

"I love you," she whispered. I hugged her back. Her body felt firm and solid in my arms.

"I love you too," I said. I closed my eyes. We had done it. We had changed our names. Deep inside my belly, I felt the beginning of another tightening, firm as a handshake, almost too strong to breathe through.

Outside the sun shone as if it had something on the rest of us, full of its own bravado. Connie and I sat on the front porch, reveling in our new names, while I thumbed through the copy of *What to Expect in the First Year* that my mother had sent me. "Oh, my gosh," I said suddenly, as I happened upon a footnote under the section on "gender differences."

"What is it?" Connie asked.

I paused as another Braxton-Hicks contraction tore through me, concentrating on breathing as deeply as possible. If this was practice, I was getting a lot of it. "Listen to this," I said. I'd finally found the only mention of homosexuality in the entire book. "It says that boys who play with dolls will become homosexuals if their fathers chastise and tell them to 'be a man.' "

"You're kidding," Connie said.

I re-read the footnote. I could feel the hairs on the back of my neck rising, like hackles on a dog. I closed the book and dropped it on the floor of the porch. Another contraction rippled through my uterus like grass fire. I was sick of these books, sick of the constant references to husbands and fathers and to babies that would all follow the same developmental patterns for their gender. I was tired of trying to sift out the relevant information while trying to overlook the fact that my existence was either wholly ignored or portrayed as something negative. I watched a robin peck for worms in the yard, while a crow hunted around the base of the forsythia as if scavenging a corpse. I was sick of being invisible. I wanted to be seen and recognized and listened to. I wanted the whole world to know that I existed, to acknowledge me as a whole human being, to pay attention to me. It didn't seem like too much to ask. I closed my eyes and breathed my way through another contraction. I was tired of politely knocking on the door—I was ready to break it down.

When I opened my eyes, Connie was studying my face. "You're

awfully pale," she said. She looked at her watch. "Maybe we should be timing these contractions."

The sun was setting before we began to wonder whether we should call the doctor. It was always so hard to know what to do. Was this really a *contraction* contraction, or just a *practice* contraction, and how could I know the difference at this point? Connie sat beside me on the couch in the back room, her watch in one hand, her open notebook in the other, writing down the times, from the start of one to the start of the next. I wondered whether I was making the whole thing up. Maybe I should just relax about it. We heard a rustle from the bushes outside. Connie looked at me. "What was that?" she asked. We both looked through the screen door into the bank of bushes that separated us from the Knights of Columbus hall next door, where the flashing lights behind the stained glass windows told us that the knights were having a party for the high school kids.

"This is where the lesbians live!" a boy's voice called from the bushes.

"Hey, shitheads!" another voice called from another place. Laughter rippled the leaves. My heartbeat quickened, even as another contraction doubled me over. Connie stood up and in one quick movement threw open the screen door.

"Who's out there?" she asked.

"Shithead!" another voice called. Somebody giggled. The darkness was spreading. We could barely see the bushes, let alone anyone behind them.

Connie stepped out onto the porch and slammed the door behind her. "Don't call me a shithead, you fucker!" she yelled. Her voice trembled. "Get the hell off my property!"

"Fucker," a voice echoed.

Connie turned around and looked at me through the screen. "I'm going in there after them," she said. Her voice was low and steady, her fists clenched at her sides. "Do we have a stick or something?" I stared at her. Who did she think she was all of a sudden, Rambo?

"Are you crazy?" I asked. "Don't go in the bushes!"

She stared at me. "Then what should we do?" she asked.

We looked at each other for a minute. "Call nine-one-one?" I asked.

By the time the police came, the woods were empty. I stood on the front lawn with Connie, the police car's red lights flashing, while the officer on duty took down our information in his note-book. I watched him write. He was young and tall and blond. For some reason he didn't feel threatening. I liked the feel of him next to me, big and full of muscle, sheltering me with his brute male strength. After he left, Connie paced the front porch. "Those little fuckers," she said. "I hope they come back!"

I glanced at the watch. Contraction after contraction tore through my stomach. "I think it might be time to call," I said.

The nurse with whom I spoke told me to lie down "and call back if they start coming every ten minutes."

I lay back on the couch for an hour, practicing my Lamaze breathing while Connie timed my contractions. In and out, fol-lowing the surge of pain, like surfing a huge wave. They weren't coming every ten minutes. I felt a swell of relief, took a deep breath, and exhaled. Then I saw that Connie was crying. "What's the matter?" I asked her.

She looked at me, her face streaked with tears. "They're coming every six to eight minutes," she said. Her voice shook.

"Go right to the OB unit at the hospital," the nurse told me. "They'll hook you up to a monitor."

By the time we got to the hospital, the contractions were coming every five minutes. "I'll call your doctor," the nurse said. The room was full of the sound of Zoe's heartbeat, rhythmic and even. I tried to take a breath, but all those Lamaze instructions seemed to have vanished from my mind. What was it I was supposed to be doing? Connie took my hand and I focused on her eyes, deep and dark in the light of the hospital room.

It was week thirty-four. "We have to stop the contractions," Dr. Gordon told me over the phone, "or we'll have to ship you up to Elmira for a premature delivery." I held the phone numbly, un-able to say anything in response. "In the meantime," he contin-ued, "we'll do a blood count and a urine catheter, to test for infection." I watched the nurse readying a syringe. "And we'll give you a sedative to try to calm your uterus."

The nurse rolled me over and swabbed my behind. "Now breathe in," she commanded and drove the needle home. I gasped with the pain, clutching Connie's hand. This was almost worse than the con-tractions. "Nubaine may burn," she added, as an afterthought. She scowled at the monitor. "You see this mountain?" she asked me, pointing at the swell of a uterine contraction on the printout. "I don't want to see any more mountains." Her dark hair clung to her face. She was Korean, her English heavily accented. I found that reassuring somehow. Like us, she was different, even though a silver cross swung from her neck. She gathered up her paraphernalia. "That baby's got to cook a little longer," she said. She looked at us both, her eyes dark and steady. "You pray now."

We spent the night in the hospital, Connie in a recliner by my side. While Connie slept, I watched the monitor registering my contractions in the form of hills and valleys. Dr. Gordon had told me he wouldn't discharge me until he'd seen a flat line for forty minutes. I watched the needle on the paper, ticking out mountain after mountain, doing my best to pray, to a god or goddess I wasn't even completely sure was really out there, much less with nothing better to do than listen to my feeble pleas.

"Irritable uterus," Dr. Gordon commented cheerfully, writing the discharge orders in my chart the following morning.

"Excuse me?" I said. It had sounded like he'd said I had an irritable uterus. I shook my head. This sedative was taking a while to wear off.

"You've got a condition called 'irritable uterus,'" he said. "Some women have it. Nobody knows why. It can cause early contractions, because your uterus doesn't want to have that baby in there." He smiled at me, his glasses glinting in the fluorescent light of the room. "If it persists, we'll have to put you on tocolytic agents to relax the uterus so you can carry to term."

I exchanged a glance with Connie. Oh great. An irritable uterus. Was there something wrong with me, that I couldn't seem to handle any aspect of this pregnancy with any grace and dignity? I pictured my uterus in there, grumpy from the task of playing hostess to some unwanted guest who'd clearly overstayed whatever welcome she'd come in with. Here I was, trying to finish out my pregnancy like a good girl, while my uterus was whining about what a bad day she was having. What did she think was going on with me—some kind of picnic?

I spent the day feeling anxious and hung over. As I tried to fall asleep the next night, I had another contraction. Fear swept through me. What if they didn't stop? What if I had to go back to the hospital and do it all over again? I pushed back the sheets and started to get up.

"Where are you going?" Connie asked groggily.

"I'm scared," I said. I could feel the tears filling my eyes. Connie sat up and put her hand on my arm.

"Come back to bed," she said. "I'll hold you."

We lay together all night, Connie putting her arms around me every time I awoke. "It'll be all right," she whispered. "Everything's going to be all right."

Connie brought me breakfast in bed the next morning, plumped up the pillows behind my shoulders, and opened the blinds to let in the sun. The morning was cool and crisp, almost like autumn, like a gift from the goddess, just to make my pregnancy more comfortable. Connie sat down beside me and opened her notebook.

"We have so much to do," she said, "with this name-changing stuff. There's our social security cards, our insurance, the hospital admittance papers, the doctor's records, the car registrations, the titles, the mortgage, the deed to the house." She lay down her notebook. "We'll never get it all done!"

I took a bite of toast and chewed it tentatively. Nothing had much taste anymore. My stomach was in a constant state of agitation and excitement, a combination of Christmas Eve and preparation for a funeral. I glanced around the bedroom. That dropped ceiling was as annoying as ever. I eyed it as I took another bite of toast. I wanted it down. I really wanted it down, before the baby was born.

At my next prenatal inspection, Dr. Gordon told me, "Her head is engaged in the pelvis now," Dr. Gordon said, doing the internal at my next prenatal visit. "Her head is really right there." His voice rang with enthusiasm. "Look," he told Connie. "I can rock her head and Louise's hips will rock from side to side right along with it."

Well, don't talk to me about it, I thought. I'm just a pod for her. Go ahead and jerk me all around the table. Privately, Connie and I referred to him as Dr. Dad. "I heard you got a friend of mine pregnant," Deborah had told him, at the receptionist's desk shortly after my successful insemination, much to the consternation of the office staff.

Dr. Gordon extended his arm and pulled me to a sitting position, supporting me as I swung my legs over the side of the table. I took a deep breath. I felt so much less pregnant now that the baby had dropped. I had so much more space to breathe and eat in.

"After one more week, she'll be OK," Dr. Gordon said, "and if you start to go into labor, we won't try to stop it anymore."

I ran my hand across my belly. My baby was in there, about to come out. A wave of excitement washed through me, swiftly followed by a surge of dread. Zoe moved a little. She had so little room now that her little foot came right through my stomach, pushing out the skin. Connie and I both stared at it. What a bizarre thing this was, carrying a live human being around inside of me. One day soon that little foot would be out in the open, that whole little body would be out in the open, free of the constraints of my grumpy uterus, out on its own, living its life. I couldn't imagine it. I just couldn't imagine it.

Once Zoe could be born safely, she showed no signs of wanting to be born anymore. The contractions dissipated into light, shimmering waves that came and went like a rainfall, while through it all Zoe slept securely, locked into place in my pelvis like a docked boat. The temperatures rose as my belly swelled to unimaginable proportions. I felt hot and huge and cranky, a woolly mammoth trudging up and down the streets of Wellsboro, just looking for a fight.

My manuscript for my second book lay in its padded envelope on the postal scale, ready to be sent to yet another agent who would probably turn out to suffer from a multiple personality disorder. "Four dollars," the postal clerk barked, hauling the envelope off the scale.

"OK," I said. "I need four dollars worth of stamps for the outside envelope and the same amount for the SASE inside."

The clerk studied me. He was an old white-haired white guy who ruled the post office from his corner window. I'd heard him say to another post office guy, laughing one of those croupy laughs that sound like he might cough up a lung in another second, "You sound like a Japanese Jew!" It was hard, so hard, to get a grip on the mentality around here. His dark eyes narrowed. "You got another envelope inside here?" he asked, as if I might be confessing to smuggling drugs.

"Yeah," I said. "And I need the same amount of postage for it." It wasn't like I didn't do this all the time. I'd sent out hundreds of manila envelopes from this post office, all with self-addressed envelopes inside for which I needed to procure extra postage, and every single time it was a problem.

"I need to take it out," the clerk said, pulling open the outside envelope, "and weigh it separately."

I looked at his hands, at his fat, meaty, pasty fingers trying to touch my manuscript. A wave of heat went through me. Mr. Post Office Man. Just let him try to get his hands inside my envelope.

"No, you don't," I said. "It's going to weigh the same. All I need is four dollars worth of stamps for it."

"I need to weigh it," the clerk persisted, trying to open his end of the envelope. I grabbed the other end and held on tight.

"No, you don't," I said menacingly. We stared at each other for a moment, each of us holding one end of the envelope. A silence fell over the post office. A few people in line behind me shifted their weight from one foot to another. "Just give me the stamps," I hissed, my teeth clenched, my fingers tight on my envelope.

"Just let me take this out," the clerk said, pulling on his end. Sweat rolled off his brow.

"GIVE ME THE STAMPS," I snarled. I pulled on my end of the envelope so hard I nearly hauled him over the counter. He let go.

"That'll be eight dollars," he said, letting go of the manuscript and opening the stamp drawer.

"And a receipt," I said, pushing the money at him. Everyone waited in silence while I took out the inside envelope, pasted on the stamps, and pushed it back in. I sealed the outside envelope and put the remaining stamps on it. "Stamp it first class," I said. My voice was level, my stomach huge. I was bigger than he. I was bigger than anyone else in that post office. I could take him; just let him try to mess with me.

He stamped the envelope. "Next," he said, avoiding my eyes. His voice shook slightly. A ripple of triumph went through me. I'd won. I'd intimidated Mr. Post Office Man. I turned and swept past the townspeople gathered there, moving like an elephant, slow and full of grace, my trunk swaying from side to side, the townspeople huddling in the corner, as if they were clearing space, praying only that they might be spared, that they alone might live.

I walked home slowly, the trees shaking with the weight of my step, traffic stopping as I crossed the street. When I got to the house, I kicked open the front door and eyed the stairs. It was time for that dropped ceiling in the bedroom to come down, and I was just the woman to do it.

Just Make Sure Your Water Isn't Leaking

O K," the painter said cheerfully, as his crew packed up their supplies. "I think we're all finished here."

I watched as they loaded up their truck, brushing the plaster dust from their pants with paint-splattered hands. "We'll send you the invoice," he said, rolling down the driver's window and backing carefully out of the driveway. "Thanks for the business."

Thanks for the business, indeed. Connie shot me a glance from the corner of her eye as we turned back to the house. Well, so, OK, I'd run out of energy halfway through the project. At least I'd managed to tear down all those ceiling tiles and take them to the dump. It wasn't until I'd looked up at that huge exposed ceiling, filled with holes and leaking plaster dust everywhere, that I'd realized I couldn't go on. I lay on the couch for the next three days with the fan on me, watching them work. I'd saved us some money, anyway, hadn't I?

"Hey," Connie said. "You want to go get some lunch?"

The flags waved up and down Main Street. It was July in Wellsboro again, and we were doing it up right. Granted, we didn't have any display of fireworks in our town for the Fourth, but we knew how to fly our flags. Nobody could say we didn't know how to put a face on things, even if we didn't pack any firepower to back it up. Between the flags and the annual Prayer Meeting on the Green, we had all the bases covered. Every year I fantasized about going to the prayer meeting myself, falling to my knees before the Winken, Blinken, and Nod fountain, and crying: "Praise Jesus, thank you for making me a lesbian!"

"Look," Connie said, as we stopped at the light. "There's Judge Anderson." I watched him crossing the street in the company of several other men, all talking and laughing, their neckties waving in the breeze.

"He looks like an actor, doesn't he?" I said, "playing the role of a good moral judge in a small town."

"That's exactly what he looks like," Connie said. "The guy in *To Kill a Mockingbird*, about to face some moral dilemma."

I watched him walk down the street, tall and thin and vital, gesturing with his hands while the other men listened with respect. Of course, I thought, suddenly. He is about to face a moral dilemma, when we petition for Connie's adoption of Zoe. An adoption by a same-sex couple had never happened in this part of Pennsylvania. The light changed, and Judge Anderson and his entourage approached the diner. I watched the door swing closed behind them. I wondered what decision he would make, when it really came down to it, when he was really faced with taking such a public stance. The name change was one thing, the adoption entirely another. Which side of the line would he end up on, when all was said and done? Connie and I headed for another diner down the street, just a little less local, just a little less visible, just that much farther from the line of waving flags reminding us of where we were.

—⊶—

"Do you want a glass of water?" Connie asked me, appearing in the screen door as I sat rocking on the porch.

"Do I look like I want a glass of water?" I snapped. What the hell did she think, I was just sitting there longing for water?

"I was just asking," Connie said, retreating quickly. Her tone was sharp. I watched her disappear through the screen, and terror seized me. What if she left me? How would I manage? How would I ever get along without her? Tears stung my eyes. I could feel them running down my cheeks. I brought my hands up to my face and sobbed. I needed her so much. I could barely get up out of the chair without help. How would I manage after she was gone? I wept and wept, until Connie had reappeared at the door, pushed it open, gathered me up into her arms, and pressed my head against her chest, until all my tears had gone.

The contractions were constant, coming and going like the sunshine, sometimes sharp and painful, sometimes a dull ache like menstrual pain. I practiced my Lamaze breathing till I felt like a pro, wondering all the time how I would ever know when I was really going into labor. Every day I looked for a sign, some indication that labor was about to start. I'd had no idea everything would be so vague. It would be so much easier if there were some kind of road sign: This Way, Ladies—Labor Starts Here!

As it was, I progressed in a constant state of confusion. One morning nineteen days before Zoe's due date I got up and found vaginal discharge on the sheets. I stared at it in wonder. The books talked about "bloody show," the rupturing of the capillaries as the cervix effaced and dilated, giving the mucus a hint of pink. Some women experienced bloody show, and others never did, the books said. Bloody show—it sounded like the punch line to a Monty Python joke. I hauled my body into the bathroom. When I went to flush the toilet I saw a glob of mucus floating around. Something tightened deep in my stomach. Was this the mucus plug? The books said that as the cervix began to thin and open, the cork of mucus sealing the opening of the uterus could become dislodged and be passed through the vagina a week or two before the first contractions. Or it could be passed just as labor started. I stared at it in panic. Which was it? Now or later? I'd read the section in the books on false labor symptoms and real labor symptoms so many times I thought I had them memorized, but now I couldn't remember anything. I stared at it more closely. Was it the mucus plug or not? I'd pictured it as larger somehow—like a great big drain stopper. According to the books, however, it could be passed in parts, through increasing discharge. I forced myself to leave the bathroom. I didn't flush, though. Maybe Connie would want to see it.

———⁂———

"Just make sure your water isn't leaking," my sister dourly admonished me over the phone. "My friend Cynthia had a constant discharge the last few weeks of her pregnancy, and it turned out that her water had been leaking all along, and by the time she went into labor, it was all dried up. You wouldn't believe the complications!"

I hung up uneasily, took my massive body into the bathroom, and felt myself carefully between the legs, as far back as I could reach. I didn't feel anything leaking, but how would I know? Probably, Cynthia hadn't felt anything either. I examined my underwear hourly for discharge. What if my water had already leaked out and inside me Zoe was slowly suffocating? Terror shot through me. She hadn't moved in a while. What if she were already dead?

The temperature climbed to 100 degrees. The weather forecasters announced cheerfully that the humidity level was more than 90 percent. My stomach grew and grew, crippling my body like a huge embrace, much too tight for comfort. I couldn't sleep, my shoulder and pelvic joints ached. When I tried to climb out of bed at night to go to the bathroom, my round ligaments seized me with a burning, throbbing pain. Nausea came and went like an unwanted house guest. My back ached down to my thighs. "Pregnancy is designed this way so that you'll feel so miserable you'll do anything to get the baby out of you when labor comes," my colleague Rhoda told me. I thought she had to be right. What was twenty to thirty hours of acute pain compared to weeks of misery? I thought that at this point I would welcome labor because at least something would be happening. Pains shot through my cervix constantly, as if Zoe's head were butting up against it.

When the letter came from the university officially granting me tenure and promotion to the rank of associate professor, I hardly cared. It was just one more thing to check off the to-do list while I waited grimly, my body settling around me, gelatinous and sullen.

The only time I felt good was when Connie rubbed me down with a cool cloth. We went swimming in the lake, and I waded deep into the water until I was nearly submerged. Water was the only place I had some sense of balance. I'd never felt so consistently sore. Another contraction rippled through me. Big fucking deal, I thought, moving slowly through the water. When was I not having a contraction? My fingers were swollen, my ankles thick by the end of the day. When we went to bed, I thought I'd never make it through another day. And I still had nine days till my due date.

"I don't know what to tell you," my mother informed me by telephone. "All my babies were born right on time."

"What the hell does that mean?" I asked Connie, as she rubbed her cool cloth along my stomach.

"Who knows?" She checked her watch, timing my contraction. We timed my contractions all the time, just for the hell of it, because they were never regular. They came and went at all hours, like a wayward adolescent, never giving us the courtesy of any notice. The full moon that the month before had sent me to the hospital for sedation came and went without producing a single contraction of note. Nine more days of waiting.

When I woke up, the clock said 1:55 A.M. Something was wrong. I raised myself up on my elbow and felt a trickle from my vagina. Was I pissing? Or—did I dare think it?

"What is it?" Connie asked, sitting up in bed.

"I don't know," I said. "Something's happening." Connie turned on the light and pushed back the sheets.

"Oh, my god," she said as a gush of fluid dampened the sheets.

I stared at it in awe. "My water broke," I said. I looked at Connie. "My water broke!" It had happened. Finally, I had my sign. My membranes had ruptured. It was official. It was 2 A.M. on July 17 and I was in labor. My stomach clenched, but it felt more like anxiety than like a contraction. I took a deep breath. "I'm in labor," I said. We both stared at the water gushing from my vagina and quickly turning pink.

"I'm getting a towel," Connie said. She rushed to the bathroom and rushed back and climbed back into bed beside me.

"What now?" I asked her. All that time for preparation, and now I felt like I had no idea what to do.

"I guess we call the hospital."

The first painful contraction came at 2:53, a combination of lower back pain and bad menstrual cramping. Panic overtook me. I'd never be able to do it. This was real pain. I'd never get through it, and it was only just beginning. "Breathe," Connie said, taking my hand. "Breathe!" I took a deep breath and the pain subsided. Of course, I thought. It was going to come and go. It wasn't going to be constant. I waited for the next swell of pain and took another breath. It felt like a wave. All I had to do was bend my knees and surf it through. Never mind that I had never surfed, it still felt like a good analogy.

"Come in now," the nurse said when we called the OB floor.

"I don't want to," I told Connie. I wanted labor to happen at home. I was so comfortable, sitting on my towel in our wet bed. The books said to put off going to the hospital as long as possible. Connie got her guitar and I got my journal. We sat on the bed for a while, slowly soaking the sheets with pink, breathing our way through the contractions. After a while I took a shower and carefully shaved my legs and dried my hair, even as I wondered what the hell I was doing. This was labor after all, not a party I was going to. We took Ned for a walk around the block and packed up our CDs and our portable CD player. It was 6 A.M. and time to go. The excitement I felt was like a pressure in my chest, threatening to explode at any moment. It was happening. She was going to be born. Zoe Constance Sullivan-Blum was about to come into the world.

We Thought Maybe You'd Changed Your Mind

Hmmph," said the night nurse when we appeared on the OB floor, our CD player, CDs, candles, and incense in hand. We must have looked like a small encampment. She glanced at her watch. "We thought maybe you'd changed your mind," she said acidly. She led us to a birthing room, clean sheets neatly folded back on the bed. "Lie down," she commanded, after I'd exchanged my clothes for the negligible coverage of a hospital gown. She snapped on a pair of gloves and lubed them up. "I'm just going to check your cervix," she said, spreading my knees and getting a fix on my vagina. She slid her finger in.

I'd had seventeen years of pap smears. Half a year of lying on my back and spreading my knees and having sperm shot toward my cervix. Nine months of various gloved fingers reaching in and checking things out to see if I was open or closed, thick or thin, ready to go or still just hanging in there. You'd think it would have been old hat by now, all this prodding into the most intimate area of my being. But nothing prepared me for what it would feel like to have somebody put their fingers up my vagina to check out my cervix when I was having a contraction. It was like having someone reach in and rip out your uterine lining with their bare hands at the height of your period. I nearly kicked her teeth out. "You're not dilated at all," she said matter-of-factly, pulling out her hand and stripping her gloves off with a distinct and barely concealed air of triumph.

A surge of annoyance shot through me. All those Braxton-Hicks contractions—and for what? Six weeks of contracting and contracting and contracting, and my cervix was still closed? What did I have in there—a brick wall? No wonder it took me so long to get pregnant. That must have been a hell of a sperm that finally made its way into my well-armored egg. The nurse strapped me to the monitor and checked the strip. It was clearly marked with my name: Louise A. Blum, July 17, 1995. OK, wrong name, not the $400 name we'd so painstakingly made sure the hospital had on our preadmission papers, but there it was. One way or another, Zoe was going to be born today to somebody. The nurse glanced at the clock on the wall.

"For some reason Doctor Gordon thinks this is going to be a quick labor," she said. Her tone implied that at any moment she might laugh out loud. She picked up her clipboard and sauntered off into the hallway, the door swinging shut behind her, final as a punctuation mark, ending the sentence of my life before children. A quick labor. Connie and I looked at each other. A swell of excitement surged through me. I swallowed quickly and tried to take a long deep breath to calm myself down. It was 6 A.M. During our last prenatal inspection Dr. Gordon had felt the contours of my stomach and said that Zoe was going to be a small baby, even if I carried to term. "Not more than seven pounds," he said. A small baby, a quick labor. What more could I ask for? I said a quick prayer, thanking the goddess for giving me Dr. Gordon, the man who had made me pregnant, seen me through my pregnancy, and who was now about to deliver my tiny speedy baby. I reached for Connie's hand. Through the windows I could see the trees swelled with green, waving gently in the breeze. Somewhere out there birds were singing, dew was clinging wetly to the grass, squirrels were chasing one another up and down the trunks of trees, the sun was gearing up for another day. Zoe was gearing up as well, preparing to tuck her head in neatly to her chest and dive into my birth canal, swiftly surfacing at the mouth of my vagina, where I would push her firmly into being, hear that first cry split the air, bring her swiftly to my chest, fix her mouth to my breast, suckle my slippery little newborn into the fullness of her life. By 9 tonight we'd all be watching *Murphy Brown* together.

Connie squeezed my hand. "Well, here we go," she said, and together we entered into labor with joy and trepidation, just as we had entered into every other phase of our lives together, since that first moment we'd laid eyes on one another so many years before.

It wasn't a quick labor. She wasn't a small baby. We never did watch *Murphy Brown*. In fact, I don't think we ever watched it again. It took me fifteen long hours to dilate to 10 centimeters, hours that seemed to have their own dimensions, existing far longer than they did in ordinary time. My insides felt like they were shredding, filling up with blood and tissue. I wanted to run, to leap up and get the hell out of there, but every movement made it worse. Connie opened the door to find a nurse, and the minute she did there was Angela—resplendent in pink scrubs, her long dark hair tied back into a ponytail, her face round and earnest, her appreciation of our musical selections immediate and honest. "I just love coming in here," she said, as the CD player resounded with the Indigo Girls, Bonnie Raitt, Mary Chapin Carpenter, the Cranberries. "The music is great in here!" she said, nodding contentedly while she slid her fingers in like a cattle prod to check my cervix. "Get out of bed," she said. "Move around."

"I can't," I moaned. I thought that I would never move again.

"You can," she said pleasantly but firmly, as she slid her arm through mine. Pain shot through my body as she helped me off the bed. I would have doubled over if I could have bent that way. I spent the transition hours in a recliner by the window, staring at a spot on the wall like they'd said to do in Lamaze, while Connie massaged me over and over and reminded me to breathe. I could only sit there, staring at my spot on the wall, concentrating on each press of Connie's fingers. Everything centered on my breathing, in and out, in and out, over and over and over, the contractions coming every three to four minutes, each one feeling like it was more than I could possibly tolerate. "When can I have something for the pain?" I asked Angela. I'd never been committed to a drug-free labor, any more than I'd ever been committed to a drug-free life in my twenties.

"We don't like to give pain relief till you're far enough along," she responded seriously, checking my cervix yet again for its lack of progress. "Or it will only slow down the process."

Even in that state I could see her logic. Who would want to spend one more minute in this hell? I braced myself for her to check my progress again, reach her carefully gloved fingers in to assault my stubborn cervix. I willed it to open, willed it to flower and let her fingers in, willed her to pry the fucking thing apart if it wouldn't cooperate. "One more centimeter," she said. The shot of Fentanyl, when it did come, injected by Angela straight into my vein, helped immediately—for about two contractions.

"We don't want to overmedicate women in labor," Dr. Gordon informed me politely, strolling into the room for one of his checks, "because it takes away from the elegance of giving birth." I stared at him in disbelief. This was elegant?

Angela convinced me to take a shower. By this time she had assumed the proportions of her name. I was convinced she had been sent there just for us, that she had not existed before she walked into our hospital room and would not exist the moment after Zoe was born. Every hour Angela became more beautiful to me. If she wanted me to shower, I would shower. I concentrated on trying to get my body to move. It was as if we were working together, my body and I, trying to work out the best way to get to our feet. As I pushed myself out of the recliner, I caught sight of Connie's face, pale and drawn. "Take a break," I urged her, in perhaps my only moment of selflessness. Or maybe it was selfish after all—I did want her to last for the duration, right?

Angela agreed. "It's going to be a long haul," she said. "You have to take care of yourself."

Amen. Somebody ought to get the hell out of this room, and it obviously wasn't going to be me.

Angela helped to ease my swollen body into the shower. The warm water beat down on my mammoth belly, while I braced myself against the tile walls and wept. My stomach felt like a huge festering wound, like a tumor whose growth would never be abated, like I carried inside me the ruins of civilization, the aftermath of war, whole battlegrounds of severed body parts strewn from hipbone to hipbone. Carry her out, I prayed to the water as it splashed off my belly and onto the tile. Just carry her out of here. Zoe could have slipped out and slid right down the drain, for all I cared at the moment.

"Get on your hands and knees at the foot of the bed," Angela told me, toweling me off, slipping me into a fresh gown, and leading me back to the mattress of torture. "I'll massage you." I assumed the position, let her fingers untie my gown and push it out of the way, felt her hands ply my flesh, knead me like dough, work against this rock hard thing along my spinal cord that felt like the muscles had spasmed into a fist.

"What is that lump sticking out of her back?" Connie asked Angela in horror as she came back into the room to find me splayed out across the foot of the bed for all the world to see. Modesty had long since vanished, leaving only a keen animal desire to rid my body of this crippling mess.

"That's the baby's head," Angela responded casually, as if she were pointing out the sprinkler on the ceiling.

That should have been our first clue, had we known anything about it, that Zoe wasn't presenting in the proper vertex position, head dutifully facing the spine. Somehow in all that twisting and turning of the final weeks she'd maneuvered herself around until she was facing the wrong direction altogether, as if she might be trying to chisel her escape route out through my vertebrae instead of taking the more conventional exit.

It was as if at any moment my back might crack right along the spinal cord and split open like a melon. Those deep breaths mattered less and less. It was as if someone were sitting on my lungs, squeezing them thin as paper plates. Somewhere, nonetheless, deep in my head, a brain wave snapped like a lasso. "Can I ask for more pain relief?" I asked Angela dumbly.

"Of course," she said, considering my request as if I'd asked for the evening's specials. "I'll phone the doctor."

Two hours later Dr. Gordon was there. He carefully administered the interthecal, a shot right to the spine (this hospital didn't do epidurals, something I still consider a potentially litigious oversight). The minute he withdrew the syringe, I dilated to 10 centimeters. The relief was tremendous, as if he had reached right in and lobotomized my pain, removed it like a frontal lobe. A driving pressure replaced the pain. I rolled over and sat up. "I feel like I have to shit," I said between clenched teeth.

Dr. Gordon paused, jotting down notes in my file. "What did she say?" he asked the nurse, as if I might not be capable of speaking for myself.

"She said," Angela repeated, her enunciation as careful as a schoolgirl's, "that she feels like she has to shit."

He pocketed his pen and delivered upon me his best and most reassuring smile. It was positively beatific. "It's time to push," he said. He patted my leg. "You'll have this baby out in fifteen minutes."

Connie and I looked at each other. It was 5 P.M. The pain was relieved; the pushing was about to begin. We could still make *Murphy Brown*. We missed any expression that might have flitted across Angela's face in the privacy of her own musings.

After four hours of pushing, Zoe was still inside me. I tried as best I could. I shook and moaned and peed, threw up again and again. "You can do it," Angela and Connie kept saying, persistent as cheerleaders. "You can do it."

I pushed. I pushed and pushed and pushed. I shook and trembled and tried to heave the contents of my belly out of me, the way you'd hurl a case of diarrhea as forcefully as you could into the toilet bowl.

"Just one more push," Angela said again and again.

"It's getting close," Connie assured me after a brief sojourn from my head down to my nether regions, which by now felt as disconnected from me as the phone lines outside the window. "She's right there. I can see her hair—it's black and thick and curly!"

"I don't care!" I snarled, my voice taking on the exact tone, I'm sure, of Linda Blair's in *The Exorcist*. Angela leaned toward me. I could see her face, round and white and framed by her long dark hair. There could have been a halo around that head. It seemed small and far away, as if it were at the end of a long tube. My whole face turned toward her, my head swaying like a brontosaurus's, until suddenly we were nose to nose. "Louise," she said, "can you reach down inside yourself and find your baby and help her out?" I stared into her dark, dark eyes and pulled myself back up to a squatting position. I seized the bars of the bed and pushed and pushed. I threw up again. Chills racked my body.

Connie no longer knew what to do for me, beyond mopping my face and neck with a cold cloth and offering me ice chips. I could have been spitting them back in her face, for all I was cognizant of. I no longer had any idea what was happening. When Dr. Gordon attempted a vacuum extraction, I thought he must have taken hold of the examination lamp and shoved it up my vagina. My head snapped up so I could look him in the face. "What . . . are . . . you . . . doing?!" I asked him slowly and deliberately, clearly enunciating each word. He looked startled. Connie informed me later that he had just finished explaining the whole process to me step by step and that I'd nodded fairly solemnly. I have no memory of the exchange, but it's an old trick of mine, to nod solemnly as if I have full understanding of the situation, when in fact my mind is a million miles away.

After three attempts at vacuum extraction Dr. Gordon put down his equipment. "We're going to have to do a C-section," he said.

"Oh, no, no, no!" I cried. I could hear my voice rising from the bed, spiraling around in the air above our heads, thinning as it rose. All I could think was that it was taking so long because I was failing, like this was the final thing, the final test of womanhood that I was failing, one more test that I just couldn't bring myself to pass, like not being able to fold sheets properly or, worse yet, even understand why it mattered how I folded them. All I could think was that I'd come so close and it was my fault somehow. I didn't know until later that Angela had taken Dr. Gordon aside and told him: "Something is wrong. No woman should have to work that hard." I didn't know that they had exchanged a look; I didn't know that I was cold, my body trembling, my teeth chattering. I felt only hot, so hot I could hardly bear it. I didn't know that Connie was so scared she could hardly breathe.

Nobody seemed to pay any attention to me. They just laid down their instruments and set about calling a surgeon and shaving my private parts, taking their good old time, as if labor might have somehow been suspended, now that the urgency of vaginal delivery was gone. The contractions continued as if they hadn't heard the news. "Should I still push?" I asked the nurse who was shaving me. She looked surprised, as if she might have thought I would have stopped talking by now. It must be so inconvenient, when patients insist on communicating with you. "I don't know," she said. "Let me check."

They took me down and left me in a room that looked like an old gymnasium, filled with lights and gurneys. I kept grabbing the anesthesiologist and saying: "Don't you think you should give me that spinal now? Don't you think you should make sure I can't feel anything when the surgeon gets here?" I didn't know that Angela had left the room to pray, that Connie was putting on scrubs so she could be with me and that she was praying too, and that Dr. Gordon was preparing to assist the surgeon, a Christian missionary doctor recently returned from Africa to cut up an American heathen for a change. All I could think was that everyone had left me, and I was all alone, with a nurse I didn't know. She turned toward me and took my hand in hers. "When you feel a contraction, squeeze my hand," she said. I looked into her eyes, and when the swell of pain came, predictable as a wave, I squeezed. Like Angela, she saved my life, and I don't even know her name.

Zoe cried while she was still inside me. "The minute they cut you open, I knew that she could never have been delivered vaginally," Dr. Gordon told me later, "because she was staring right at me, screaming her head off." Not only was she facing the wrong direction, but instead of tucking her head in neatly, my daughter had thrown it back, wedging her brow into my pelvis so tightly that the surgeon had to wrench her out of my pelvic cavity. The whole table rocked. I lay there, so drugged from the spinal I never noticed. Connie sat on a stool at my side, holding my hand, hers shaking so hard that I no longer knew who was supposed to be giving comfort to whom. I heard Zoe's screams, dimly at first, then they grew louder and louder. Why doesn't that mother pick up her baby? I wondered to myself. Only later did I realize that she was my baby and that I was the mother in question.

When Angela brought Zoe over to me, clean and dry, I couldn't have cared less. "Look!" Angela said. Her eyes were wet with excitement. She pinched the fat on the baby's leg. "Eight pounds, four ounces!" Her voice rang with triumph. But none of it made any impression on me. All I could think was that this was the last straw—eight pounds, four ounces. I'd never believe anything Dr. Gordon said to me again.

The baby in her arms looked down at me, her eyes a deep black violet, dark as the irises that framed our front steps. Her hair was black and wild, lifting off her head in a pouf that made her look like Elvis in his less fashionable period. Her lips were parted slightly, her gaze level and directed right at me. I could hear her question clear as day: Who the hell are you, and what are you doing lying down?

I didn't have an answer. I just looked back at her for a moment, wondering who the hell *she* was, and then the surgeon sent a gush of sedative surging through my veins so strong it knocked me out, so he could start the process of stitching me together, to send me on my way, launch me into motherhood, like sending a rocket off toward a distant planet, armed only with the vaguest of coordinates.

Connie, meanwhile, wept and wept. When they asked her if she wanted to cut the cord, she could only shake her head. When they asked her if she wanted to hold the baby, she was trembling too hard to trust herself. By the time Connie was ready, Zoe had already been taken upstairs and placed under the lights, in the charge of a stranger, a nurse we didn't know. She refused to let Connie hold the baby. She wasn't the one who gave birth, after all, and she obviously wasn't the father. It was Dr. Gordon who ultimately procured the baby from the nursery and placed her in Connie's arms. She sat beside me after they brought me back from the recovery room and held Zoe in her arms so our baby wouldn't have to spend her first night untouched. Connie stared into her sleeping face, trying to welcome her as best she could.

"You'll have to grieve the C-section," Dr. Gordon told me when he appeared at the foot of my bed the following morning. I lay against the pillows, bruised and sore. I couldn't even swing my legs over the side of the bed. I was still catheterized, still hooked up to the

IV, still on Demerol. Apparently, they didn't mind giving you pain relief once the baby was out of you. Connie was gone, having finally pried herself away from my side long enough to go home and get a shower. I didn't say anything; I knew that if I opened my mouth I would begin to cry. I held myself still, the way I used to hold myself in childhood, forcing back the tears with every ounce of strength I had, waiting to cry till no one was around to witness it. When he left the room, I closed my eyes. Despair welled up in me. I clenched the sheet with both hands. My body spilled out around me on the bed, my belly a saggy, cushiony pillow that didn't even have the weight of fat. It was just an empty flap of skin. I missed my pregnant belly, huge and solid beneath my hands, full of someone else's presence. I missed the feel of her kicks inside me, the constant company she'd been. When I began to cry, I couldn't stop. It was as if Dr. Gordon had given me permission to grieve. I grieved the C-section. I grieved the loss of that moment I'd dreamed of, having my baby placed on my chest immediately following the birth and putting her to my breast, looking deep into her eyes, having her know exactly who I was.

I had told my mother not to come. "You'll need time to bond as a family," a friend had told me shortly after the birth of her own baby. "Tell her to come later." Alone in my hospital bed now, I suddenly wanted my mother more than I had ever wanted her. But she was back in Ohio, respecting my decision. "Well," my sister said upon hearing the details of Zoe's birth, "it all sounds very *dramatic*."

When I told her I'd pushed for four hours, she responded: "I pushed for three, and"—she paused for emphasis—"*Cynthia* pushed for five." Cynthia again—my sister's friend with all the complications.

Well, there was no beating Cynthia, in any way, ever. I lay alone in my hospital bed, my face turned to the wall. I'd asked my mother not to come—why did I now want her so much?

I wept and wept. The tears fell like afterbirth, simultaneously pried from my body and descending of their own accord. When the door opened, I turned my face away, tried to pull myself together. The nurse glanced at me, then glanced away, checked my pulse, and slipped back out the door. I lay my head against the pillow and turned my face to the window. The trees sparkled in the sunlight. The door opened again. The nurse was back, Zoe in her arms. "I know it might feel like a lot right now," she said, "but do you think you could hold your baby?"

I took a deep breath and held out my arms.

"Now hold her like this, that's right, support her head with your arm." The nurse leaned in toward me and helped me get Zoe into position. "Now guide your nipple into her mouth." Beside me, Connie, who'd come back just in time, leaned forward, watching eagerly. I'd seen a lot of pictures of happy nursing babies. How hard could it be? "Be sure you get your areola into her mouth too," the nurse said. "That's it." Zoe's little mouth clamped shut around my nipple. A jolt went through my body like an electric shock. My toes curled, my uterus contracted, my breath stopped. It was like labor, all over again.

"This can't be right," I gasped between clenched teeth. "This has got to be wrong."

"Nope," the nurse said, leaning in to check. "It's perfect."

"Breathe," Connie said, massaging my shoulders as she had massaged my body through the hell of transition the day before. "Just breathe." The milk burned as it left my breast. I fought to hold the baby gently as her little mouth sucked urgently, sucking me as if she could suck the chrome off a trailer hitch, to borrow a line from a guy in *The Electric Cowboy*, who hadn't been talking about breast-feeding.

"She's a real barracuda," the nurse said admiringly. I pictured Zoe's body winding through the sea, baring her teeth, looking for prey, finding my nipple, and sinking her gums into my flesh as if in another moment she would swallow me whole.

"She knows how to do it," the nurse said. I looked down at her curly little Elvis head. Maybe she knew, but did I? I'd thought this process would be more natural—you put the baby on your breast, it sucks, the milk flows. What was with this pain? But then, again, I'd thought pregnancy would be natural.

"Slip your finger in her mouth to break the suction," the nurse told me, and I eased her off my breast. Blood ran from my nipple. The air-conditioned air stung my flesh. The skin was cracked and bleeding, like a scraped knee. I took a deep breath. Zoe turned her head to the side, her eyes closed, her mouth opening, seeking out my breast as if by smell. I stared at her, fascinated. She looked like a blind rat. "Put her on your other breast," the nurse prompted me. I looked at her beseechingly. My nipple throbbed. My other breast was still a virgin, still tender and untouched. I knew what it would look like when she was finished.

"Remember what the book said," Connie consoled me. "It'll only hurt the first twenty times or so."

And that was supposed to be comforting? I took a long deep breath, guided Zoe's mouth to my breast, and exhaled as her lips snapped shut around it, locking into place like a Venus flytrap, sucking it deep into her throat. I closed my eyes. My Caesarean incision burned. My shoulders ached. My whole body felt like I'd been run over by a truck.

"You're doing really well," the nurse said, patting my shoulder.

I opened my eyes and looked at her. Really? I was doing this well? So far it felt just like labor had, like an endeavor I had no talent for.

"It always hurts at first," she said, gathering up her equipment to leave the room.

I watched Zoe, eyes closed, sucking away. I took another deep breath against the pain. It always hurts at first. I was doing this well. I looked at Connie, sought out her eyes. We were doing this. We had our baby. We had our lives. It was always going to hurt at first, but we were doing it well. We were always going to do it well.

Zoe flopped off my breast, her mouth still open, her breathing deep and even. I stared into her round wrinkled face, her mass of wild hair.

It was like seeing God.

⸺ ∞ ⸺

It's been several years since Zoe's birth. She's sleeping now, a sweaty bundle of energy, forced to rest against her will, her fists clenched, her head still thrown back, the way she must have held it in the womb, like a runner crossing the finish line, her dark hair strewn across her pillow. I watch her sleep, and my heart softens in my chest like butter.

Nothing has been easy. Not the breastfeeding, with the cracked and bleeding nipples, the recurring mastitis, the biting when her teeth came in, the nursing strike in the tenth month, the endless sleepless nights. Not the sleeping, which for years she did in our bed, wedged between us, taking up far more than her fair share of room, continuing to wake several times a night to nurse. Not the months of colic, for which we could only walk her back and forth across the room in endless shifts, cradled close to our bodies in our ever-present sling, while I eliminated everything from my diet I could think of—milk, wheat, onions, garlic, tomatoes—in case their presence in my breastmilk was causing her this pain. Not her health, with the first ear infection at six weeks and followed by another every month, interspersed with tonsilitis and strep and scarlet fever and stomach flus. Certainly not her surgeries, one to put in ear tubes and another to remove her adenoids. Not the time she broke her foot in a collision with the dog or splashed sand from a cigarette receptacle into her eyes. "You'll get so much writing done," people told me. "Babies sleep all the time."

I don't even know who those people were anymore.

Any fantasy I might have had that Zoe's existence would make us more palatable to this small town has been dashed. I think I used to feel that a baby would make people realize, finally, that we are just like them—with one small difference. But if anything, Zoe's presence only caused the harassment to increase, because now there was an additional target. Shortly before her third birthday, three male high school students stole her sandbox and toys from our backyard in the middle of the night, breaking her heart, and making one of my worst fears come to pass—that in Wellsboro our child would be persecuted because of who her parents are.

Paradoxically, our adoption went through smoothly; Judge Anderson did come through for us, and we became her legal parents without incident. Shortly after granting our adoption, however, the state of Pennsylvania changed its legislation, due largely to Clinton's signing The Defense of Marriage Act in 1996. It is now difficult if not impossible for a same-sex couple to adopt in Pennsylvania.

I think I know by now that nothing about this process will ever be easy, that the moment I think I know how to do something, I'll have some new challenge to contend with. I think I don't care anymore if it's easy, or if I'm doing it right, or if things are going the way they are supposed to be going. I just want them to keep going.

Every morning I drop Zoe off at preschool and then go to teach, or go back to my desk to write. When I think of her throughout the day, I feel this flutter of excitement in my chest that is not unlike the feeling I had when I first met Connie, when I wasn't quite sure of her or how far we were going to take this thing. When I go back to pick Zoe up, I hesitate at the door for just a moment and look in through the window while my hand still rests on the knob. I look for her. I look for her in a sea of small and bobbing heads, and my first sensation is always one of fear; my chest tightens as I try to pick her out. What if she is gone? What if someone came into the room and stole her, what if she wandered off on one of their walks to the park and disappeared, what if there was an accident and they've taken her to the emergency room, what if something tore her from my life? Every day I stop at the threshold and search for Zoe, in a mad scramble of small people who are all her height, with the same mannerisms, identical cries. I look for her, and this ache inside me swells to fill my chest. What if I do not find her?

Then I see her. There she is—sitting on top of the slide, in the corner reading a book, at the table, having a snack, poised, my little scrapper, to push the first kid that gets in her way when she sees me enter the room. "My mommy," the other kids will say, to tease her. "*My* mommy!" she'll respond, shielding my legs with her arm and looking around, ready to take on the first kid that dares to challenge her claim. My mommy. Everytime I see her, I fall in love with her all over again, as if I'd never seen her before, as if all this were new, uncharted territory.

∞

We go for a drive into the hills, the three of us, Connie and I in the front, Zoe in the back, kicking her feet against our seats. The Chenille Sisters are singing children's songs on the cassette player; we are all singing along, Zoe's voice exuberant, the words barely recognizable, the tone wholly off-pitch, much, I realize now, like my own. The lilacs are in full bloom, huge trees thick with blossoms, languid in the soft damp air. Someone must have planted them a hundred years ago for them to be so big. What an act of faith. What a gift to leave for future generations. I slow down as we pass the Methodist church on our way out of town, the one that had invited passers-by to come meet Jesus at a spaghetti dinner. The old message is gone. In its place, framed by the lilacs that bloom all around it, is a new one. "Thank You, God," the sign says simply.

Yes, I think, tightening my hands around the wheel. I press my foot against the accelerator and speed up again, sailing off along my country roads, the roads that I have come to claim, pressing deeper into God's Country. Exactly. Thank you, God. Thank you, whoever you are, for everything I am.